"This is a stunning document of genocide ⸺ account of his experiences in and around Urfa in eastern Anatolia provides a window onto the destruction of the Armenian Christian population, including the suffering of the deported Kurdish communities of the Ottoman Empire during the First World War under policies of the Committee of Union and Progress-led Ottoman regime. In addition to his detailed testimony to the horrors of the genocide, it also records the behavior of some of the key perpetrators both on local and provincial level as well as indicts the many ordinary people who participated in or profited from the crime, and honors the acts of humanity by those Ottoman subjects who helped to rescue or hide the victims. *In the Land of Blood and Tears* never succumbs to the temptations of sensationalism or prurience. Künzler's writing is measured, his prose spare, and the resulting litany of horror and tragedy is the more disturbing for it. To the author's self-sacrifice in the cause of saving lives in the most onerous of circumstances, to his endeavors to help rebuild the shattered remnant of the Armenian community in the aftermath of genocide, this book, too, is ample testament."

— Donald Bloxham,
Reader in History at the University of Edinburgh

"Stationed in the 'Swiss Hospital' from 1899-1922 in the multiethnic city of Urfa on the crossroads for the Armenian 'death caravans' on their way to the Syrian desert, Künzler and his wife witnessed the destruction of the Armenians at close hand and tried their best to alleviate their suffering. Künzler's book is a sober account of his war experiences. The first hand information from many sources, among them local government circles, lends Künzler's report a special authenticity. As disturbing as his report is, at the same time it is a declaration of love for a turbulent land of different languages, religions, and the people who live there."

— Hans-Lukas Kieser,
Historian and Privadozent of Modern History,
University of Zürich

"Künzler's book is a very unique source. As a neutral Swiss, he was one of very few foreign observers allowed to stay in Turkey throughout the entire war. His eyewitness accounts are essential for both the Armenian and Assyrian genocides."

— David Gaunt,
Södertörn University College, Stockholm

Im Lande des Blutes und der Tränen

Erlebnisse in Mesopotamien während des Weltkrieges

von

Jacob Künzler

1921.
Tempel-Verlag in Potsdam

Cover of the original German Edition, 1921.

IN THE LAND OF BLOOD AND TEARS

Experiences in Mesopotamia During the World War (1914–1918)

By

Jakob Künzler

Edited with a Preface by Ara Ghazarians
Foreword by Vahakn N. Dadrian
Introduction by Hans-Lukas Kieser
Editor 1999 German edition

Translated from the 1999 German edition

ARMENIAN CULTURAL FOUNDATION
ARLINGTON, MASSACHUSETTS
2007

In the Land of Blood and Tears
Experiences in Mesopotamia During the World War (1914-1918)
By Jakob Künzler

Published in 2007 by
Armenian Cultural Foundation
441 Mystic Street, Arlington, Massachusetts 02474-1108

Originally published in German as *Im Lande des Blutes und Tränen. Erlebnisse in
Mesopotamien während des Weltkrieges*, by Tempel-Verlag, 1921.
Reprinted in German by Chronos Verlag, 1999.
© 1999 Chronos Verlag, Zürich, 2. Auflage 2004
First published in English by the Armenian Cultural Foundation, 2007.

English translation by Geoffrey Steinherz

Cover & Book Design by
Arrow Graphics, Inc., Watertown, Massachusetts
info@arrow1.com
Printed in the United States of America

Library of Congress Cataloging-in-Publication Data

Künzler, Jakob, b. 1871.
[Im Lande des Blutes und Tränen.
Erlebnisse in Mesopotamien während des Weltkrieges (1914-1918) English]
In the land of blood and tears : experiences in Mesopotamia during the World War
(1914-1918) / by Jakob Künzler ; edited by Ara Ghazarians ;
translation from the 1999 German edition edited by Dr. Hans-Lukas Kieser ;
with a Foreword by Dr. Vahakn N. Dadrian.
p. cm.
Summary: "Presents information regarding the Armenian massacres in Urfa,
Ottoman Turkey during the World War I. Includes maps, illustrations,
two selected bibliographies, and two introductory articles"--Provided by publisher.
Includes bibliographical references.
ISBN 13: 978-0-9674621-8-9
ISBN 10: 0-9674621-8-5
1. Künzler, Jakob, b. 1871.
2. World War, 1914-1918--Personal narratives, Swiss.
3. Armenian massacres, 1915-1923--Turkey--Urfa.
4. Armenians--Turkey--Urfa--History.
I. Ghazareans, Ara, 1954-
II. Kieser, Hans-Lukas.
III. Title.

D640.K94813 2007
956.6'20154--dc22   2007018810

SPONSORS

*This book was published through the generosity of
Mr. and Mrs. Mesrob and Anne Bchakjian of Clifton, New Jersey.
The Armenian Cultural Foundation expresses its deepest
gratitude for their vision and unconditional
support of this invaluable project*

Acknowledgements

I would like to express my deepest gratitude, first and fore-most, to Mr. and Mrs. Mesrob and Anne Bchakjian for their generosity in sponsoring the publication of this invaluable doc-ument, and Dr. Robert Mirak, president of the Armenian Cul-tural Foundation for granting me the opportunity and privilege of working on this book, and his thoughtful comments and suggestions in the course of this project.

A few individuals rendered me their assistance in navigating through several aspects of the text, which helped me to dis-cover new sources and information on the Künzler's experi-ence. On language matters, I would like to thank Arman Derian for his help with the Turkish terms and phrases, and Ms. Hei-demarie Floerke and Dr. Rudolph Storch for their assistance in the translation of the German terms and Dominique Abdi for proofreading them. My special thanks to Dr. Ara Sanjian, Director of the Armenian Research Center, University of Michigan-Dearborn, for introducing and sharing with me an invaluable source document on the legacy of the Künzlers, which led to discovering unexplored aspects of their service to Armenian orphans in Syria and Lebanon.

I am deeply indebted to Missak Kelechian of Beirut, Lebanon, a researcher with zeal and passion, for his uncondi-tional support and help, who went out of his way to locate his-toric sites and items, document invaluable resources and materials on the Künzlers and the Near East Relief's activities in Lebanon and share priceless photographs from his personal collection, some of which are being published in this book for the first time. Karekin Dickran, a private archivist of Århus,

Denmark, shared valuable information and bibliographic sources on Danish missionary Karen Jeppe. My thanks to Mrs. Danette Hein-Snider, great-niece of American missionary Effie Chambers, who provided me with biographical information and pictures on her great-aunt. Also, thanks to Aram Sargisian of the Armenian Memorial Church in Watertown, Massachusetts for providing documents on the history of Armenian Missionary movement in Urfa, to Mrs. A. Weilenmann and Ms. Bleuler of Schweizerische Nationalbibliothek for their help in retrieving information on German language resources in their institution, to also, Roseanna A. Sommers for her assistance in retrieving primary sources on Jakob Künzler and other missionaries in the Near East Foundation archives.

The realization of this project would not have been possible without the skilful services of Geoffrey Steinherz, who translated this work in a very short period of time.

My special thanks to Alvart Badalian and Aramais Andonian of Arrow Graphics for their professionalism in the preparation of this manuscript, and their patience, and DJ Hall for her professional and meticulous copy-editing of this book. Also my gratitude to Rev. Joanne E. Gulezian Hartunian, Suzanne Pearce, and Ara Nazarian for reading and commenting on the text. Last but not least, I would like to thank Ms. Monika Bucheli of the Chronos Publishing House, and Dr. Hans-Lukas Kieser, who from the earliest days of this project cooperated with me and rendered their advise on various aspects of the book.

Contents

Maps

1. Map of Urfa / *82*
2. Map of Historical Armenia:
Armenian-populated provinces of the Ottoman Empire / *189*
3. The 1915 Armenian Genocide in the Turkish Empire / *191*
4. Transportation and relocation routes of the Armenian orphans
through the Near East (1922–1923) / *193*

"He Who Saves a Life, Saves the Whole World"[1]

Ara Ghazarians[*]

I n every human catastrophe, when despair overcomes hope, there always emerge souls of exceptional qualities who revive shattered lives and communities and restore faith. Jakob Künzler, the author of this book, was one such individual. His five decades-long calling to attend to and save the lives of thousands of Armenians and other minorities during the World War I genocide and after is testimony to the human spirit. In 1899, Künzler arrived in Urfa[2], a polyglot and multi-ethnic,[3] wealthy Ottoman commercial and agricultural city. Later in Syria and Lebanon, Jakob Künzler stood by his adopted people, the Armenians, as their "guardian angel." Today, more than a century after his arrival in Urfa, the legacy of this "apostle of our times"[4] is cherished and immortalized in the memories of thousands of survivors of the Armenian Genocide and their descendents.

Künzler's first exposure to the East and the Armenians was based on his reading in 1897 of *Am dunkeln Strom* [On the Banks of the Dark River] by the American Deborah Alcock.[5] Based on real-life characters and events, it vividly portrays the suffering of the Armenian people during the Hamidian massacres of 1894-1896 and the Armenian massacres and holocaust,[6] particularly in Urfa in December 1895. The book left a lasting impression on the young Künzler. In May 1899, while an employee at the Basel municipal hospital,[7] Künzler was offered a job at the Deutsche Orient-Mission[8] hospital in Urfa, which was established by the renowned German physician and humanitarian Johannes Lepsius. Künzler accepted it unhesitatingly. On November 10, 1899, after an emotional homage to his mother's gravesite,[9] Künzler departed his native Switzerland for Urfa, a city with deep biblical roots on the fringes of the Mesopotamian desert. Jakob Künzler's journey to the East turned out to be remarkable. Unlike many other missionaries whose assignments are relatively uneventful and short-term, Künzler's proved to be tumultuous and lasted a lifetime.

Upon his arrival, Künzler immediately and enthusiastically assumed his medical responsibilities under two Swiss nationals, Dr. Hermann Christ, the chief physician of the mission, and his future successor, Dr. Andreas Vischer. Heading an Armenian staff[10] of physicians, pharmacists, and nurses, Künzler assumed the directorship of the mission hospital upon the departure of Dr. Vischer. On November 7, 1905, in Safed, he married Elisabeth Bender, the daughter of a German missionary.[11] A trained and skilled nurse, she became not just a lifelong companion to Künzler but also a staunch supporter and comrade with whom he weathered many storms and challenges.

Two distinct periods can be identified in Künzler's life as a missionary and medical doctor in the East: the Urfa years (1899-1922) and the Lebanon years (1923-1949). The record of Künzler's accomplishments in Urfa is impressive and rich. Conversant in Turkish, Arabic, Kurdish, and Armenian, he bridged many communities with his dedicated service, outgoing character, and integrity. Like many who banked on the promises ushered in by the Young Turk revolution of 1908, Künzler also became disappointed as the true intentions of the new leaders of the Ottoman Empire began to surface. After the Adana massacres of 1909, it became clear to him that new calamities were looming on the horizon.

With the reform programs mandated by the Treaty of Berlin (1878) dissipated, World War I provided the great opportunity for the Young Turk leadership to implement the Armenian

Genocide. As the "final solution" to the Armenian Question got underway throughout entire eastern Anatolia, streams of orphans and widows began flooding onto the streets of Urfa, a transfer point to the Mesopotamian desert. Despite all the obstacles created for him by the local Turkish authorities, Künzler continued to direct the mission hospital as well as establish an orphanage in Urfa[12] with perseverance and iron will. Over the years, orphaned Armenian children and young girls freed from the Istanbul harems after a decree in 1918 found refuge in the orphanage. Künzler, his wife, and other missionaries— prominent among them the Danish Karen Jeppe[13] and the Americans Corinna Shattuck[14] and Effie Chambers[15]—endangered their lives assisting the refugees wandering in the streets of Urfa. Künzler's wife and others also conducted many search-and-rescue missions to collect Armenian orphans and hide them under their own roofs. At the height of the massacres throughout the Ottoman Empire, Künzler also witnessed the heroic Armenian resistance of Urfa (September 29-October 23, 1915), which concluded with the destruction, plundering, and virtual extermination of the Armenian community.[16]

The armistice of 1918 and the defeat of the Central Powers, of which the Ottoman Empire was a member, did not end the suffering of the Armenians. An enormous challenge was emerging: the saving and protection of more than 132,000[17] orphans—mainly Armenian[18] but also Assyrian, Syrian, Greek, and Kurdish—scattered throughout Asia Minor and the Near East.

In 1920, after a short retreat to Switzerland, the Künzlers responded to their calling again. Upon their return to Urfa, they organized and carried out the evacuation of more than 8,000 Armenian orphans[19] to safety in Syrian towns, some of which constitute part of present-day Lebanon. It was during this heroic undertaking that the couple was nicknamed *Papa* and *Mama* Künzler, terms of endearment that they cherished and carried for the rest of their lives. This major humanitarian operation marked the beginning of the second period of the Künzlers' life service, this time under the auspices of the American Near East Relief (NER) organization.[20]

Referring to this chapter of his life as the "most precious and rewarding," Künzler and his wife attended to the needs of tens of thousands of Armenian orphans and widows. As the NER representative, he canvassed the entire Lebanese countryside. He assumed the directorship of the American orphanage in Ghazir,[21] where an estimated 1,400 orphans, mostly girls, were sheltered. Simultaneously, the Künzlers initiated and engaged in a series of projects, including houses for the blind[22] in Ghazir (1922) and Maameltein (1923); infirmary in Azouniyeh; summer retreat projects for orphans in Zahleh; residential buildings in Ashrafiyeh (1930-1939); and the School for the Deaf and Mute (1946).[23] His many duties included relocating refugees from tent cities, providing medical and educational programs about malaria and tuberculosis, and running soup kitchens[24] for orphans and widows. In the late 1920s, Künzler also supervised water supply canalization from Rihaniyeh to Nor Marash to Aleppo to Shtora in Lebanon, where the foundation of new Armenian villages were taking shape.[25] Furthermore, Künzler also engaged in procuring and providing the needy with thousands of tons of flour and seedlings of various crops.[26] Künzler even assumed the responsibility of procuring and distributing Gambusa affinis— in various tributaries in Lebanon, known for having the Anopheles as its diet—which protected the waters from malaria-breeding mosquitoes.[27]

Aware of the challenges facing his "children's" future, Künzler also developed vocational training for the younger orphans. As early as 1923, with the help of an Armenian friend from Urfa,[28] Künzler established a rug factory. In six years, the Armenian orphans (mostly young girls) produced 3,240 rugs. In appreciation of the unconditional support and assistance of Americans, 400 orphan girls worked eighteen months to weave what came to be called the Ghazir Rug,[29] which was presented to President Calvin Coolidge on Christmas Day in 1925 by Dr. John Finlay, the vice president of the NER.[30] The publicity generated by the presentation of the Ghazir Rug resulted in contributions of $4 million[31] in one day, couple of weeks after the annual international fundraiser, Golden Rule Sunday,[32] and it doubled the amount collected in previous years. The rug factory, the first of its kind in Lebanon, was visited by the president of Lebanon, who bestowed upon Künzler the Lebanese Order of Merit, one of several honors and awards by various countries he received in his lifetime.

In addition to the administrative aspects of his projects, Künzler also undertook the difficult task of raising funds for the institutions entrusted to him. Prior to World War I, the Swiss-Armenian Friendship Society [*Bund schweizerischer Armenierfreunde*] provided funds to sustain Künzler's services. With its entry onto the scene in 1915, the Near East Relief organization alleviated most of the Künzlers' financial concerns into the post-War years. When the Near East Relief operation ceased in 1930, Künzler appealed to his comrades-in-faith at the Swiss-Armenian Friendship Society and other missionary circles in Europe to sustain a number of projects in Lebanon.[33] With the help of several notable people—including Dr. Emanuel Riggenbach, the executive secretary of the Swiss-Armenian Friendship Society—the group played a major role in alleviating Künzler's heavy financial burdens. In a period of about eleven years (1932-1944), Künzler was able to raise about 320,000 in Lebanese gold, an average of 26,000 per year.[34] Künzler also generated donations during his travels around Switzerland and through the numerous articles and essays he wrote. Most of those funds were allocated for the relocation of Armenian refugees from tent cities into newly built structures. Künzler built more than 300 units.

On May 19, 1939, in recognition of the Künzlers' four decades-long humanitarian service, the Armenian community of Beirut paid tribute to this exceptional couple. A jubilee, organized by representatives from all segments of the Armenian population and institutions, was held at the Memorial Hall. It was attended by the Künzlers' German, Swiss, and Lebanese colleagues; representatives of the Armenian churches; community leaders; and survivors of the Armenian genocide. One after the other, speakers highlighted the fruits of the Künzlers' accomplishments with words of gratitude for their invaluable humanitarian mission. At the conclusion of the evening, Künzler spoke briefly in Armenian, English, and German, thanking many by name and sharing an encounter with the Armenians shortly upon his arrival in Urfa in 1899. It epitomizes his feelings and belief in the Armenian people. He said:

> After what I experienced, I had felt that I had been summoned from the Heavens . . . The Lord had shown me the path . . . [and] led me to a people, who, despite all adversities and miseries, had resolved to remain faithful to their God and the Lord . . . Isn't this the same people who just a couple of years ago [1894-1896] had been subjected to horrible massacres? Their villages razed, plundered, and tens of thousands massacred. And yet, this very people, with resolute faith in God, continue to remain hopeful that better days are yet to come and that they will be more felicitous. God dispatched me to such a people so that I can attend to their wounds as their true brother.
>
> Thus, I resolved to serve that people as a true brother. Ever since, I have come to deeply believe that *all barbaric schemes to destroy the Armenian people will always be destined to fail.*[35]

Jakob Künzler died on January 15, 1949, surrounded by his immediate family in Ghazir, thousands of miles away from his native Switzerland. Two days later, as a terrible storm raged outside, throngs of people—schoolchildren; the blind; friends, young and old; and representatives of the government, embassies, missions, churches, and relief organizations—assembled at the Presbyterian Anglo-American Church in Beirut to pay their final respects to an extraordinary figure.[36] Multilingual eulogies (read in Arabic, Armenian, German, English, and French) speak to the greatness of Jakob Künzler and his humanitarian service, life, and legacy; and the gratitude and deep appreciation of a multi-ethnic community for a modest and yet noble life lived to the fullest.[37] Künzler's wife,

Elisabeth, continued their work for two more decades. She died on January 9, 1968, at ninety-three.

In the Land of Blood and Tears

My first encounter with Jakob Künzler took place a few years ago when I came across *Papa Kuenzler and the Armenians*, a biographical narrative written by Ida Alamuddin, one of the Künzlers' daughters. The more I read, the more I became fascinated with his character and heroic efforts in Urfa during the Armenian Genocide and his Herculean and invaluable services to the needy and destitute survivors.

Although I was aware of the humanitarian deeds of several missionaries, travelers, diplomats, and journalists of various nationalities, Künzler's experience stood out for its remarkable achievements. Unlike many, he stayed with the genocide survivors and helped them build their lives in the post-World War I Middle East.

My curiosity led me to further research on Künzler and his legacy, which guided me to the discovery of his *Im Lande des Blutes und Tränen* [In the Land of Blood and Tears], which was published in 1921. Upon inquiries from scholars in the field, it soon became evident that *Im Lande des Blutes und Tränen* is perhaps one of the most important works available in the German language.[38] Künzler's narrative occupies a special place among other first-person accounts. It stands out for its clarity and objectivity and is testimony to the premeditated nature of the Armenian Genocide, first perpetrated in the early decades of the twentieth century by the Young Turks and concluded in the formative years of the Turkish republic.

This first English edition of *In the Land of Blood and Tears* is based on the second and third German editions published in Switzerland in 1999 and 2004.[39] Künzler guides the reader through various stages of the developments in Urfa: before, during, and after World War I. Through a selective portrayal of encounters with people from different walks of life—commoners, government officials, and community leaders—Künzler immortalizes thousands of lives, those who perished and those who survived. Künzler also provides insight into the mentality of the Armenians as a people and offers his thoughts and recommendations to overcome their shortcomings. He describes the racist mentality, laced with religious fanaticism, of the ruling Young Turk elite and its representatives, who brought the millennia-old civilization of the Armenian people to the brink of extinction.

Two pieces precede the main text. The first, an introduction by Swiss historian and scholar Dr. Hans-Lukas Kieser, provides a brief biography of Jakob Künzler and sheds light on the activities of the missions stationed in Urfa during World War I and the various aspects of the Armenian Genocide. The second, an essay by Dr. Vahakn N. Dadrian, examines the Armenian resistance in Urfa, its heroic beginnings and tragic fate; and he sheds light on the premeditated nature of the genocide as the "final solution" to the Armenian Question.

A few supplementary materials accompany the text. These include original photographs from the life and experiences of the Künzlers from Switzerland to Urfa and Ghazir, Lebanon. A set of four maps include: the administrative divisions of the Ottoman Empire with a focus on the Armenian-populated provinces; The Armenian Genocide in the Ottoman Empire; the collection and transportation route of the Armenian orphans and their settlement in Lebanon; and the map of Urfa around 1900, prior to its destruction. Two bibliographies include, first, selected works on Urfa in Armenian, German, Turkish, and English; and a second presents books and articles by Jakob Künzler. Hopefully they will stimulate further research on Künzler's life and legacy and the Armenian Genocide in general, and the fate of the Urfa Armenians in particular. The Armenian names mentioned in the text are in Western Armenian; the Turkish person and place names are in Turkish transliteration styles. The annotations, other than those marked with *(JK)* for Jakob Künzler and *(G)* for Goltz, are those of the editor.

It has been almost sixty years since the passing of Jakob Künzler. He lived a turbulent and uncommonly rewarding life.

He saw the demise of the Ottoman Empire and emergence of the Turkish Republic. Living in Urfa for a quarter of a century (1899-1922), including the World War I years, Künzler was an eyewitness to the Armenian Genocide, the uprooting of an entire nation from its three millennia-old ancestral homeland, death marches, and deportations.

Today, Urfa, like hundreds of once-thriving Armenian communities in Turkey, is void of its Armenian population: its historical and religious sites desecrated and destroyed; its villages razed; and the remnants of its population forcefully proselytized and deported. All bear testimony to the darkest depths of "man's inhumanity to man." Despite all adversities and with unshakable faith and iron determination, Künzler remained loyal to his calling and supreme principles: the unbound and indiscriminate love and service to humanity. Absent in body, Jakob Künzler and his wife Elisabeth are present in spirit and live through the lives of countless descendents of the Armenian Genocide survivors who owe their gift of life to the couple. Their memory and legacy shall live in the hearts and minds of the Armenian people for generations to come.

* Ara Ghazarians, curator of the Armenian Cultural Foundaiton in Arlington, holds a PhD in sociology from Northeastern University in Boston, Massachusetts. He has worked as an editorial assistant and manager for the *Armenian Review* (1987-91), and director of resources and archives at the Zoryan Institute (1989-90). He has compiled bibliographies and translated several articles and books, including *Hakob Karapents' Bibliography* (1999), and *Bibliography of Armenian Periodicals, Monographic Series and Resources Materials* (2000); *International Trade and the Armenian Merchants in the Seventeenth Century* by Vahan Baibourtian (2004); edited works, including *Armenia 1915: What the German Imperial Government Concealed from Its Subjects; The Slaughter of a Civilized People at the Hands of the Turks* by Heinrich Vierbücher (2006); *Murad of Sepastia* by Mikayel Varandian (2006); and *The Widening Circle and Other Early Short Stories* by Hakob Karapents (2007).

Notes

[1] The title, a paraphrase, extols us to save lives unconditionally and without any limitations as stated in two major sacred Scriptures. In the Babylonian Talmud, Tractate Sanhedrin 4:C: "If a person saves a single soul, Scripture imputes to him/her as though he/she had saved the whole world;" and in the Qu'ran Sura 5:32: "And if anyone saved a life, it would be as if he saved the life of all mankind."

[2] Urfa, Urha, Al-Ruha, ancient Edessa, and presently Sanliurfa (Urfa the Glorious) is known as the City of Prophets and located between the Tigris and Euphrates rivers in the southeast of present-day Turkey, about twenty miles north of the biblical city of Harran. For more on the origins and history of ancient Urfa, see H. S. Ep'rikian, *Patkerazard Bnashkharhik Bararan, hator arajin* [Illustrated Geographical Dictionary, Volume 1]. (Venetik-S. Ghazar, 1903-1905), 647-54; and Rev. Ephraim Jernazian, *Judgment Unto Truth: Witnessing the Armenian Genocide* (New Brunswick, 1990), 35-37.

[3] Under Greek rule, Urfa was a predominantly Muslim city and home to a number of ethnic groups, including Armenians, Syrian Christians (Süryani), Jews, and Kurds. Population estimates vary. According to Vital Cuinet [*La Turquie d'Asie*] (Paris, 1892), the Christian community numbered no fewer than 12,000. Based on missionary reports, the city's population in the late nineteenth century is estimated to have been about 30,000 Muslims and 20,000 Christians. Of the Christians, missionaries approximated that about 12,000, were Armenian Orthodox; 1,200, Armenian Catholics; 2,000, Armenian Protestants; and 5,000 of Syriac faith, about 1,000 of whom were Jacobite rite. See Hans-Lukas Kieser, "Le petit monde autour d'un hôpital missionnaire à Urfa, 1897– 1922", in François Georgeon et Pal Dumont (eds.), *Vivre dans l'Empire ottoman. Sociabilités et relations intercommunautaires (XVIII–XXe siècles)* [Life in the Ottoman Empire: Socialization and Intercommunal Relations (18th-20th centuries)]. (Paris, Editions l'Harmatan, 1997), 213-36.

[4] His Holiness Catholicos Karekin I of the Great See of Cilicia delivered a message of gratitude on the occasion of the 40th jubilee celebration held for Jakob Künzler in Beirut on May 19, 1939. For the complete text of the message, see *Zuits'erats'i hayaser Eagop K'iwnts'ler ir hayanpast gortsuneut'ean 40 ameakin art'iw* [Swiss Armenophile Jakob Künzler: On the Occasion of the 40th Jubilee of His Benevolent Service to the Armenians] (Peyrut'-Halep: Tparan "Rot'os", 1946), 1-2.

[5] Deborah Alcock, *Am dunkeln Strom*. Translated by E. von Feilitzsch. Berlin-Westend: Verlag der akademischen Buchhandlung, W. Faber & Co.) [1897].

[6] For eyewitness accounts of the Urfa massacre, see Karapet Kilejian, *Edesioy soskali depk'ě* [The Horrible Incident of Edessia]. (Bulgaria,

1904); *Diwts'aznakan Urfa ew ir hayordinerĕ* [Heroic Urfa and Her Armenian Offsprings] (Beirut: Tparan Atlas, 1955), 341-423; Edwin Munsell Bliss, *Turkey and the Armenian Atrocities: A Reign of Terror. From Tartar Huts to Constantinople Palaces. Centuries of Oppression—Moslem and Christian—Sultan and Patriarch—Broken Pledges Followed by Massacre and Outrage* (New York: Hibbard & Young, 1896); Frederick Davis Greene, *Armenian Massacres or the Sword of Mohammed, Containing a Complete and Thrilling Account of the Terrible Atrocities and Wholesale Murders Committed in Armenia by Mohammedan Fanatics, Including a Full Account of the Turkish People, Their History, Government, Manners, Customs and Strange Religious Belief,* ed. Henry Davenport Northrop (Philadelphia: National Publishing Co., 1896), 340-44; and "A Dreadful Massacre," *London Daily Telegraph,* January 18, 1896.

[7] At the time of Lepsius' visit, Künzler had been working for four years as an orderly-nurse at the Basel municipal hospital. *Zuits'erats'i hayaser,* 234.

[8] Uwe Feigel, *Das evangelische Deutschland und Armenien: die Armenierhilfe deutscher evangelischer Christen seit dem Ende des 19. Jahrhunderts im Kontext der deutsch-türkischen Beziehungen* [Evangelical Germany and Armenia: The German Evangelical Aid to Armenian Christians Since the End of the 1900s in the Context of German-Turkish Relations] (Göttingen: Vandenhoeck & Ruprecht, 1989).

[9] For more details on Künzler's visit to his mother's grave, see his *Dreissig Jahre Dienst am Orient* [Thirty Years in the Service of the East] (Basel, 1933).

[10] Some of the dedicated personnel who worked with Künzler included Drs. Avetis Jebejian, E. Aroyan, S. Mgrdichian, Tigran Gassabian, A. Abuhayatian, and H. Balian, most of whom were dispersed after the outbreak of WWI—some to the front and others to prison.

[11] Elisabeth Bender received her early education at the Talitha Kumi School in Jerusalem and later trained to be a nurse at the Royal Infirmary in Perth, Scotland. She was the youngest of four children (Maria, Marta, and Gotlieb) of Christian Friedrich Bender from Gernsbach, Germany, a lay missionary and a master road builder who, having been imprisoned in Ethiopia by Emperor Tewodros II, was forced to build cannons, guns, and roads until he was rescued by the British Raj in 1868. Her mother was Yeshimabet Desta "Princess", the daughter of the prominent German botanist, Georg Wilhem Schimper, known for his discoveries in the world of Ethiopian flora and fauna, and Mirtsit, believed to be the daughter of Ras Wube, the ruler of Tigray, with family roots traced back to the Ethiopian Solomonic dynasty. Elisabeth and Jakob Künzler met for the first time in Aleppo during an excursion arranged by the Swiss Consul and married seven years later in Safed on 7 November 1905. The Künzlers were blessed with five children (Arnold, Marie, Ida, Marta and Elibet) and Rosa, an adopted Armenian orphan. Source: The Bender-Künzler Family Tree, cour-

tesy of Künzler family archive and an interview conducted in Arlington, Massachusetts (14 September 2007). Also, Ida Alamuddin, *Papa Kuenzler and the Armenians*. (London: Heinemann, 1970).

[12] Lucia Gassabian, a native of Urfa, became a close confident of the Künzlers. She moved with the Künzlers to Beirut, working at Ghazir and caring for 1,400 Armenian orphans for more than thirty years. *Zuits'eratsi hayaser Eakop K'iwnts'ler*, 238-39.

[13] Karen Jeppe (1876-1935), a Danish missionary of the Johannes Lepsius' Deutsch Orient-Mission, assumed the responsibility of caring for Armenian children in the Millet Khan German Orphanage after the 1895 Urfa massacres. She worked closely with Jakob Künzler and American missionaries stationed in Urfa. Later, she moved to Syria, where she was the representative of the League of Nations in Aleppo (1922-1927), taking care of Armenian Genocide survivors, mostly orphans and widows. She established three workshops in Aleppo to teach various skills to the orphans so they could become self-supportive. On October 25, 1947, Karen Jeppe College was established in Aleppo. See Jeppe's correspondence and other material, December 5, 1922-November 4, 1948, Church National Archives of the Armenian Prelacy of Syria; Karekin Dickran, Danish-Armenian Archives: Photographs (94) from the Karen Jeppe Archives, Gylling, Denmark; Mihran Herardian, "Karen Ep'p'e hayĕ," [Karen Jeppe the Armenian] in *Diwts'aznakan Urfan ew ir hayordinerĕ*, 518-30; Artashes Abeghian, "Arak'elatip Kinĕ" [The Venerable Woman] *Arewelk' Daily* [Aleppo], August 6-8, 1948; Jonas Kauffeldt, "Danes, Orientalism and the Modern Middle East: Perspectives from the Nordic Periphery," Chapter 4 in "Aid Worker to a Devastated People: Karen Jeppe and the Armenians" (doctoral dissertation, Florida State University, 2006), 23-56; and Perchuhi Awetian, *Mis Ep'p'e mayrikĕ* [Miss Jeppe the Mother] (Beirut, 2007).

[14] Corinna Shattuck (1848-1910) was born in Louisville, Kentucky, and worked as a missionary in Syria and Turkey for three years before arriving in Urfa in 1892. Upon witnessing the condition of the destitute remnants of the Armenian community subsequent to the December 1895 Urfa massacre, she single-handedly raised 15,000 in Turkish gold from her friends and associates. She established coed orphanages for 200-300 children and provided them with an education, and she founded a school for 30-40 blind girls. She also set up workshops for 800-1,000 orphans and widows who learned skills, particularly design, needlework, and embroidery. Their goods were sold in England and America, and the income generated helped sustain charitable and educational operations in Urfa. Even Turkish officials respected her enough to call her *Urfanum Meleyi* [Angel of Urfa]. She died on May 22, 1910, shortly upon her return to Boston, Massachusetts. For more on her life and legacy, see Emily C. Peabody, *Corinna Shattuck Missionary Heroine* (Chicago, Illinois: The Woman's Board of Missions of the Interior, 1913); "Corinna Shattuck—Missionary Heroine of Oorfa," *Lives Worth Living: Studies of Women, Biblical and Modern, Especially*

Adapted for Groups of Young Women in Churches and Clubs (Chicago: Chicago University Press, 1915), 130-44.

[15] Mary Effie Chambers (1863-1947), was born in Fremont County, Iowa, and sent by the Congregational Board of Foreign Missions to Kessab, Syria, in 1893. Chambers worked for Corinna Shattuck in Urfa. She returned to the United States in 1912, lectured for the cause of foreign missions, and taught Sunday school in Iowa. See *A Century of Faith 1852-1952*, pamphlet Congregational Church, Tabor, Iowa; "A Letter from Effie Chambers," *The Tabor Beacon (IA)*, January 27, 1910; and *Diwts'aznakan Urfan ew ir hayordinerĕ*, 485-88.

[16] Many surviving Armenians and Syrian Christians returned to Urfa in 1919 and 1920, only to discover that local war and expropriation commissions had transferred their possessions to local Muslim merchants or Kurdish tribal leaders; and they found the character and demography of their native town drastically changed. See Stanford J. Shaw and Ezet K. Shaw, "Resettlement of Refugees in Anatolia," *Turkish Studies Association Bulletin* 22, 1 (1998): 58-90, and Mary C. Holmes, *Between the Lines in Asia Minor* (New York: Fleming H. Revel Company, 1923), 30-32. According to other sources, Armenian and Syrian Christians lived in Urfa until the 1970s. The last Armenian in the city was reported to be a medical doctor who died and was buried there. See, Kerem Öktem, "Creating the Turk's Homeland: Modernizatin, Nationalism and Geography in Southeast Turkey in the Late 19th and 20th Centuries," (paper, Socrates Kokhalis Graduate Workshop, University of Oxford, 2003), 23. According to Öktem at least "200 families of Armenian origin [Islamicized with Turkish names], probably more, live in Urfa," cf. 24.

[17] Alamuddin, *Papa Kuenzler,* 115.

[18] According to Künzler, an "army" of 400 administrative staff, consisting of doctors and nurses, was mobilized to implement this huge undertaking supported by money and material from New York. See Künzler, *Dreissig Jahre Dienst am Orient.*

[19] Of the 8,000 orphans, about 1,000 were from Urfa, 1,000 from Mardin, and 5,000 from Harput (Kharberd). See Künzler, *Dreissig Jahre Dienst am Orient.*

[20] At the urging of Ambassador Henry Morgenthau Sr., the Near East Relief organization was incorporated by an act of the 66th Congress in August 1919 "to prevent the complete destruction of the Armenian population." Between 1915 and 1930, when it ended operations, NER administered $117 million in assistance, delivering food, clothing, and shelter materials and setting up refugee camps, clinics, hospitals, orphanages, and vocational training centers. NER is credited with having cared for 132,000 Armenian orphans scattered from Tbilisi and Yerevan to Constantinople, Beirut, Damascus, and Jerusalem. For a comprehensive history of NER, see

Robert L. Barton, *Story of Near East Relief* (New York: Macmillan, 1930) and the Near East Foundation Web site *www.neareast.org*.

[21] The name Ghazir, "meaning separated area" in the Syrian language, reflects the geographical position of the town east of coastal Jouniyeh and about forty miles north of Beirut.The American orphanage, under the auspices of the Near East Relief agency, operated for about a decade and was closed in 1930 by Congressional mandate. The Danish mission in Jebail and Dr. Lepsius' German Orient-Mission assumed the responsibility of caring for the remaining few hundred orphans.

[22] One source estimated 4,000 cases of blindness in Syria. Most cases are attributed to various diseases, such as trachoma, and exposure to poisonous gases during World War I. See "Ghaziri kuranots'e" [The Ghazir House for the Blind] in *Zuits'erats'i hayaser Eakop K'iwnts'ler*, 166-71. Künzler and his colleagues cared for the blind, educated them using Braille, and helped them develop skills. His colleagues established schools for the blind in Urfa, Malatya, Harput, Adana, and Maameltein. In 1926 the Swiss-Armenian Friendship Society assumed the responsibility of caring for more than 200 blind people under the supervision of Theodore Wieser. Later, a number of handicapped were put under the Society's care. See *Zuits'erats'i hayaser Eakop K'iwnts'ler*, 173-75, and "Blind Refugees in Aleppo: 100 Armenian Children Make 500 Mile Trip from Harput," *New York Times*, September 7, 1922.

[23] The Künzlers, with the support of the Swiss-Armenian Friendship Society president Dr. Emanuel Riggenbach, led in the construction of housing units for Armenian Genocide survivors. The League of Nations initiated house-building projects in Beirut, Damascus, Aleppo, and Alexandrette. From 1931 to 1946, hundreds of one- and two-room units were built. These housing blocks carried such names as Maria Magdalena (named after a paper published in Switzerland); villages in Switzerland; children of various benefactors; and Society officers. See reports and pictures on the project in *Mitteilungen über Armenien*, Dr. E. Riggenbach, ed. Also see *Zuits'erats'i hayaser Eakop K'iwnts'ler*, 182-99.

[24] From 1932-1943, Elisabeth Künzler administered the free-lunch program for 1,500 children in the Nor Marash neighborhood of Beirut, where she had established a nursery school. *Zuits'erats'i hayaser Eakop K'iwnts'ler*, 196-97.

[25] Ibid., 198-99.

[26] Ibid., 200-21.

[27] Ibid., 202-03.

[28] Hovhannes Tashjian, one of Künzler's colleagues from Urfa and a rug expert, introduced the idea of establishing a rug factory. Künzler saw it as a way of guaranteeing jobs and economic future for the mostly girl orphans, who would also be able to support their husbands upon marriage.

Künzler received $400 from the NER as seed money to launch the project. See *Zuits'erats'i hayaser Eakop K'iwnts'ler*, 162-66.

[29] The Coolidge or Ghazir rug was modeled after a Persian Isfahan rug in the Dresden Museum collection in Germany. The rug was eleven-feet-seven inches by eighteen-feet-five-inches. See Hagop Martin Deranian, "Calvin Coolidge and the Armenian Orphan Rug" (paper, Armenian Rug Society Symposium, New York, 1982) and reprinted in *Congressional Record* 130, no. 49 (April 24, 1984): S4715-16.

[30] See letter from President Coolidge to Near East Relief, December 4, 1925, in Alamuddin, *Papa Kuenzler*, 137-38.

[31] Ibid., 165.

[32] Relief worker Charles C. Vickery initiated the idea of the Golden Rule Sunday, designating December 5 as the day for making contributions to the International Golden Rule Sunday Committee. The project, which lasted from 1923 to1929, asked Americans to eat only a one-course meal, similar to "a simple orphanage meal" on Golden Rule Sunday and to contribute the money saved to the NER fund. See Suzanne S. Moranian, "The American Missionaries and the Armenian Question: 1915-1925" (doctoral dissertation, University of Wisconsin-Madison, 1994), 214-25; Vickery, "Golden Rule Sunday: Earthquakes and Orphans in Armenia; A Thanksgiving Season in America," *The American Review of Review* 74 (December 1926): 591-99; and Mabell S. C. Smith, "Civic Cooperation in the International Golden Rule Campaign," *The American City Magazine* 31 (November 1924): 482-85. The publicity also led to large orders for the rug factory in Ghazir. See Alamuddin, *Papa Kuenzler*, 137-38.

[33] Jakob Künzler's "Husk' bank," [Closing Words], *Zuits'erats'i hayaser Eakop K'iwnts'ler*, 41.

[34] Ibid., 232.

[35] Ibid., 233-34.

[36] The main eulogy at Künzler's funeral was delivered by Bishop Khoren Paroyian (who would become Catholicos Khoren I) on behalf of the Armenian Catholicosate of the Holy See of Cilicia. Eulogies were also delivered by representatives from the Protestant, Protestant-Armenian, and Catholic Armenian communities. See "Mah ew mahagrut'iwn Dokt'. Eagop K'iwnts'leri," [Death Notice and Obituary of Doc. Jakob Künzler] *Hask* 18, t'iw 1, (Hunuar, 1949): 29-30; *Zart'onk'*, 20 Hunuar 1949; and "Hamazgayin hugharkaworut'iwn ew t'aghum Tk't'. Eak'op K'iwnts'leri," [National Funeral and Interrment of Doc. Jakob Künzler], *Aztag Orat'ert'*, January 19, 1949.

[37] Künzler is buried in the French Evangelical Church Cemetery on Rue Damas [Damascus Road], which has graves that date back to 1870. Künzler's headstone is adorned with an Armenian cross and engraved:

"Diakon Jacob Kuenzler (Papa Kuenzler), Father of the Armenian Orphans —Born in Hundwill Switzerland 8 March 1871, Died in Ghazir, Lebanon 15 January 1949." It includes a Bible verse: "Blessed are the Dead in the Lord. They rest from their labor and their works do follow them, Revelation 14:13."

[38] Among other German-speaking witnesses were Heinrich Vierbücher (1893-1933), an activist, lecturer, and member of the German Peace Society, who lived and served in wartime Ottoman Turkey in 1914-1917. As the interpreter for German Field Marshal Otto Liman von Sanders in Constantinople, he traveled throughout Turkey and was an eyewitness to the Armenian Genocide. Vierbücher provides in vivid colors and condemns with the strongest language the Turkish government's slaughter of more than 1.5 million Armenians and the "co-responsibility" and complicity of the Imperial German war government. See Vierbücher, *Armenien 1915: Was die kaiserliche Regierung den deutschen Untertanen verschwiegen hat: die Abschlachtung eines Kulturvolkes durch die Türken* (Hamburg-Bergedorf: Fackelreiter-Verlag, 1930). On his legacy and the German pacifist movements see, Helmut Donat, "Heinrich Vierbücher and the Armenian Massacres as Seen by the German and International Peace Movement (1895-1933)," in Vierbücher, *Armenia 1915: What the German Imperial Government Concealed from Its Subjects; The Slaughter of a Civilized People at the Hands of the Turks.* (Arlington, Massachusetts: Armenian Cultural Foundation, 2006), 99-128.

[39] Künzler, *Im Lande*, 2nd and 3rd ed., Hans-Lukas Kieser, editor, (Zürich, Switzerland: Chronos, 1999 and 2004).

This edition of
In the Land of Blood and Tears

Hans-Lukas Kieser*

After the 1980 military putsch in Turkey many fled to Switzerland. I was then a student of history in Basel and met many young refugees, Turks and Kurds, who lived in the same quarter as I. At the same time I came across a small, yellowing book in the estate of my father. The author was the Swiss orderly Jakob Künzler, who had been made an honorary doctor of medicine by the University of Basel in late 1947 and died in 1949. In Künzler I had found a fellow Swiss with impressive experience in the multiethnic and multireligious community of Armenians, Turks, and Kurds. He lived almost a quarter century in the Ottoman city of Urfa (1899–1922) and afterwards, until his death, in Lebanon (1923–1949). Urfa is in the north of Mesopotamia and the southeast of Turkey, near today's Syrian border. The city and the region of Urfa were marked by many cultures in Ottoman times: Turkish, Armenian, Kurdish, Arabic, and Syrian-Christian as well as small Jewish and Greek communities. In the winter of 1919-1920, during his vacation back home in Basel, Künzler wrote his Experiences [*Erlebnisse*] in wartime Urfa. From a sense of responsibility, which he felt as a unique witness to the terrible events in this region, he decided in the spring of 1920—despite the opposition of close relatives who feared a reprisal—to publish them. The Tempel Publishing House in Potsdam published them a year later.[1]

In the Land of Blood and Tears tells the story of war and suffering as it was experienced in the vicinity of Urfa. It is the
unedited record of a politically neutral observer of the first
genocide organized with modern means against its own
nationals, namely that of the new Turkish wartime government against Ottoman Armenians in 1915. The historic significance of this document is, therefore, great because it describes
from up close the meaning of the bureaucratic term "systematic deportations," which were telegraphically guided and
watched over by the commissars of the central authority. As in
Nazi Germany, the term did not mean the resettling of a people
from the region they inhabited. It meant simply their extermination. Künzler's eyewitness account soberly documents the
regional and local implementation of a concealed policy of
destruction. In contrast to the *Shoah* (Jewish Holocaust) in the
prevailing European historiography, the fact of the Armenian
genocide has not been generally accepted and openly declared
to be a fact. The almost total neglect of the subject in German
school textbooks is a cause for concern.[2]

Künzler's Path Through Crisis Shaken Turkey

Jakob Künzler was born in 1871 in Hundwil, Appenzell Ausser-
rhoden. His family was without means; and as a child he often
worked. His father died when he was six and his mother when
he was eleven, after which he grew up with relatives. After an
apprenticeship as a carpenter, he went to Basel, where he
received training as an orderly. Through the mediation of the
Basel physician Hermann Christ, who had traveled to Urfa in
1898, the Berlin missionary Rev. Johannes Lepsius approached
Künzler and won him over for his Armenian Relief Organization. Jakob Künzler went to Urfa in 1899 as a relief organization worker, who assisted Hermann Christ in his medical
work. That same year Lepsius re-established the organization
directed by him with headquarters in Berlin as the Deutsche
Orient-Mission [German Mission of the East]. Künzler's clinic,
which was set up in 1897 by the Zürich physician Josephine

Zürcher, became the bay of tranquility for medical work in Urfa. The "Swiss Hospital" was a part of the Deutsche Orient-Mission until the end of the war and remained a Swiss institution until it was dissolved in 1922. The hospital was only able to pursue its work thanks to the substantial Swiss support it received from philanthropic circles in Basel.

Anti-Armenian pogroms were the reason for the European relief organization activity in "interior Turkey." In Urfa at the end of 1895, there already was, as the American missionary Corinna Shattuck called it at the time, a "holocaust," in which 3,000 Armenians were doused with kerosene and burned in the large municipal cathedral. A similar number of men fell victim at the same time to butchery in the streets and houses. The Jews were charged with the macabre task of removing the bodies from the city.[3] The news of pogroms in which 100,000 fell victim in the Ottoman eastern provinces created a storm of outrage in broad circles of the European and Anglo-Saxon world in 1895 and 1896. This led to no foreign policy decisions, but it created for the first time a formative impression of Turkey. The shock of the 1895 pogroms provoked stereotypical, long-acting images of a "bloodthirsty sultan," "barbaric Islam," and "brutal Turkdom" among many Europeans and Americans. Some others, namely German propagandists, represented the Armenians as a "degenerate race" and the "Jews of the Orient" who plotted conspiracies and made noise in the international arena against the fighting, patriotic majority in Turkey.[4] The horror of that experience motivated a relatively small group of people (like Lepsius, Zürcher, Christ, and Künzler) to sustained activity and a lasting commitment to human rights, minorities, and addressing religious conflicts in Ottoman Turkey. This group displayed a relatively different perception, which was fed by their own experiences in the area. They were connected with the Middle East for a lifetime.

In Great Britain and Switzerland in 1896, it was almost considered de rigueur to belong to the transconfessional, pro-Armenian movement. Many Swiss local politicians and church and state officials profiled themselves at the many events presented throughout the country. Free-church circles, Jewish personalities (among them at least one rabbi), socialists, and Freemasons expressed solidarity with the movement. Behind their support were common values and views, as well as a marked internationalist human-rights impulse directed against racial hatred, nationalism, and imperialism. But in 1896-1897, representatives sent out from the newly founded relief organizations met with no effective support for their activities from diplomats, with the exception of the British. German diplomats refused any protection for those Germans who were involved with the politically delicate subject of Armenians and who traveled through the Ottoman eastern provinces. In contrast, a few years later they took pains to rein in the missions posts, like the one in Urfa, which were created for their mission policy.[5]

Jakob Künzler became a mainstay of the small mission of Johannes Lepsius, which, at the urging of the American Protestant mission in 1896, had selected Urfa as its center. With his pragmatism and dependability, Künzler provided the counterbalance to the restless idealist and publicist Lepsius. For three decades, Lepsius not only provided aid for victims with great personal dedication, he also achieved an inestimable publicity for the Armenian cause.[6] Künzler was also a talented writer. His strength lay in the direct portrayal of personal experience, whose meaning went far beyond the personal sphere. Künzler published countless articles in the mission organ, *Der Christliche Orient*, but also in other newspapers and magazines as well as a dozen books and brochures.[7] He spoke Turkish, Kurdish, Armenian, and Arabic. As an outgoing human being, he made contact with people from the most varied groups in the lively and tension-filled region of Urfa. In 1901, for instance, we meet him as a guest in the tent of the transregionally dominant Kurdish leader Ibrahim Paşa.[8] He founded a school for the Süryani (Syrian Christians) (Chapter 1). He had close friends among Kurds, Turks, Arabs, Süryani, and, naturally, the Armenians who were the primary beneficiaries of his work. His texts are not free of the stereotypes of the time, but they are generally distinguished by an open view toward the religious, social, or ethnically *other*, a perspective and perceptions unencumbered by party and ideology. And they contain rich details about daily life.

In spite of the thoroughly bloody fin de siècle and its anti-Armenian sentiment, life among Christians and Muslims in Urfa, as in the rest of Ottoman Turkey, settled back to normal—at least on the surface. The mission hospital under Swiss direction acted explicitly as a place of peacemaking and interreligious encounter, but not conversion. It soon was visited by women, men, and children of various groups and circles. On the eve of World War I, Urfa had about 60,000 inhabitants, with a two-thirds Muslim majority consisting of Turks, Kurds, and Arabs; and a Christian minority of Armenians and Süryani. Of the minorities, more than 2,000 belonged to the Protestant community, more than 1,000 were Catholic, and the overwhelming majority were members of the Armenian Apostolic (13,000) and Syrian Christian (4,000)[9] churches.

In 1908 the previously clandestine-operating Young Turks (Unionists) dethroned the Sultan and reinstated the Ottoman constitution of 1876. The Armenian Dashnak Party, against whose splinter groups Abdul Hamid had reacted with extreme violence, was suddenly a legal party. They formed an electoral alliance with the Unionists, and their revolutionaries were now considered heroes of freedom. The Young Turks expressed remorse for the massacres of the 1890s; they could brand them as the infamous deeds of the ancien régime. A vision was nurtured of a common future with equal rights in a modern, constitutional Ottoman Empire. The reaction of Islamist forces was not long in coming. They felt themselves challenged by the equality, the self-confident conduct, and the economic-cultural dynamic of the Christian "wards" (*zimmi*) who had been subordinate for hundreds of years and, as in 1895, would strive for dominance in the eastern provinces and in Cilicia (Adana). The pogroms of spring 1909 were limited to the region of Adana but threatened to become a conflagration were it not for the decisive Young Turk intervention against the reactionaries in the capital and, especially, in Urfa. In contrast, the official behavior in Adana and other cities was ambivalent and raised uncomfortable questions with respect to future Turkish-Armenian coexistence. However, in spite of nagging doubts, hardly anyone could have guessed that the Young Turk party would set genocide in motion six years later. The Unionists of 1908 were no liberal fighters for the constitution and civil rights; they were power-hungry patriots, who were no longer interested in a multiethnic "Ottomanism" but strove increasingly for an uncompromising Turkish nationalism. The territorial losses of the empire in the Balkans and the Maghreb [northwestern Africa] led to a dramatic hardening of the regime. From 1913 on, the Unionists ruled dictatorially. Some party members began, as Künzler witnessed (Chapter 2), to talk blithely about the "necessary elimination of the Armenians" because they would stand in the way of the creation of a homogeneous national sphere in Asia Minor, which the rulers saw as their best alternative.

Contemporary Witness of the Genocide Against the Armenians

This is where *In the Land of Blood and Tears* begins. Künzler and, especially, his American mission colleagues, followed with great concern the massive war build-up of the government. Naturally, they were not informed about the secret German-Ottoman agreement, which was signed on August 2, 1914, and viewed by the Young Turk regime with great pride as a prestigious partnership. The agreement provided for Turkish entry into combat in case of a German-Russia war, which had been declared the day before! The regime was looking for war for several reasons. One main reason was thwarting the internationally approved 1914 reforms in the mainly Kurdish and Armenian eastern provinces. These so-called "Armenian Reforms" had been a recurring, but never completed, subject of the Orient policy since the Congress of Berlin (1878). The European inspectors-general for the reforms mentioned by

Künzler were already expelled from the country in August (Chapter 1). In addition to the general mobilization, requisitions, and abolition of the capitulations (special rights for foreigners), there was also a rigorously organized propaganda campaign in preparation for war. These measures did not popularize the war. But in some locations, as in Urfa, they poisoned the interethnic climate. The war propaganda struck an anti-Armenian note early on. At the end of October 1914, under German pressure, the regime provoked the outbreak of war with attacks against Russian Black Sea cities. In December Enver Paşa began an ambitious Russian campaign, which was intended to realize the Great Turkic dream of reuniting the Muslims in Asia Minor and the Caucasus. It widened into a military and human catastrophe. With distorted releases about the Armenian resistance in Van at the end of April 1915 and the Armenians' collaboration with the Russians, the Young Turk regime whipped up the Muslim majority against the Armenian community. In the rear of the unexpectedly difficult Eastern Front, the blanket elimination of the Armenians as internal enemies began.

The recently available teletype messages of the Interior Ministry in the Ottoman State Archive in Istanbul document the telegraphically guided system of the "deportations," which went into effect in spring 1915 in almost all of Asia Minor, far beyond the war zones. For decades the state rationale for the evacuation had been that it was an uncontested military and even humanitarian necessity. While the Interior Ministry correspondence documents general deportations, witnesses on the scene, like Künzler, documented what really happened. These witnesses are therefore of central importance because the archives of the responsible Unionists and their Special Organization [Teşkilatı Mahsusa] were either destroyed or lost. Secret instructions that accompanied the deportation orders can only be circumstantially reconstructed. In contrast to Germany after the Shoah, there has never been unconditional access to the archives. Künzler exposed the decisive roles of officers Halil and Ahmed Bey, who were sent by the Unionist central authority to organize and carry out the destruction of the Armenians in Urfa with the aid of the gendarmes and military and irregular forces (beginning in Chapter 5). There are analogous reports from witnesses in other cities. The deportations were planned as grueling marches accompanied by all kinds of brutality, including sexual, along deliberately labyrinthine routes with the Syrian Desert as a goal. The female witnesses, like those cited by Künzler as credible (Chapter 8), were only able to confide in other women. For Künzler and other witnesses, the death marches were more terrible and "dehumanizing" than all other types of death, especially for the men, who, as a rule, were separated from the women and children, and were the victims of other forms of death. "Without a doubt, the plan and the will were for all the people from Urfa to die in the desert. They were led back and forth so long, that finally there was no one left to be transported" (Chapter 19).

The genocide against the Armenians took place primarily in the summer and fall months of 1915 in the eastern provinces, between the Black Sea and the Syrian Desert. Arnold Toynbee, who as a young historian during World War I had been involved with the fate of the Armenians on behalf of the British government, wrote, at an advanced age, in 1967: "The deportations were deliberately conducted with a brutality that was calculated to take the maximum toll of lives en route. This was the CUP's [Committee for Union and Progress] crime; the deportations were carried out willfully and with calculated brutality, in order to cause the maximum number of deaths. That was the crime of the Unionists. My study left an impression on my mind that was not effaced by the still more cold-blooded genocide, on a far larger scale, that was committed during the Second World War by the Nazis."[10] One must assume a magnitude of a million victims of genocide in 1915-1916.

The modern, mass extermination of life started in the summer of 1915 at Gölcük Lake near Harput, 150 kilometers north of Urfa. There were collective killings there alone of more than 10,000 men, women, and children. Officials hired local Sunni

Kurds as slaughterers with cold weapons, while the Alevi Kurds from the northern-lying Dersim made their autonomous territory into the only collective asylum for the persecuted. Not Künzler, but his American mission colleagues (with whom he was in contact in those years) and the American Consul Leslie Davis, have in writing and with photographs documented the Harput extermination and death camp, as they called them.[11] A people lay "on the slaughtering block," as the highest Armenian cleric of Urfa described to Künzler in tears (Chapter 5). In spite of urgent and unmistakable pleas from missionaries like Künzler, who had turned early on to the consuls in Aleppo (Chapter 4), the European states were preoccupied with the World War and did little or nothing.

Künzler was, as he emphasizes at the beginning of his book, the only neutral eyewitness of wartime Urfa, through which the deportation caravans from the north passed. Like his Danish colleague Karen Jeppe (also an employee of the Deutsche Orient-Mission), he stood in "close contact" not only with the Armenians, but also with official representatives and Kurdish, Arab, Turkish, and Christian-Syrian circles. These manifold connections and insights give his account an unusually broad basis of information. He could draw on his own diaries and probably those of his wife for additional detail (Chapter 4). Künzler's report as well as those of his mission colleague Bruno Eckart (the brother of the director of the German carpet factory, Franz Eckart) and Syrian-Christian Rev. Ephraim Jernazian (who had to act as the Armenian translator for the war tribunal) provide a clear, indelible picture of those years in Urfa.[12]

Besides Zeytun, Van, and Jebel Musa (Musa Dağ), Urfa was practically the only location where the Armenians could put up armed resistance. In contrast to Van, they did so in a desperate, hopeless situation. Most of their leadership had already been murdered. The missionaries strove in vain to make this circumstance clear to the officials, especially the German officer Eberhard Count Wolfskeel von Reichenberg, who led the artillery bombardment (Chapter 18). They were met with silence. The presence of German officers—not only in Urfa—created the impression in the eyes of the population that, in the final analysis, the Germans were responsible for the Turkish participation in the war as well as the elimination of the Armenians. This rumor could only please the Young Turk war regime.

Künzler, Jernazian, and Bruno Eckart recorded their evidence independently from each other. There is a striking difference in the attitude toward the Muslim refugees from the Eastern Front. While Jernazian describes them in a cool and somewhat disrespectful way, Künzler has warm words for them. In fact, in 1916 he started an impressive, large-scale rescue operation to do something about Kurdish suffering. Not without a quiet reproach, he remarked that, indeed, not one European newspaper had taken note of the Kurdish deportations (Chapter 31). Künzler's solidarity with the Kurds, which continued after his departure from Urfa, is often forgotten in the shadow of his main involvement with the Armenians. Jakob Künzler understood his role as a "helper of harried existence in the whole world."[13]

The aid given by the Künzler couple, the Arab servant Ali, Karen Jeppe, Bruno Eckart, the Capuchin monks, and others to the detested Armenians put their lives at stake during the worst of times. Elisabeth Künzler (1875–1968) belonged especially to those courageous "lady missionaries"—teachers, nurses, station leaders, orphan mothers—who, during World War I, displayed an impressive initiative. The universal acclaim accorded Jakob Künzler's service concealed the lesser-known efforts of his wife. If he became despondent, she bolstered him (Chapter 15). On her own initiative when the war began, she gathered money for the Red Crescent with a group of women, including an Armenian, a Turk, a Kurd, and an Arab from Urfa. The Künzlers bought medicine and bandages and sent them to the Eastern Front.[14] Like the Künzlers' later relief operation for the Kurdish evacuees, this initiative also helped to increase the prestige of the gâvur [infidels] from Europe and thereby created more leeway for their own activities. In the eyes of the

Muslim majority, the missionaries had created suspicion for their too exclusive involvement with the Christian minorities.

Beginning in the summer of 1915, Jakob and Elisabeth Künzler operated independently of each other for reasons of their own security. The husband was much more involved with the officials and therefore happy not to know about the often forbidden activities of his wife. She organized a search-and-rescue mission for runaway Armenian girls to Aleppo. With the aid of a Turkish woman friend, she rented two houses and set up an illegal orphanage in 1917 (Chapter 33).[15] Until the hospital was closed by officials, her husband devoted his time to the "medical practice for the poorest," which had assumed "enormous dimensions" since the summer of 1915.[16] His main task from the summer of 1916 on was the care of about 2,500 needy deportees, who had found shelter in and around Urfa. Almost half of the financial support for them came from Basel.

The oppressive burden of witness, the fear of persecution by the gendarmes, and the excess of improvised relief operations were a drain on the health and nerves of the Urfa missionaries. The young American friend of Künzler, Rev. Francis H. Leslie, was the first victim. By June 1915 the news about the extermination of the Armenian people had become a certainty; and the report of the American mission doctor Smith, who had been expelled from Diyarbakır, was in large part responsible. "Mr. Leslie had no peace from that moment on." The gendarmes' interrogation after the elimination of the Armenian district where he had been trapped, the official confiscation of Armenian possessions that had been entrusted to him, and the daily sight of the extermination of Armenians in the streets and on the squares of Urfa drove the young missionary to suicide (Chapter 17). The Danish woman Karen Jeppe risked death when she hid young Armenian men in her house. The Urfa Capuchins paid for the same risk with imprisonment and deportation (Chapter 24). In 1917 Künzler went to Istanbul, accompanying Karen Jeppe, who suffered a nervous breakdown, and Beatrice Rohner from Basel, whose orphanage in Aleppo was shut down by officials. In a letter delivered by a

German officer to the mission directors in Berlin, he [Leslie] wrote wearily on August 8, 1917: "I have been harassed enough for the last two years, I was just four days in jail, and I want to be the first to leave."[17]

With his tribute to the *kadı* [chief justice] of Urfa, Künzler corrected the general impression of the "gruesome Turks" and Muslims. This man, whom Künzler characterized as his best friend, even brother, had had the courage to take a public stance against atrocities committed against Armenians, and he illegally took in Armenian refugees (Chapter 24).

New Approaches and Disappointments

The end of the war in 1918 appeared to bring a chance for a hopeful reconstruction in Urfa and all of Anatolia, where the surviving Armenians who had suffered the most were to be reserved an appropriate homeland (Chapter 43). Künzler also hoped for this (letter to Lepsius, pp. 155-56). The Peace Treaty of Sèvres (August 10, 1920) foresaw an independent Armenia with a substantial Anatolian component. However, different factors made impossible the creation of an internationally approved, multiethnic order in Asia Minor: imperialistic greed, unrealistic Greater Armenia demands, and the concern for a strong Turkey as a bulwark against Bolshevism. Above all, however, was that despite the Turkish defeat in the war, the Young Turk secret organizations in the eastern provinces had an untouched military and administrative base at their disposal. General [Mustafa] Kemal Paşa (Atatürk) organized the Turkish nationalist liberation war, which he represented as a battle of Muslims against foreign invaders and internal traitors, in order to win Kurdish support.

The occupation of Urfa by the British in March 1919 brought with it six months of peace and rapid reconstruction (Chapter 46). Their relief by French troops was not greeted with approval by the Muslims. Künzler's book does not cover those months from fall 1919 to spring 1920, when the Turkish nationalist armed forces wore down the inferior French occupation detachment. From the summer of 1919 on, the Künzlers spent a year in Switzerland. The report by the Basel mission doctor, Andreas Vischer, and the diary of his wife Gertrud Vischer-Oeri fill in these gaps of perception and perspection from the Swiss hospital.[18] They show realities that surprise no one and are not flattering for the myth of national heroism. The main effect of the identification with the "war of liberation" was the final exclusion of the non-Muslim groups from Urfa and almost all of Anatolia as well as the implementation of a monoethnic nationalism that is still fraught with conflict today.

When Künzler returned to Urfa in August 1920, the Kemalist "guerrillas" had the say, and the Christians were intimidated again. Künzler was subjected to gendarmes' persecutions for—imaginary—espionage. Thanks to the regional reservoir of trust that the Künzlers enjoyed, they could set up again, but only preliminarily. Künzler's dream, to continue to work as a self-employed general practitioner in Urfa, failed to clear the very high hurdle set by the government in Ankara (Chapter 64). For years he had performed the work of a doctor and enjoyed the prestige that encompasses it. In addition, one spoke of him as "Dr. Künzler;" Jernazian also calls him that in his book. He signed his own letters with "Br. Jakob Künzler," whereby the "Br." looked remarkably like a "Dr." However, the future of the couple lay in the orphanage work of the Near East Relief financed by the American relief organization in Ghazir, Lebanon. They did this until 1931. Afterwards, they were involved in the care of Armenian widows and in setting up a sanatorium. They stayed in Lebanon for the rest of their lives. "The non-Armenian, who was most often named in our interviews, was Papa Künzler," wrote Donald Miller and Lorna Touryan Miller in their book that tells the story of the genocide against the Armenians from reports of survivors. They are convinced that the Armenians will continue to be thankful for the love and care that Jakob and Elisabeth Künzler bestowed on the poorest of the poor.[19]

The present edition is based on the original text of 1921 and supplemented with four articles by Jakob Künzler from the

Lepsius' newspapers *Der Orient* and *Der Christliche Orient*,[20] two of which were explicitly declared as continuations of the book. These appear in the present edition with sequel chapters numbers in brackets (Chapters 54–64). They cover the last two years of the Urfa Swiss hospital (1920–1922) and the time after the Künzlers' return from home leave. In addition to his service at the hospital, Künzler worked on behalf of the Near East Relief on the transportation of Christian orphans from Turkey to Syria.

The article called "For the Red Crescent" has already been mentioned. In the previously unpublished article, "The Turks and the Armenians: A New Phase" from 1928, Künzler posed the question of reconciliation against the backdrop of the genocide. The—justifiably!—rejected draft of this issue of the magazine *Der Orient*, from which it comes, had the title "Dedicated to the Turks and the Armenians!" Whoever reads it will become aware of how difficult it was, even for the well-informed authors, to handle convincingly the subject of the Armeno-Turkish relations, the genocide, and the question of guilt. The time, not only in Turkey but also in Germany, was not yet ripe for a profound discussion. Even Künzler's article contains questionable trains of thought, which throw a revealing light on the discussions of the time. He uses the terms "punishment," "complicity," and political "loyalty" with questionable simplification and still uses, completely anachronistically, the multiethnic term "Ottoman" for a Turkey which, in 1928 more than ever, celebrated a primitive ethno-nationalism. He rightfully speaks of an "urgently necessary change in the Turkish policy," which, with its "elimination of non-Turkish elements, "instead of reconstruction lead always back to decay."

Künzler's view of Turks and Armenians as brothers and sisters is remarkable, even provocative. Their relationship could be restored simply with an "unprejudiced answer of the question of guilt" and the "absolutely necessary confession." He tellingly asks the question about "such confessors" in Turkey without indicating an answer. Although he is aware of the utopian dimension, he expresses belief in a forgiveness of the two peoples who, since the World War I, have "infinitely with-drawn from each other." Künzler's confession that his highly praised achievement of safely transporting 8,000 Christian orphans to Syria in 1921-1922 was "not the right way" is remarkable. He himself had characterized the work a few years earlier as the most beautiful in his life (see Chapters 57–62). But the right way would have been the construction of a common future on Anatolian soil and thereby the creation of a new basis of trust (Chapter 2). "Every people has a right to exist. Namely, in the place where they are born. Whoever vio-lates this right, commits injustice, which will sooner or later be avenged."

* Hans-Lukas Kieser is an independant historian and Privadozent of Mod-ern History at the University of Zürich. His books include *Turkey Beyond Nationalism* (London: I.B. Tauris, 2006). *Der Völkermord an den Arme-niern, die Türkei und Europa* [The Armenian Genocide, Turkey and Europe] in collaboration with Elmar Plozza. (Zürich: Chronos, 2006). *Der Völkermord an den Armeniern und die Shoah* [The Armenian genocide and the Shoah] in collaboration with Dominik J. Schaller. (Zürich: Chronos, 2003); *Der verpasste Friede: Mission, Ethnie und Staat in den Ostprovinzen der Türkei 1839-1938* [The Missed Peace: Mission, Ethnicity and State in Eastern Provinces of Turkey (1839-1938)] (Zürich: Chronos, 2000).

Notes

[1] According to Hermann Goltz, the title *In the Land of Blood and Tears* was proposed by (General-) Secretary Richard Schäfer, one of the most trusted co-workers of Johannes Lepsius in the "office work" of the Armenian relief organizations and the German Orient Mission.

[2] Concerning the question of official recognition by Switzerland, compare ArbeitsKreis Armenien (pub.), *Völkermord und Verdrängung. Der Genozid an den Armeniern –Die Schweiz und die Shoah* [Mass Murder and Expulsion: The Genocide of the Armenians – Switzerland and the Holo-caust] (Zürich: Chronos, 1998). Fortunately, the situation has substan-tially changed since this introduction was written in 1999. Hans-Lukas Kieser, Elmar Plozza, eds., *Der Völkermord an den Armeniern, die Türkei und Europa* [The Armenian Genocide, Turkey and Europe] (Zürich: Chronos, 2006).

³ Letter from Corinna Shattuck from Urfa on January 24, 1896, to Julia S. Conant, American Board of Commissioners for Foreign Missions, Individual Biographies 54: 21, Houghton Library, Harvard University, Cambridge, Massachusetts. For rich insights into the historical Urfa, see Richard G. Hovannisian, ed., *Armenian Tigranakert/Diarbekir and Edessa/Urfa* [Historic Armenian Cities and Provinces] vol. 6. (Costa Mesa, California: Mazda Publishers, 2006). On the late Ottoman Urfa, including World War I, see my article in the above-mentioned volume entitled "Ottoman Urfa and its Missionary Witnesses," pp. 399-466.

⁴ Compare, for instance, Hans Barth, *Türke, wehre Dich!* [Turk! Defend Yourself] (Leipzig, 1898).

⁵ Compare Hans-Lukas Kieser, ed., *Die armenische Frage und die Schweiz/ La question arménienne et la Suisse (1896–1923),* [The Armenian Question and Switzerland: 1896-1923] (Zürich: Chronos, 1999), and Hans-Lukas Kieser, *Der verpasste Friede. Mission, Ethnic und Staat in den Ostprovinzen der Türkie 1839-1938* [The Missed Peace: Mission, Ethnicity and State in Eastern Provinces of Turkey 1839-1938] (Zürich: Chronos, 2000). Also, in Turkish, *Iskalanmiş Bariş Doğu Vilayetleri'nde Misyonerlik, Etnik Kimlik ve Devlet 1839-1938.* (Istanbul: Iletisim, 2005).

⁶ German-patriotic excesses, especially in 1914, could not diminish his services for long. Among Lepsius' most important publications were: *Armenien und Europa. Eine Anklageschrift wider die christlichen Grossmächte und ein Aufruf an das christliche Deutschland* [Armenia and Europe: An Indictment against the Christian Great Powers and an Appeal to Christian Germany] (Berlin, 1896). *Bericht über die Lage des Armenischen Volkes in der Türkei* [Report about the Atrocities of the Armenian People in Turkey] (Potsdam: Tempel-Verlag, 1916); and the documents collection *Deutschland und Armenien 1914–1918* [Germany and Armenia: 1914-1918] (Potsdam, Tempel-Verlag, 1919).

⁷ Compare the selected bibliography in this book.

⁸ *Der Christliche Orient*, 3 (1902): 65–70.

⁹ Compare *Der Christliche Orient*, 14 (1913): 174. f. The demographic sources are fraught with considerable uncertainty. Compare Raymond H. Kévorkian and Paul P. Paboudjian, *Les Arméniens dans l'Empire Ottoman à la veille du génocide,* [The Armenians in the Ottoman Empire on the Eve of the Genocide] (Paris: Editions d'art et d'histoire, 1992), p. 325.

¹⁰ Arnold J. Toynbee, *Acquaintances* (London: Oxford University Press, 1967), p. 241 f.

¹¹ Among the recently published works are: Leslie A. Davis, *The Slaughterhouse Province: An American Diplomat's Report on the Armenian Genocide, 1915–1917*, edited with an introduction and notes by Susan K. Blair (New Rochelle, New York: A.D. Caratzas, 1989). Henry H. Riggs,

Days of Tragedy in Armenia. Personal Experiences in Harpoot, 1915-1917. (Michigan: Gomidas Institute, 1997).

[12] Ephraim K. Jernazian, *Judgment Unto Truth: Witnessing the Armenian Genocide* (New Brunswick and London: Transaction Publishers, 1990). Bruno Eckart, *Meine Erlebnisse in Urfa* [My Experiences in Urfa] (Potsdam: Tempel-Verlag, 1922). Also in *Der Orient*, (1921): 54–58, 119–26, 133–46, 154–60; and (1922): 20–24.

[13] Compare the dedication of his autobiography published by Paul Schütz in 1951. Its original title *Köbi, Der Lückenbüsser, im Dienste des Lebens* [Köbi: The Stopgap in the Service of the Life] was in the following edition in *Köbi—Vater der Armenier* [Köbi: Father of the Armenians] unchanged. Künzler's daughter Ida wrote in her book about her father: "With the Kurds he had always felt an affinity; like himself, they were of mountain stock; they were natural and unspoilt, a happy people, whose language he had learned and with whom he found it easy to go on." Ida Alamuddin, *Papa Kuenzler and the Armenians* (London: Heinemann, 1970), p. 41.

[14] Compare the article "Für den roten Halbmond" [For the Red Crescent] from 1920 on p. 140 of this book.

[15] The goal of the state orphanages, which in those years were booming, was to turkify and Islamicize the children, regardless of where they came from.

[16] *Der Christliche Orient,* 16 (Oktober 1915): 76.

[17] Lepsius-Archiv Halle, 9028, p. 3. With thanks to Professor Hermann Goltz for making available the letter.

[18] Andreas Vischer, *Erlebnisse eines Schweizerarztes bei den türkischen Nationalisten,* [Experiences of a Swiss Doctor with the Turkish Nationalists] (Basel: Baselr Nachrichten, 1921). Gertrud Vischer-Oeri, *Erinnerungen an Urfa* [Remembrances of Urfa] hectographed, (Riehen, 1967, Universitätsbibliothek Basel).

[19] Donald E. Miller and Lorna Touryan Miller, *Survivors. An Oral History of the Armenian Genocide.* (Los Angeles: University of California Press, 1999), pp. 121 and 130–32.

[20] "Letzte Erlebnisse in der Türkei " [Last Experiences in Turkey], *Der Orient,* (1925): 60–64, 85–91; "Die Türken und die Armenier, eine neue Phase," [The Turks and Armenians: A New Phase] from a draft from the Nr. 5 of *Der Orient* (1928) (Universitätsbibliothek Basel, Lieb Z 256); "Für den roten Halbmond" [For the Red Crescent], *Der Christliche Orient* (1920): 42–44.

Jakob Künzler:
Witness to the Armenian Genocide and Resistance in Urfa

Vahakn N. Dadrian[*]

In December 1899, Jakob Künzler, a Swiss orderly and later physician, arrived in Urfa, (historic Edessa.)[1] For the next quarter century, Künzler and his wife lived through the genocide inflicted on the Armenians of Urfa; ministered to the sick, wounded, and orphaned; and sought to alleviate, through pleadings with local Turkish authorities, the sufferings of the local Armenian population. With his riveting account of his life in Urfa, Künzler represents one of the most powerful extant witnesses to the Turkish atrocities, the characters in charge, and the reasons for the genocide and the Armenian resistance in Urfa.

Künzler's account is invaluable because as a Swiss national he was a neutral. He was also closely associated with Turkish leaders of the region, and his testimony is fully corroborated by other contemporary accounts. In addition, Künzler points out that the Armenian genocide was not conceived as a result of Armenian uprisings or the exigencies of World War I, but was long in the making. To be sure, some historians have expressed doubts about prior deliberation and planning. Precisely for this reason, Künzler's testimony is of exceptional value. To give one example: In order to take care of the sprained foot of one of its members, he, as a "medical doctor," was invited to accompany a small Turkish Expeditionary Force on its way from Urfa all the way to Baghdad. As a result, he became embroiled in an exchange with the leader of the group, Major Nefiz, who categorically declared, "We Turks must either exterminate the Armenians wholesale [*samt und sonders*] or force them to exodus. A coexistence with them in our Empire is totally out of the question." The declaration is most significant because Nefiz was no ordinary officer. He was, in fact, one of those politically committed, namely "politicized," Turkish military officers who, as the taskmasters of the ruling Young Turk party—the Committee of Union and Progress or CUP—had participated in the overthrow of the despotic ruler Sultan Abdul Hamid and thereby had ushered in the new CUP regime. Nefiz also had actively participated in the suppression of the subsequent March 31-April 13, 1908, anti-CUP counterrevolution. Second, and more significant, the above-cited exchange took place in mid-December 1914. In other words, long before the occurrence of such debacles as the Turkish military defeats at Sarıkamiş and Van in January and May 1915, respectively, and skirmishes at Zeytun in February 1915 (for which the Armenians were blamed and which, admittedly, were grave enough to precipitate the genocidal anti-Armenian measures) the idea of the urgency of such measures was already germinating in the thinking of the CUP leaders.

Although Künzler's account of the genocide in Urfa is without rival, understanding the events of 1915 requires a review of the historical context that framed these events. Indeed, the World War I massacre at Urfa emerges as the culmination of a process involving a series of antecedent massacres, notably those of 1894-96. According to British Vice-Consul Gerard H. Fitzmaurice, in the spring of 1915 Urfa Armenians remembered with terror the horrors of the twin massacres of December 28 and 29, 1895, when some 8,000 Armenians perished. Especially gruesome was the fate of an estimated 2,500 Armenians, practically all of them women and children, who had taken refuge in the sanctuary of the Armenian cathedral of Urfa. To kill and immolate the terrified victims, on December 29 the perpetrators brought in thirty cans of kerosene and set the entire edifice on fire, thereby incinerating the trapped refuge-seekers. As usual, the victims were assured, just before the unleashing of that holocaust, that the government would ensure their safety. In another part of the city:

> . . . a certain Sheikh ordered followers to bring as many stalwart young Armenians as they could find. They were to the number of about a hundred thrown on their back, and held down by their hands and feet, while the Sheikh, with a combination of fanaticism and cruelty, proceeded, while reciting verses of the Quran, to cut their throats after the Mecca rite of sacrificing sheep. When it was all over, Ali, Urfa's *müfti* (a senior religious authority) and Hüseyin Paşa, a notable and a principal architect of the Urfa massacres, accompanied by other notables, and preceded by music, went round the quarter announcing that the massacres were at an end (*paydos*).[2]

In the perspective in which the series of wholesale massacres, including those of World War I, are seen as being organically and historically interconnected, militant Islam, evidently, emerges as an overarching factor.[3] Fitzmaurice, cited above in connection with the 1895 massacres, provides an explanation for the critical importance of this religious factor. Speaking of the Muslim "Shariat Law" Fitzmaurice wrote:

> That law prescribes that if the '*rayah*'[4] Christian attempts by having recourse (*dehalet*) to foreign powers to overstep the limits of "privileges" (*berat*) allowed to them by their Musulman masters, and free themselves from their bondage, their lives and properties are to be forfeited and are at the mercy of the Musulmans. To the Turkish mind the Armenians had tried to overstep those limits by appealing to foreign powers, especially England. They therefore considered it their religious duty and a righteous thing to destroy and seize the lives and property of the Armenians, and they jumped at the further gratuitous conclusion that the Armenians and English had become enemies of Islam...[5]

In fact while destroying religious objects, the mob kept screaming, "mockingly calling on Christ to prove himself a greater prophet than Mohammed." Alive to this religious dimension of the Urfa massacre, the prominent British lawyer Sir Edwin Pears, who for more than four decades (1873-1915) had practiced law in the Ottoman capital, lamented:

> This was the deliberate sacrifice of a cathedral full of people. The hideous holocaust will not and ought not to be forgotten. The ugly barn-like cathedral, like the mountain of sacrifice of Mexico, like the Bridge of Sighs of Venice and the other mountains of man's inhumanity to man, ought to be religiously preserved as a memorial of the stiff-necked determination of the Armenians to die rather than change their religion, and of the infernal brutality which can be practiced in the name of religion.[6]

It is worth noting that Fitzmaurice ends his most detailed report, compiled on the spot in Urfa on March 16, 1896, (some ten weeks after the cataclysm) with the following observation:

> Though the secret and terrorizing methods of the Turkish Administration do not always permit the production of the evidence usually required by a European Court, I have been at great pains to sift carefully my information, the greater portion of which I have obtained direct from Musulman sources, or have had confirmed by Musulman authority.[7]

In his report Fitzmaurice also indicates that prior to the twin December 1895 massacres, another set of twin massacres, albeit on a smaller scale, was committed in Urfa, namely on October 28 and 29, 1895. He indicates also that of the 2,500 Urfa Cathedral victims, 1,800 were administered the last sacraments by the priest there; and the total figure of the entire carnage most likely was 9,000 or 10,000 out of an estimated total of 20,000 Urfa Armenians.[8]

Next to vivid historical memories enveloping the psyche of the victim population, another factor that imparted a distinct character to the World War I genocidal fate of Urfa's Armenian population (as noted above) bore the spectacle of misery and despair of deportee convoys passing through Urfa in the summer of 1915 on their way to their ultimate peril. The stories of untold atrocities that these remnants of decimated Armenian convoys related to Urfa Armenians, who were yet to be targeted wholesale, animated a broad segment of the latter to resist and die fighting instead of being butchered like sheep. In his November 16, 1915, report, Germany's consul to Aleppo, Walter Rössler, confirms this consideration. In the same report, Ahmed Celal, the Turkish governor-general of Aleppo province, which encompassed the independent district of Urfa, is quoted as saying, "When trampled upon, a worm will bend and twist."[9]

The outbreak of the insurrection was preceded by a series of harsh and often deadly measures that the authorities inflicted upon the Urfa Armenians. As early as May 27, 1915, for example, the police raided the St. Sarkis Monastery, arresting its school director and his assistant and confiscating their papers and other belongings. On the morning of June 8, eighteen notables and political leaders of Urfa's Armenian community were placed under arrest; together with their families, they were deported two days later to Rakka, one of the principal extermination camps in the Mesopotamian deserts. (Some members of this group were weeks later recalled to Urfa and were subjected to a new investigation punctuated by torture). On June 25 after very careful preparations, the remaining elites of the Armenian community were arrested by recourse to tricks and slyness; the authorities were thus able to decapitate in a matter of few hours the targeted victim population—or so they believed. Among the 200 arrestees were party leaders, prominent businessmen, intellectuals, and other notables. On July 10, the Very Rev. Ardavazd Galemkerian, the primate of Urfa Armenians, was given an ultimatum to collect and deliver within forty-eight hours all weapons in the possession of Urfa Armenians. On July 26, the primate was once more summoned by the government, but this time he was ushered into prison. On July 28, the 200 arrestees mentioned above were massacred at Şeytan Deresi [Satan's Valley]. On August 19, a general massacre was launched against the entire Armenian population of the city of Urfa. This atrocity served as a triggering mechanism for the completion of the preparations for the Armenian uprising.

For Urfa Armenians the final die was cast when two chieftains of the murderous Special Organization [*Teşkilatı Mahsusa*] arrived in Urfa on August 10, 1915. Barely on the scene, Major Çerkez Ahmed and Lieutenant Halil, took over control of the arrangements relative to the liquidation of the area's Armenian population. When Colonel Sadık, the local military commander, refused to cooperate with them in this murderous undertaking, they roundly thrashed him. They then proceeded to carry out their exterminatory scheme. First they ordered the immediate deportation of the Armenians already incarcerated in local prisons. They then collected a bribe of 6,000 Turkish pounds (approximately $27,000) under false promises. The series of deportations and associated massacres that ensued were initiated by a two-tier massacre, whereby two Armenian labor battalions, all together some 1,500 young Armenians, were killed.[10] The standard method used for this exterminatory procedure, according to a survivor, was first to order the victims to disrobe (allowing them to keep only their shirts), then march them two-by-two with their hands tied together up to the edge of the cliff, and then dispatch them into the abyss with a deadly sword strike.

Having thus disposed of a potential obstacle, brigand leaders Ahmed and Halil proceeded to the principal task of their mission: the wholesale liquidation of Urfa's Armenian population. But there was an ancillary mission to be taken care of first. It involved the perfidious murder of Vartkes and Zohrab, the two preeminent Armenian deputies of the lower house of the Ottoman Parliament. Under the pretense of taking them to Diyarbakır for court-martial on fabricated charges, their carriage was stopped outside the city of Urfa as Ahmed and Halil, who were lying in wait, pounced on the two deputies and killed them forthwith.[11] Throughout these operations, Ali Haydar, Urfa's district governor, and an operative of the Special Organization, worked hand in hand with those two Special Organization brigand chieftains. There is considerable information about one of them, Major Ahmed.[12] All three of these CUP potentates oversaw the manifold tortures that were inflicted upon some 200 leaders of the Armenian community prior to the general deportations and massacres. As elsewhere throughout wartime Turkey, these captives were subjected to excruciating tortures so as to compel them to reveal hidden caches of weapons.

The detailed examination of the genocide and the ensuing Armenian uprising (September 29–October 23, 1915), which, as noted above, clearly was a last-ditch effort to die fighting rather than face preordained extermination, is beyond the pale of this introductory essay. The tolling of the bells of Urfa's two Armenian churches was to signal the outbreak of the insurrection. This act was precipitated by the attempt of the Turkish police to arrest on September 29 the couple of Armenian labor battalion soldiers who had miraculously survived the above-mentioned Kudama massacre (see note 9) and escaped. By all accounts, the resistance was, against very heavy odds, a defensive insurrection on an epic scale in which elements of despair and uncommon heroism were entwined. However, unlike the case of the other three major uprisings of this kind—Van (April 20-May 17, 1915), Şabin Karahisar (June 6–July 4, 1915), and Musa Dağ (July 30–September 12, 1915)—in the Urfa case, many boys 10-14 and particularly dozens of female teenagers, proved themselves intrepid fighters. Their death-defying bravery reportedly astounded General Fahri, the commander of the 13th Army Corps who was in charge of suppressing the insurrection. It is worth citing here the case of the young Armenian girl Ms. Ketenjian, a graduate of Harput's American College, who was in command of the three squads of female fighters comprising several dozen girls and young women. They captured a large number of prisoners and destroyed dozens of assaulting policemen, gendarmes, regular army officers and soldiers, and countless elements from the mob and rabble. All this evidence is corroborated by Turkish military officers and policemen recounting their experiences in post-war narratives.[13]

Two names are indelibly attached to the saga of Urfa. One of them belongs to General Fahreddin (or Fahri) Türkkan, the commanding officer of the 12th Army Corps, who was tasked to crush the insurrection. Unable initially to achieve that goal, he not only sought and obtained a series of reinforcements, thereby assembling a corpus of some 7,000 fighters, but more importantly, he requested and obtained the services of Major Graf Eberhard Wolfskeel von Reichenberg, a skilled German artillery officer, whose intervention proved decisive for the ultimate defeat of the insurgents. Von Reichenberg, in fact, managed to reduce the insurgents with overwhelming fire-power, involving the use of six large-caliber artillery pieces. In the end, many of the despairing male and female fighters, often together with their families, committed suicide through a variety of methods. On the other hand, all captured male insurgents were executed on the spot; of the 112 that were hanged, 34 of them were young women. When told that the Armenians were being subjected to "foul" abuses [*schandtaten*], the general, after patiently listening to the horrors, is reported to have retorted with a shrug of the shoulders: "Turkish nature" [*Türklük*].[14] After the war, when Turkey was lying prostrate and defeated, this general was arrested by the British and, along with other perpetrators of the Armenian Genocide, was exiled to Malta to await criminal prosecution,[15] which did not materialize because, among other reasons, of the rise of a defiant Kemalist challenge.

The Armenian counterpart of General Fahri was Mgrdich Yotneghbayrian, the thirty-one-year-old resourceful and highly ingenious Dashnak[16] party architect of the Armenian insurrection at Urfa, an insurrection which he organized, supervised, and directed with great discipline, authority, and infectious leadership. Conversant in several Near Eastern languages and adept at detective work, daredevil reconnaissance, and impersonation by using a variety of Turkish military uniforms, he was able to carefully plan the insurrection. Namely, he amassed a significant stockpile of weapons and ammunition from Turkish military depots; countless Ottoman-Turkish military uniforms (which were used with great skill to produce confusion and thereby cripple the onslaughts of Turkish army units); and components for a makeshift military hospital for use within the confines of Armenian defense positions. Severely wounded, with his right knee shattered by shrapnel, Mgrdich continued to direct the insurrection on a stretcher until the very last moment. By all accounts, he was indeed a legend, a rare specimen of a hero.[17]

The insurrection failed, and the carnage continued through Urfa and the south.

Künzler is aghast at the magnitude of "unnatural" [*widernatürlich*] crimes perpetrated against Armenian boys—"hundreds, yes thousands of whom," he says, fell victim to their homosexual Turkish tormentors. He also inveighs against Turkish officers who committed, he says, "unbelievable and unspeakable" offenses, especially in dealing with Armenian girls who were "bartered away."[18] Urfa's great Cathedral, where the convoys in transit were taken to, was reduced to a bordello.[19]

Notwithstanding, Künzler points out that there were kind Muslims, especially female ones, who saved many children and who also sheltered a number of other Armenians. Those who did so for selfish [*selbstsucht*] reasons were mostly villagers who even dared to shelter men in order to benefit from their labor, which often was offered gratis. Of the 1,000 orphans who were Islamized and received Muslim names, 200 survived. Künzler's greatest praise, "you can't find a nobler soul," goes to Mustafa Şevket, the Muslim judge [*kadı*] of Urfa. He was an inordinately devout Muslim, filled with sentiments of genuine compassion, charity, and above all, righteousness. He stood up to Fahri Paşa, the general in charge of suppressing the Armenian uprising and who demanded from him a *fetva* [the issuance of an authoritative opinion] meant to sanction his military operations, including the massive bombardments of the Armenian quarter; the kadı steadfastly refused, thereby angering the general. Having been transferred from Erzincan, where he likewise had angered the authorities by objecting to the ongoing anti-Armenian atrocities, this religious leader continued to shelter many Armenians in Urfa. The Muslim Turks nicknamed him "the Armenian priest" [*Ermeni papazı*]. At the end of the war, he tried to restore to the Armenians their properties. Another case of civil courage of this kind involves a Turkish lieutenant who was in charge of one of the labor battalion contingents, who were subsequently massacred wholesale. When one of the two Special Organization chieftains in question demanded the surrender of that contingent and he refused, this intrepid Turkish officer was shot dead by the chieftain who then proceeded with the scheme of wholesale liquidation of the unarmed Armenian soldiers.[20] An example of some measure of chivalry relates to the treatment of a seventeen-year-old "very attractive" [*bildhübsch*] Armenian girl who, refusing to surrender, kept fighting[21] until she was gravely wounded. She had been shot through her abdomen. With a sense of admiration of her bravery, the Turkish soldiers took the trouble of carrying her for treatment at Künzler's hospital, where she soon died.

In offering some comments and interpretations on the entire episode in which murderous designs and associated butcheries are entwined with multitudes of examples of resistance through self-sacrifice, death-defying heroism, and ultimate demise, Künzler conveys his views on the Armenians as the victim component of that episode. While deploring the half dozen or so Armenian informers who betrayed their compatriots in the hope of saving themselves, he proceeds to offer a diagnosis of what he considers to be the root causes of the tragedy befalling the Armenians. Granting that the bulk of the victim population (80% to 90%) consisted of harmless peasants and farmers and that sustained tragedy and suffering in certain respects adversely affected Armenian national character, "nevertheless," he maintains that certain flaws in Armenian national character are, and should be, amenable to modification if not correction. Foremost, among them is, he says, the proverbial Armenian penchant for discord and disunity. Furthermore, alive to what he calls the "unspeakable" crimes that were perpetrated against the Armenians and wondering whether "any pen can describe" them adequately, Künzler still believes that Armenians will have to extricate themselves from the shackles of "deep-seated emotions of revenge and retaliation . . . Free Armenia may not forget that all around her country many Mohammedans live, while they are just a small people . . ."

For the Armenians, however, the problem was much more complicated. Generally speaking, conditions of national discord and disunity are intrinsic to all political processes involving personal ambition, interpersonal competition, and rivalry. In complete disregard of this fundamental fact, Armenians with consuming envy—and as if confirming Künzler's judgment—persist in negatively comparing themselves with the Turks, their historical nemesis. Yet, by way of just focusing on one single episode of modern history, namely the creation and establishment of the modern Republic of Turkey, one may easily discern a critical factor at work here that may significantly explain the difference in question. Mustafa Kemal, the principal founder of that Republic, was also constantly embroiled in interpersonal and political conflicts with his Turkish opponents and rivals while directing the consuming Turkish War of Independence for three consecutive years. That notwithstanding, he received substantial indirect help from the Italians and the French, Turkey's wartime enemies, and direct help from Lenin's Bolsheviks.

What the Turks amply possessed, and the Armenians patently lacked, however, was, on the one hand, historically cumulative experiences in state craft, and, on the other, battle-tested armies led by professionally trained staff officers and field commanders. More often than not, wherever such capabilities are at hand, problems involving human sentiments (such as collective vindictiveness and retaliatory impulses against another country or people) tend to become eclipsed as they are harnessed and ultimately channeled into the realms of overall national desiderata and policy issues under the watch of circumspect governmental authorities.

The Armenian uprising at Urfa, just like the other major wartime uprisings at Van, Musa Dağ, and Şabin Karahisar, was a last-ditch, improvised, and disjointed undertaking.[22] However sublime in inspiration and heroic in execution, they were episodes that dramatically and tragically reveal the fatal consequences of the minority status of a population whose vulnerability became even more compounded by the additional, and far more important, fact that the victim population was deprived of the potentially protective shield of a parent state entity.

* Dr. Vahakn N. Dadrian is the Director of Genocide Research with the Zoryan Institute in Toronto, and a member of the Academy of Sciences of the Republic of Armenia. He is the author of numerous groundbreaking scientific books and articles on the Armenian Genocide. For several years, he was engaged as director of a large genocide study project sponsored by the H. F. Guggenheim Foundation. His major works include an extensive volume, *The History of the Armenian Genocide: Ethnic Conflict from the Balkans to Anatolia to the Caucasus* (Oxford & Providence, RI, 1995); *German Responsibility in the Armenian Genocide: A Review of the Historical Evidence of German Complicity* (Cambridge, MA, 1996); and *Warrant for Genocide: The Key Elements of the Turko-Armenian Conflict* (London & New Brunswick, NJ, 1999). His latest work is *Key Elements in the Turkish Denial of the Armenian Genocide: A Case Study of Distortion and Falsification* (Cambridge, MA and Toronto, 1999). A serialized collection of his works in the Turkish language have appeared through the efforts of and editorship of Attila Tuygan, entitled *Ermeni Soykırımında Kurumsal Roller. Toplu Makaleler 1*. [The Role of Institutions in the Armenian Genocide] (Istanbul: Belge Publishers, 2004), *Türk Kaynaklarında Ermeni Soykırımı. Toplu Makaleler 2* [The Armenian Genocide in Turkish Sources] (Istanbul: Belge Publishers, 2005). For more on the academic career and accomplishments of Dr. Dadrian and a complete bibliography of his works, readers are advised to log on to *www.zoryaninstitute.org*.

Notes

[1] Situated north of the Aleppo-Baghdad railway on the lower slopes of a range of hills known as the Nemrut (Nemruth) mountains, Urfa had the status of a "district" [*sancak*] in the Ottoman provincial administrative setup,

thus nominally subject to the jurisdiction of Aleppo province. However, prior to the outbreak of World War I, it had acquired the status of an "independent" district [*müstakil*], very similar to the status of the nine other independent districts. Out of an estimated total population of 65,000, about 20,000 were Armenians, the heirs of a long-cherished military as well as a religious-cultural legacy spanning centuries. The prolific medieval Armenian Church luminary Nerses Shnorhali (Nerses the Graceful), who in 1166 was elected Catholicos (the Supreme Patriarch of the Armenian Apostolic Church) and authored numerous theological, philosophical, pedagogical, and even patriotic tracts, wrote his "Eulogy of Edessa" [*Oghb Edesioy*] (Erevan: HSSH GA Hratarakch'ut'yun, 1973) in Urfa, where he is buried. In it, he lamented the destruction of the city in 1144 by the invading hordes from Mosul. In brief, Urfa, located halfway between Gaziantep and Mardin in present-day Turkey, had, up to 1915, a continuous Armenian presence. That presence was shattered for the first time during the 1894-96 Abdul Hamid-era serial massacres. Vahakn N. Dadrian, *The History of the Armenian Genocide: Ethnic Conflict from the Balkans to Anatolia to the Caucasus*, 8th ed. (New York, Oxford: Berghahn Books, 2007), p. 240.

[2] This forty-two page, comprehensive report is filed in the archives of the *British Foreign Office*, F.O. 195/1930, X/L05446, pp. 30-72, or folios 185-206. Fitzmaurice had arrived in Urfa on March 10, 1896, and his report from Urfa is dated March 16. It is addressed to Sir Philip Curie (British ambassador to the Ottoman Empire), who had authorized the on-the-spot investigation. As British vice consul and first dragoman [an interpreter, translator or guide in Turkish, Arabic and Persian-speaking countries] he had ample latitude to carry out broad-based inquiries, in the course of which he was able to co-opt several governmental officials and secure ample Muslim eyewitness testimony. This comprehensive report is printed in its entirety in *Blue Book*, Turkey no. 5 (1896), pp. 2-17, an enclosure in Ambassador Curie's April 27, 1896, report. Here are the respective page numbers for the references from Fitzmaurice's report in *Blue Book*: Urfa's Armenian population estimate, p. 31; the earlier October massacres, p. 32; the reference to Islamic Sharia law relative to *rayahs* [a Christian subject under an Ottoman ruler], p. 34; the author's dismissing of the "stereotyped official version" of the cataclysm, which "must be received with great reserve, if not incredulity," p. 41; the premeditated and purposively engineered incidents precipitating the massacres, p. 49; the role of Nezif Paşa, the commander of the troops participating in the massacres, p. 47; the role of Captain Abdul Kerim in lulling the anxious and fearful Armenians in the Cathedral, p. 52; the cut-throat and prayerful sheikh and his hundred Armenian victims, p. 56; the holocaust in the Cathedral and the administration of sacraments, pp. 57-83; on mocking the Christian faith of the Armenians and Christ himself, p. 59; igniting the holocaust through thirty

cans of kerosene, p. 59; the declaration of ceasefire [*paydos*], p. 60; "the criminal misrepresentation . . . regarding the Armenians" by local authorities and Istanbul's "false and unstatemanlike attitude," p. 66; "between 400 and 500 Urfa Armenians, out of mortal fear, became Muslims," p. 70; and Fitzmaurice carefully sifted evidence before ascertaining facts, pp. 71-72.

[3] This is particularly relevant as far as popular participation of mobs is concerned. When on November 23, 1914, the Proclamation of Holy War [*Beyannamei Cihad*] was issued, the Armenians in Istanbul became the mob's first targets. Furthermore, according to the same source, the men, mostly gendarmes, escorting the countless and doomed Armenian deportee convoys were influenced by the deadly injunctions of Holy War [*cihad*] when attacking and destroying them. The source in question was Marshal Liman von Sanders, the head of the German Military Mission to Turkey and successively commander-in-chief of several Turkish Armies during World War I.

[4] *Rayah*, a Christian subject under an Ottoman ruler.

[5] Fitzmaurice, *Blue Book,* p. 34.

[6] Sir Edwin Pears, *Turkey and its People*, 2nd ed. (London: Methuen and Co., 1912), p. 283. On p. 284, Fitzmaurice is portrayed as "a keen observer who has long been known for his skill in gaining the confidence of Moslems and Christians alike and for his habitual good faith." In his *Forty Days in Constantinople* (New York: Appleton, 1916), p. 344, Pears underscores Fitzmaurice's "general intelligence, knowledge of Turkey, of its Ministers and people, and especially of the Turkish language . . ." And on p. 138, Fitzmaurice is described as a diplomat possessing "exceptional knowledge of men and affairs, . . . passing a considerable portion of his time in the really Turkish cafés . . . frequented almost exclusively by Turks or Turkish subjects . . . acquired . . . colloquial Turkish . . ."

[7] Fitzmaurice, *Blue Book*, p. 34.

[8] Fitzmaurice, ibid, casualty figures, p. 62; on Major Hasan, mayor of gendarmerie and arch organizer of the October 28 massacre, p. 65; "the criminal misrepresentation . . . regarding the Armenians" by local authorities, and Istanbul's "false and unstatemanlike attitude," p. 66; "between 400 and 500 Urfa Armenians, out of mortal fear, became Muslims," p. 70; and Fitzmaurice carefully sifted evidence before ascertaining facts, pp. 71-72.

[9] German Foreign Ministry archives, R14089. More details are provided in Bruno Eckart, *Meine Erlebnisse in Urfa* [My Experiences in Urfa] (Berlin-Potsdam, Tempel-Verlag, 1922), pp. 25-27, 28, 29. For this kind of display of understanding and companion benevolence, Vali Celal was subsequently relieved of his post and transferred to Konya. For British

Prime Minister William Ewert Gladstone (1808-1898), who was aghast at the infernal character of the Abdul Hamid-era massacres, that "trampling" involved "outrages that the powers of language hardly suffice to describe what has been done and is being done in Armenia, and the exaggeration is almost beyond power." *Life of Abdul Hamit* (London: Constable and Co., 1917), p. 253.

10 The first batch of 400 was massacred on August 19 at the Kurdish village of Yedikuyu, located an hour north of Urfa near Karaköprü; the second batch was likewise dispatched on August 22 at Kudama. Eckart, likewise describes the wholesale liquidation of these disarmed Armenian soldiers, *Meine Erlebnisse*, p. 16.

11 Despite their parliamentary immunity, the two Armenian deputies were illegally arrested on May 20, 1915, without any requisite formality or any explanation. They were ordered by Interior Minister Talât to be court-martialed in Diyarbakır instead of Istanbul or anywhere else. In line with this method of chicanery, Talât then arranged for Tahsin, Urfa's municipal physician, to issue a false certificate. In it, Dr. Tahsin falsely certified that Deputy Zohrab succumbed to sudden heart failure. Talât and his co-conspirators were subsequently impelled, if not compelled, however, to allow the truth to surface and become a matter of public record. Indeed, on November 28, 1916, Adil, the president of the Chamber of Deputies, read an official declaration issued by the office of the grand vezirate, admitting that Zohrab and Vartkes were in fact murdered. Arshag A. Alboyadjian, *Anhetats'ogh Demk'er, Krikor Zohrab* [Vanishing Personages: Krikor Zohrab] (Istanbul: Der Nersessian Eghbayrk', 1919), pp. 247-50. Besides Ahmed and Halil, the band of criminals included Police Chief Şakir; Sargeant-Major Abdurrahman; Brigand Chief Mustafa, son of Haci Reşid; and two gendarmes accompanying the coach in which the victims were riding. Abdurrahman was subsequently promoted to commander of gendarmes in Nisibin. The murder was carried out at Karaköprü, some half hour away from Urfa, harboring 120 houses and a bridge, near Kasabtaşı Rock. The coach drivers were Kücük Muslim, who was Klo Muhammed's son, and Khallo. According to a document found in the archives of the Armenian Patriarchate of Jerusalem, Fazıl, a police commissar, was dispatched by Talât to Diyarbakır two days after the exile of the two Armenian deputies. Under the guise of an appointment at the Treasury of Diyarbakır, he was to supervise the murder operation.

12 See "Documentation of the Armenian Genocide in Turkish Sources," compiled by Vahakn N. Dadrian, in Israel W. Charney, ed., *Genocide: A Critical Bibliographic Review* (London: Mensell, 1991), pp. 118-19, 120. Reprinted as a separate booklet by Zoryan Institute, Toronto, Canada, 1981.

[13] All the pertinent data were culled from the massive and comprehensive 1,368 page (plus 132-page supplement) compendium, Aram Sahakian, ed., *Diwts'aznakan Urfan ew ir hayordinerě* [Heroic Urfa and Her Armenian Offsprings] (Beirut: Atlas, 1955). The epic Urfa resistance is recorded pp. 917-28; and testimonies of Turkish police officers, military officers, a brigand chieftain, and Halef Mahmud, a Turkish civilian combatant pp. 929-38. A very useful companion volume is Lut'er, [Aram Sahakian], *Urfayi Herosamartě* [The Heroic Battle of Urfa] (Beirut: Aztag, 1933), 264 pp. Lut'er estimates total Turkish losses to exceed 2,000 dead and wounded, p. 151.

[14] Eckart, *Meine Erlebnisse*, p. 27.

[15] F.O. 371/6500, folio 199/463 ff.

[16] Reference is to the Armenian Revolutionary Federation, one of the three traditional Armenian political parties, established in Tbilisi in 1890. Most of the other leaders, including their female counterparts, were likewise Dashnak.

[17] For a biography and details of his incredulous exploits see *Diwts'aznakan Urfan ew ir hayordinerě*, pp. 998-1027 and Lut'er, *Urfayi Herosamartě*, pp. 165-98.

[18] For details of this problem, see Vahakn N. Dadrian "Children as Victims of Genocide: The Armenian Case," *Journal of Genocide Research* 5, no. 3 (September 2003): 421-37.

[19] Eckart, *Meine Erlebnisse*, pp. 18-19.

[20] Ibid., p. 17.

[21] As one Kemalist deputy underscores in his memoirs, "whether in the market, the streets, or in the stores, all kinds of weapons were freely available for sale . . . Town criers and traveling salesmen peddling their arms with loud voices were part of this picture." Damar Arıkoğlu. *Hatıralarım* [My Memoirs] (Istanbul: Tan Publishing House, 1961), pp. 45, 47. Cemal Paşa, a member of the ruling Young Turk troika, says the same thing in his *Hatıralar* [Memoirs] (Istanbul: Cağdaş, 1977), p. 427. This volume is edited by Behçet Cemal, his son.

[22] These descriptions are with emphasis confirmed by Rössler, Aleppo's German consul, in his January 3, 1916, report to his ambassador in Istanbul. He states that an Urfa deportee convoy had the following treks to endure: 1. Urfa to Tel Abyad, 2. Tel Abyad to Rakka, 3. Rakka to Tel Abyad, 4. Tel Abyad to Rakka. See note 1. The noted British historian Arnold Toynbee, too, underscores this fact. Arnold J. Toynbee, *Acquaintances* (London: Oxford University Press), pp. 240-41.

Jakob Künzler

In the Land of Blood and Tears

Experiences in Mesopotamia
During the World War (1914–1918)

1. The War Begins

As I get ready to write down my experiences and observations in Urfa during the Great War,[1] I do so in the first instance because I am the only neutral party to have seen from beginning to end all the terrible events that occurred in Urfa more than any other Turkish city.

Miss Karen Jeppe, a Danish woman, was also there until the end of 1917. She was in close contact with the Armenians.

At the outbreak of war I was with my family in Galilee for the summer holidays. With a certain premonition that great events were about to occur and therefore that it would be better to be on duty in Urfa than in Galilee, I decided to return sooner.

I had not been deceived; the war had really begun. The tensions were also very high in Turkey from the beginning. The rail traffic between Aleppo and Damascus was barred for private persons. I just got through with on the last train through Damascus to Aleppo.

On the way from Aleppo to Urfa I met two parliamentarians from Urfa who were responding to the sudden call to travel to the imperial headquarters. They asked me if I thought it would be good if Turkey would enter the war on the side of Germany. My answer was that it was best not to be drawn into a war at all, either on the German side or the side of the Entente.

When I visited one of the two parliamentarians in Constantinople in December 1917, he alluded to our exchange, saying that, in his opinion, Turkey would have been better served if she had conducted herself as I suggested. That was the judgment of a dyed-in-the-wool Young Turk who, along with many like-minded colleagues, had used the isolation of Turkey to carry out the undisturbed extermination of the Armenian people.

The outbreak of war awoke an inner conflict in me from the very beginning. As a German-speaking Swiss, I felt German and remained German in my thinking until the end of the other war. A factor in my loyalty to Germany might have been that I had nothing to read other than German and Turkish magazines.

When I arrived in Urfa, the mobilization of the troops was in full swing. The youngest recruits, including the Christians, were already in arms. A general registration of all men from fifteen to fifty years of age had begun; failure to register was punishable by death.

The general registration could only, of course, pertain to subjects with a fixed abode. Although the nomadic tribes of inner Turkey had been called up, they did not bother with the demands of officials. The armed troops were soon shipped out. Although the music, which was always played on such occasions, was supposed to generate great enthusiasm among the departing troops and population, the mood cannot be described as enthusiastic.

The two European inspectors-general—the Norwegian [Nicolai] Hoff and the Belgian [Louis Constant] Westenenk,[2] whom the great powers had forced on Turkey in order to create a model for order in the six east Anatolian provinces—had come in the spring of 1914 in order to start their work. They traveled back to their countries shortly after the war broke out. One of them came through Urfa. The town military commander escorted him. The Turks had apparently sent these men home. They had no more business in Turkey now that the great powers were fighting each other.

At the end of August 1914, one heard in Urfa that the Armenians from Zeytun had resisted the conscription in their district.[3]

This rumor was circulated in order to create suspicion in the Muslim population. They said to themselves that if the Armenians in Urfa also wanted to revolt like that, it would not bode well for the Mohammedans[4] there. Although the Mohammedans in the city of Urfa were in the majority, about twice as many as the Christians, they also considered themselves inferior to the Christians in courage and especially in sophistication.

When German victories were announced in Urfa at the end of August, Mohammedans greeted every announcement of victory with jubilation and looked with Argus[5] eyes at the Armenians. Did they share the joy or could one sense an inner rejection? One could draw his conclusion one way or the other. Individual Armenians made no secret of their opinion that the Germans could never win the war because they were such a small minority. That did not improve the already suspicious attitude toward them, and one could soon hear that the Mohammedans talking about the Armenians as the "Traitorous Armenian Nation" ["*Melun ermeni millet*"].

On September 10 [1914], the repeal of the capitulations[6] was announced and celebrated the next day by the Mohammedans as if the repeal of the rights of the Europeans in Turkey meant that the Turks had won a great victory.

In spite of many efforts, our German mission hospital in Urfa, over which I presided at the time, was still operating without official permission from the Turkish government, so I had to try to acquire official recognition with a new application. Since our hospital was a German institution, which had existed de facto for two decades, the work of a friendly and allied nation, would be recognized by the Turks without any misgivings; but I would like to say right away that I was disappointed in this expectation. However, since the Turkish officials never answered the request for permission to function, the hospital was neither licensed nor forbidden. At any rate, we conducted ourselves as if the hospital were licensed.

On the day that the German consul in Aleppo telegraphed the Germans in Urfa the news of the [Paul von] Hindenburg victory on the Mazurian Lakes, the leaders of the Urfa Armenians were in the courtyard of the German hospital. I told them about the victory message, but they advised me not to believe such news. A German victory, especially, should not be mentioned if Turkey would also now enter the war on her side. I felt compelled to advise these people, all of whom were my friends, that in this or in a similar case, as subjects of the Turkish state, they should apply greater political discretion.

It could fare badly for them and their people. The Entente was far away yet the Turkish sword terribly near; and the suspicious Muslims in their flush of victory could be easily excited. It would be better, therefore, to be cautious and restrained than to somehow let it be known that one could not share the joy for the Turkish success.

Before Turkey officially entered the war, many soldiers had fled from the barracks; but they were almost all Mohammedans. As hard as it was to perform the lowest tasks for the hate-filled Mohammedans, the young Armenians who were already under arms remained in their units in the beginning. Here is an example of what the Christians had to endure in the Turkish army:

The teacher of the Germans in a school founded by me was called up. As a former student teacher in the Syrian orphanage in Jerusalem, he had good pre-training for military instruction. In fact, he could have assumed an officer's rank from the beginning. He was assigned to direct the gymnastic exercises for the recruits. In the barracks, his corporal, who could neither read nor write, harassed him and had a penchant for deploying him to cleaning the privy pit. Under such widespread conditions, it is understandable that the Christians grew weary of their initial readiness for military duty. Soon, many sought to free themselves from service or simply deserted. The previously mentioned teacher was in the barracks in Ayntab. From there he found his way back to Urfa as a deserter and hid for a few days. Afterwards, I was able to find a position for him in the construction of the Baghdad [rail] line. Since he too carelessly postponed his departure, the gendarmes seized him and only let him go after a payment of a *bahşiş*[7] of 200 francs. But he proved himself in the rail line construction. Although he could have surely served his country better as a soldier, he worked until the end of the war as the chief accountant for the Taurus construction division.

2. On the Trail of Diplomacy

In the second half of December 1914, two Persian princes[8] accompanied by Turkish officers and soldiers appeared in Urfa. One of them, Prince R. el-Sultan el-Dowleh, sprained his ankle while riding. It was my duty to treat him. When the princes traveled on, I accompanied them as their doctor. I was supposed to travel with them to Baghdad; they were sent by the Germans to Persia. As members of the Qajar[9] tribe, they were supposed to win over Persia—especially their large tribe—for the holy war on the side of the Central Powers. The two princes had spent the last eight years in Switzerland. The Russian government had banished them from Persia because they seemed too dangerous. With 4,000 francs[10] per month from the Russians, they could live in Switzerland in luxury. In the Persian War of liberation in 1912, unbeknownst to the Russians, one of them, Saleh el-Sultan el-Dowleh, had returned to his homeland disguised as a dervish and supported the Persian War of liberation in 1912. When he arrived in his homeland, he sought out his friends and urged the monarchy-inclined Persians to fight against the constitutionalists, who were led by the Armenian Ephrem Khan.[11] Although the monarchists stood with 30,000 men against 3,000 constitutionalists, the prince lost.

Our journey to Baghdad went slowly, certainly not with the haste that the Germans wanted. During the journey, Major Nefiz Bey,[12] the head of our expedition, discussed the Armenian question one evening. He was a leader of the Young Turks and had made a name for himself during the storming of the Taşkışla barracks in Constantinople in 1908. Therefore, his remarks were of special interest to me.

"We Turks," he explained, "must either exterminate the Armenians utterly and completely or force them to emigrate. Life with them within the boundaries of our empire is completely out of the question."

Since, in the course of the discussion, Prince Saleh had something similar to say—perhaps remembering his defeat at the hands of Eprem Khan—I allowed myself a word on the subject.

"All people," I said, "have a right to exist—namely, in the place where they are born. Whoever violates this right commits injustice, which will sooner or later be avenged. Since the Young Turks had reconciled themselves with the freedom-loving Armenians in 1908, they should have kept the peace with the most intelligent part of the population, the Armenians, if only for reasons of self-preservation . . . And you, royal highness," I said to the Prince, "I wish that you would not go to Persia because you also entertain questionable thoughts about the Armenian people. Isn't Persia also the birthplace of a hundred thousand Armenians?"

The next morning the prince asked me to join him on his morning ride. During the ride he broached the discussion of the day before about the Armenians.

"Of course," he declared, "the Armenians have a right to live where they are born, in Turkey as well as in Persia. I only expressed the opposite opinion yesterday in order to please the Turkish major [Nefiz Bey], who does not exactly have the best education."

The two princes never reached Persia. In Fallujah, the last stop before Baghdad, they were stopped. A courier from Baghdad came with orders from the military commanders that the princes should not continue on their journey but instead return. Whether this interdiction was issued in consultation with the Germans—there were already some German officers on the Baghdad front—was beyond my knowledge; and I could not find out anything about it. Major Nefiz Bey, who went to Baghdad the next day and returned two days later, did not reveal from whom the order to return had come. It was a hard blow for the princes who were so close to the borders of their homeland but yet had to return. After we had been traveling a day, going the same way we had come, the princes confided in me that they had decided on an escape plan. I was supposed to participate or at least help in its execution. They wanted to reach Persia directly over the steppe without running into the Turks and without going through Baghdad. But Prince Saleh's wife was expecting and therefore could not risk such a grueling journey through the steppe. In case I decided not to accompany the princes, I could at least take the princess with me to Urfa where she could spend her confinement; and then she could be brought to Persia later. Without my participation, the plan would not be possible. I urgently advised the princes against it. We had to assume that the Germans, and not the Turks, were in charge of the princes, and the best thing would be to resign themselves to the circumstances. I felt an inner compulsion to give this advice. Throughout the entire journey Prince Saleh had cheered Field Marshal Hindenburg. He shouted over and over: "Vive Hindenburg!" and I had to listen each time. It was clear that this Oriental, once he was in Persia, would just as well take the side of the Entente. He took my advice to resign himself, and we arrived back at Der Zor.[13] The princes had to await further instructions there. I took my leave because my duty had been fulfilled, I traveled back to Urfa. I later learned that the princes had been interned in Konya, but I do not know what became of them.

3. Requisitions

What the Turkish officers requisitioned at the beginning of the war is most unbelievable. For many of them, it was a glorious time. There was nothing in storage that was not vital for the war and, which therefore, could not be requisitioned by the officers. The parties involved received handwritten slips of paper as receipts. Most of the requisitioned goods ended up in the private homes of the officers. Therefore, not only was wartime materiel picked up but everything that was pleasing and had value, such as carpets, portraits, and many similar objects. I have to tell a little story here. An officer requisitioned seven sacks of sugar from a warehouse. He called a servant and ordered him to carry them to his house. When the officer came home that evening, he asked his wife whether the seven sacks of sugar had been delivered. His wife answered, no, only six had been delivered. The following morning the officer met the servant again and asked him what had happened to the seventh sack. He answered mockingly: "Six for you and one for me for transport wages."

Every day during the Baghdad journey, requisitioning took place. Although that was only for really necessary things, every salesman knew that the slip of paper left behind as a receipt could be torn up because the goods would never be paid for.

In the first two years of the war, much wheat and other grains were requisitioned. The farmers often had to drag them to the train stations themselves. In the absence of storage bins, the grains were stored outdoors. Then came the winter; it rained on the exposed supplies, and the grains began to germinate, rot, and pollute the air in the general vicinity. At the same time, there were bread shortages on the front. Only where there were German officers present were the provisions stored in time and available on the front.

4. Evil Prospects

On the journey to Baghdad with the princes, it became clear to me that the war would bring bad times for the Armenian people. The Young Turks had anticipated their destruction. Without a doubt, they would now exploit the war when the opposing great powers were checked in their influence on Turkish soil, or, with the exception of America, completely preoccupied with the war effort. No one would find time to deal with the Armenian Question.

In March and April 1915 there were Turkish victory celebrations in Urfa, often with great ceremony. The Armenians conducted themselves very coolly, which must have severely aggravated the Turks. Some Armenians were seized at that time just because they did not participate in the jubilation. Cool-headed Turks also did not hesitate to say that they did not believe in such celebrations, but nothing happened to them.

The desertion of Turkish and Armenian soldiers continued. I will cite here a telling entry from my diary:

"February 1915. A few days ago, 400 recruits, among them a number of Armenians, set off for Ayntab. Of the 400 who arrived in Ayntab, exactly *four* arrived in the barracks and these were all *Armenians*. The officer who received them laughed and ordered the honest four to leave also."

At that time, the Armenians in Urfa held male assemblies in their cathedral every Sunday, when people spoke about the events of the war. I was able to give a speech twice during these assemblies. At all of these meetings, the Armenians also discussed their difficult situation. It was said that if the Turks were defeated in the Balkan War by four small peoples, how, one justifiably asked, should they now successfully withstand the armies of the Great Powers? The Turks in the city threatened the Armenians almost every day. They said it openly: "Woe to you Armenians if the enemies of Turkey succeed in setting foot on Turkish territory! No Armenians in the interior will survive; we will see to that."

Under such circumstances, the task of the Armenian people was to protect themselves, in the worst case, from destruction if Turkey was defeated; and they had to hold out as long as possible until the army of the Entente had taken possession of the interior of the country. Wherever Armenians gathered, secret preparations of this type were being made. Can one blame them? But the Turks got wind of these preparations. Many Armenians rejoiced when their younger generation returned as deserters. But fearful spirits deplored their return. They could only lead to undesirable investigations by the gendarmes.

One evening in April, there was great unrest in the Armenian district in Urfa. It was said that the Armenian teachers were to be arrested the next day. An assembly was immediately held in the church. The younger generation counseled resistance, which the elders opposed. It was decided to wait.

The next day the teachers were taken as prisoners. In addition, several houses were searched for weapons and documents.

A few days later, the gendarmes in Garmuj,[14] the only Armenian town near Urfa, wanted to capture Armenians who had deserted from the military. The Armenians fled to a nearby mountain and entrenched themselves. The Armenians fired on the gendarmes who had to leave some dead behind. Only after reinforcements were called in from a neighboring city could some of the deserters be captured.

The situation of the Urfa Armenians deteriorated significantly because of this event. In mid-May, eighteen of the most respectable families in Urfa were banished to Rakka,[15] a little town on the Euphrates River, 150 kilometers to the south. They were allowed to travel in wagons, which they rented themselves. They arrived safely; but after a few days, the men were brought back to Urfa and thrown into prison along with many prominent people. They were treated there to liberal doses of the bastinado.[16] Torture was back on the agenda. One of my friends asked me to bring him a soothing salve because he had many wounds from three consecutive bastinados. The imprisoned Armenians were supposed to tell where their weapons were and turn them in. But every Armenian had a weapon; and every other city dweller had a weapon. In the Orient, one cannot travel unarmed to the next little town even in times of peace. The general insecurity, which one cannot forget in judging the Orient, makes the possession of a weapon a duty for every reasonable person.

At the end of April 1915, I lay sick with spotted fever. In spite of the fact that I was still convalescing—I could barely walk a few steps—the head of the Armenian parish [*vardapet*[17]] bade me to quickly set out for Aleppo and to report to the European consuls on the Armenian situation, which had been my intention before I became ill. In mid-June I was in Aleppo. I spoke there first with the German consul and urged him, for the sake of the good reputation of the Germans, to do everything to stop the threatened demise of the Armenian people. If this would not happen, the entire civilized world would accuse Germany of complicity in the murder of the Armenian people.

I also addressed the same subject in the Austrian and American consulates. In Aleppo, I met Baron Max von Oppenheim,[18] who greeted me like a friend. I also gave him a written report on the situation of the Armenian people. I knew that the baron had come to Turkey on a diplomatic mission. I, therefore, hoped that the step I had taken would be effective. I had known the baron personally for years but not as a friend of the Armenians.

Oppenheim's task at the time was, in the interest of the Central Powers, to set up information centers in all of the larger towns in the Turkish Empire. He, therefore, gave me a sum of money, which I was to dispense to the Germans in Urfa to set up a center where pictures, telegrams, and newspapers could be distributed.

5. Fatal Hours

Upon my return to Urfa at the beginning of July, I ran across Armenian corpses that had already been eaten by animals. They were deportees who had fallen by the wayside; it was a sure sign that the greatest suffering of that poor people had begun.

When I arrived in Urfa, I didn't see our pharmacist. A few days earlier, the police had taken him from the pharmacy and imprisoned him. As an advisor to the government, this man had been active on behalf of the Turkish state, which he could do because I had allowed him to scale back his work in the pharmacy to one hour per day just so the government would not be deprived of his great discretion and competence. He was never interrogated in the jail and never received the bastinado. He was just incarcerated until he fell victim to the knife on August 12. I later heard from a Turkish gossip that he had been foreseen as the provisional governor of Urfa in an Armenian revolt that was supposedly being planned. Whether this had a basis in fact was beyond me.

Two well-known Armenians, members of parliament Vartkes [Serenkiwlian][19] and [Krikor] Zohrab,[20] came through Urfa as prisoners. They were allowed to continue in a sprung carriage. However, they met their fate an hour outside Urfa. A Turkish officer escorting them shot them. The municipal doctor from Urfa had to ride out and write up a death certificate. This said that both men died of typhus. Why was there such a concern for a medical certification? Because of the high insurance payments that the government wanted to appropriate, it was said.

The court-martial that had been set up in Urfa since January was replaced by another in July. The members of the first were

Urfa Turks and, therefore, not hard enough against the Armenians. The newly named members were Turks from outside and carried out business more to the liking of the Young Turks.

In order to review the mountain of documents seized in Armenian houses, the court-martial needed two translators. The Syrian Protestant Aghnatheos and the Syrian Protestant pastor Ephraim [K. Jernazian][21] were appointed. The former understood no European language, only Armenian; and the latter, in addition to his Armenian mother tongue, spoke Turkish, English, and some French. It is indicative that this pastor, an Armenian, was forced to do this work. In the murder trial against the Armenian people, the judges were assigned an *Armenian*, who was forced to help implement the official plan to exterminate his own people.

How very Turkish!

Ephraim, the pastor, was, of course, not seen as an Armenian by the government. Since he was a pastor of the *Syrian* parish, officials considered him a Syrian. Since he was a very high-strung Christian, he told the police director that he was an Armenian. The police director cursed him: He should shut his mouth if he knew what was good for him.

In July (when it was already known that the fateful hour for the Armenians of Urfa had arrived) at the urging of the women, some Armenians fervently agitated for a conversion to Islam as the only way to rescue their lives. But the success was minimal. The great majority of the Armenians preferred death to profession of the hated religion of Mohammed.

Already at the end of June, the first deportation trains from Harput and Erzurum in the north had arrived in Urfa. Those unfortunates who could hide in the Christian houses in the city in order to escape the farther journey into the desert described terrible experiences that they had had on the journey. The most appalling thing was that only women and children had arrived in Urfa. Where were the men who were there when the trains departed? No one knew—or to be correct, everyone knew but wanted to deny the reality—that the heinous machinery of a blind government had separated the men from the women and had beaten masses of them to death in the Taurus Mountains between Malatya and Samsat. The lamenting women, the defenseless mothers, the helpless children! They were the next to die or to be beaten to death on the next leg of the journey.

More evacuations of Armenians followed at the end of July. This time they were not allowed to take their own carriages and had to march through the steppe on foot. Those who were driven to the north in the direction of Diyarbakır[22] did not get far. The Turkish knives were most often waiting for them outside the city walls. Those who were driven to the district capital (Aleppo) could hope to arrive somewhat safely.

The highest cleric of the Armenians in Urfa still enjoyed complete freedom until the beginning of August. He summoned me in order to describe the great danger and hardship.

"Everything is finished. My people are on the slaughtering block. I have no one to help me. We Armenians are the children of death. I also only have a few days to live."

These words were spoken in a flood of tears by a broken man. He implored me to go to Europe and to try to see that something be done for the dying people. His one hope was that if the European powers were to receive a reliable account of the terrible situation of the Armenian people, they would take some step or other to help them. I earnestly considered such a trip. Above all others, I would have gone to the Armenians' most reliable friend, Dr. [Johannes] Lepsius, because if there was anyone in a position to do something, it was he. That is what I considered doing in that hour of reflection. I did not have any money for the journey. If the Turks would let me travel to Europe at all, which was highly questionable, I would arrive too late. Additionally, the events were rushing ahead. And the experience of the next months showed that I could better serve the unfortunate people by staying in Urfa than if I had risked a journey to Europe with the prospect of gaining little or nothing.

In the last days of July, gruesome rumors made the rounds. It was said that men and boys down to the age of twelve had been slaughtered.

On August 10 two ranking members of the Young Turk Committees for Unity and Progress, Ahmed and Halil Bey, appeared in Urfa. One of them was a relative of Vice-Generalissimo, Enver Paşa. It was reported that they had come from Constantinople to travel throughout Anatolia to order the killing of Armenian men and older boys and the evacuation of the remaining women and children. The Armenians of Urfa were now at the mercy of these hangman's assistants. The unfortunate people of Urfa would now get a taste of what had happened in other locations. The first deed of the two Young Turks in Urfa was to evacuate the many Armenians who were still in prison. Ahmed and Halil Bey boldly pushed aside the Urfa officials and acted as if they were in charge. Armenians from the city came to them and pleaded with them to evacuate prisoners as planned to Aleppo and not to Diyarbakır. The two promised to do that in exchange for a large sum of money. On the evening of August 11, they received a payment of 60,000 francs. But the next morning, the prisoners were sent on their way to Diyarbakır. The next day it was already known in Urfa that none of them had survived.

6. Away with the Labor Battalions

The Turks succeeded in the course of the last months in gradually pulling out another 1,000 Armenian men, who were deployed as a labor battalion building streets near the city. One battalion worked in Karaköprü [Black Bridge][23] an hour north, and the other in Kudama, five hours south of Urfa. The people were industrious, and impressive stretches of road had already been built. The two Young Turks now ordered the slaughter of this worker battalion. The first to go was the group from Karaköprü. An Armenian who was in the battalion was able to escape. He told me what happened. I will let him speak for himself:

> "I was working for several weeks with about four hundred of my countrymen in the work battalion on the road to Karaköprü. On August 15 two members of

our battalion went to Urfa without permission. When they showed up a few days later, Kurdish villagers from Karaköprü shot at them right next to our tent. One died immediately, the other was only wounded and was able to save himself beneath our tents. On the evening of that day, 180 of us were ordered to get ready to set out in the night to prepare a section of road for the transport of cannons a few hours away. After supper, we were ordered to play music, which we often had to do, but it also often created joy in our soldiers' lives. At nine o'clock, evening taps were sounded. Two hours later we set out. The necessary tools were on a carriage. Some Turkish gendarmes, who were constantly guarding us while we did the road work, went along. After a two–hour march, we stopped and were allowed to smoke cigarettes. Up until that point we had no idea what would happen to us. We had known for a long time that our fate was getting worse from day to day. Every day at work we saw long lines of deportees traveling past us, and we often had to dig makeshift graves for the bodies of murdered Armenians.

"We had hardly rested for fifteen minutes when about forty mounted gendarmes from the city came up to us. They brought with them fifteen Armenians chained together. The gendarmes surrounded us. Then came the order to tie us together. Now we knew that our hour had come. I whispered to my comrades in Armenian not to let themselves be tied together. But we were already looking at loaded rifles, so we thought it would have been in vain to resist. Then the murderers ran out of rope. About sixty of us remained to be tied, including myself. Now we marched farther on our way to death. In the morning, we arrived in the Kurdish village of Yedikuyu, where we were distributed among different houses. The comrades and I who were not tied were brought to a large courtyard, where we were closely guarded. In the course of the morning, some notorious Turks came from the city and looked us over. Apparently, they wanted to take part in the shooting. It was midday when the call suddenly rang out: Get moving!

"We were led from the village under heavy arms. We came across a pile of clothing that we recognized as having belonged to our comrades. We were now ordered to take off our clothes. We were only permitted to keep a shirt. Then we were tied together, two at a time, with bloody ropes. That was hardly done when the order to march was given. After a march of a few minutes over a pile of massacred comrades, some of whom were still in death throes, they led us to the ledge of a cliff. Now the constables and the Turks who had come from the city mocked us as 'traitors.'

"They took off the ropes from the two in the front. One after the other they had to jump off the cliff, but not before running between two gendarmes armed with long knives, each of whom stabbed the victim. When it was my turn, I was able to inconspicuously loosen my rope; and as we were ordered to step to the front, I quickly grabbed a large rock and threw it against the chest of one constable so that he fell. I didn't wait for the other constable to stab me but jumped off the cliff without hurting myself. A shot rang out behind me, but it missed. I found protection under the overhanging cliffs for the time being.

"After all sixty comrades were thrown from the cliffs, the gendarmes and the Turks came down to see who had survived this leap of death. Each victim was tied by the foot and dragged away from the pile. Blows with an axe and individual shots were intended to ensure that no one escaped death. I lay on my face and pretended to be dead. As they dragged me away, one of the gendarmes said: "This looks like the dog who tried to get away." They shot me once, and I felt the warm blood running down my back. When the corpses had all been removed and the executioners wanted to leave, one of them said that one of the victims was still breathing. They were talking about me. I immediately received a blow of the axe on my neck.

"The band of murderers finally departed. A short time later, a Kurd appeared. He cried 'Bedo, Bedo!' Bedo was one of us who was still alive and who now moved a little in response to this call. The Kurd whispered to him that he should hide behind a large rock because he could not rescue him by daylight. Bedo was in fact severely wounded, but the Kurd, who was a business friend, wanted to rescue him. I don't know if he succeeded. After the Kurd left, I tried to stand up. There were fifteen of us who, although severely wounded, could still move about. We discussed what we could do. I suggested that we return to the city by night. Most of them did not have enough energy to do that, so only three of us left in the night. In a nearby garden, we fortified ourselves by enjoying some melons.

"After marching a few hours in the night, we heard a large crowd of people coming toward us. We sought protection in a nearby vineyard. Who were they? Then we recognized them: 200 comrades from our battalion who had stayed behind yesterday in Karaköprü. They were now going the same way we had gone.

I could not go any farther that night, and my two companions were also exhausted. We decided to hide in the vineyard under the vines. We were only able to reach Urfa the next night. That was on August 19. We saw bludgeoned victims lying in the streets. A massacre had also taken place there. I had to stand in front of my house and knock and call for a long time. Finally, my wife recognized my voice and let me in. So much for the Armenians."

The other labor battalion that was working in Kudama did not fare any better. Their day of reckoning was August 22. Unfortunately, I never saw any Armenians from this battalion again, although there were reports that some of them were able to escape. There were also Syrians in that Kudama battalion. I will let one of them report on what happened there:

"In the evening," the Syrian said, "a large band of well-armed gendarmes arrived from the city. They immediately ordered the separation of the Armenians from the Syrians. About fifteen minutes later, the Armenians were tied together and led away. Soon, one could hear a lot of shooting. From the distance we could only see a big pile of people. But it was clear to us that our Armenian comrades were now being slaughtered. From the surrounding Arab villages, we saw Arabs riding toward the pile. Between shots we heard the powerful "lilililili"of the Arab women. We knew these cries, which are usually heard among Mohammedans in battle. Mohammedan women do it in order to fire up their husbands for the killing of Christians. A while later we saw a group of people fleeing toward the mountains and the Turks were shooting at them. The shooting only stopped when darkness came.

"When the gendarmes returned to the village, we Syrians thought that it was now our turn. We had to take lanterns and go off in the direction of the slaughter. When we arrived, we received the order to pull a dead Turkish officer and two dead gendarmes from among the twitching bodies and take them back to the village. On the following morning, the three dead Turks were loaded on a carriage and taken to the city. We still had to throw the murdered Armenians in a deep well. Among them were several who were still breathing; and one who could walk jumped into the well by himself. When the dead and the half-dead were sunk, we had to wall in the well and throw dirt and ash on it. We learned from the gendarmes guarding us what had happened the day before. When the slaughter began and it was the turn of some strong Garmuj Armenians, they threw stones with their free hands at the gendarme, who was busy with the slaughter. He fell down, and in an instant, they tore his knife away from him and cut through the rope. Then they took away his loaded rifle and shot an officer and two gendarmes. In the next moment, they were killed by the other gendarmes. This unexpected incident enabled the other waiting Armenians to cut through their ropes, and a great number fled to the nearby mountain. Those were the fleeing troops that we had seen from the distance."

7. August 19th

On August 19 Turkish police conducted house searches in the Armenian city district. They were looking for Armenians who had deserted. The police were suddenly fired upon from an ambush. One policeman fell, and two others fled and alerted the police station. As soon as the two Young Turk functionaries from Constantinople heard of the incident, they gave the orders to the mob: "Down with the *gâvurs*,[24] what are you waiting for?"

This call was only too gladly received. Those who weren't carrying weapons hurried home to get them, and those who had them immediately participated in the destruction of Christians by attacking the first ones they could find. From the hospital, I could see how the Kurds in their district—which like our hospital lay outside the city—hurried home; in a few moments they came back armed and ran to the market. As many Christians as possible would be sent to their deaths before sunset. After the first shots, most of the Armenians had fortunately shut down their stands in the market. Others were urged by well-meaning Mohammedans to go home as quickly as possible. Unfortunately, not everyone got the news in time about the looming danger; some, who were on their way home, had the surprise of their lives before they arrived. It was a gruesome hunt for human beings, an appalling slaughter.

The tailor Kevork and his four journeymen were so preoccupied with their work in his shop on the market that they did not notice the uncanny preparations by the Kurds and Turks. His workshop was on a street leading from the market. The mob had to get there first. It did not take long before the executioners arrived. Before Kevork could even understand what the danger was, his throat was cut with a sharp knife. Not one of his journeymen could escape. Not one of them even thought of defending himself with scissors. Blood streamed over the threshold of the peaceful tailor shop. I could still see a pool of blood on the street a few days later. The five dead bodies lay in the completely plundered shop. Many Syrians lost their lives on that day because the murderers did not distinguish between Syrians and Armenians; they were both Christians, and non-believers. When there were no more Christians on the street, the mob hurried in the night to the Armenian quarter. Shots rang out from the Armenian houses. That brought the massacre to a close for the day.

I was still in the hospital at twilight. I had not ridden as usual to the vineyard, about an hour away, where my family lived. The Armenians in the German mission hospital needed my protection and comfort.

In the vicinity of the mission hospital was a large, fortress-like house that belonged to the butcher Shiko and his large family. Shiko had seven grown-up sons, two of whom had been sent to their deaths in Diyarbakır. That evening, after they were finished with their bloody work at the market and were returning to the city, the Kurdish mob turned to his house. But the two large gates withstood their attempt to force their way in. The band knew that outside of the old man Shiko and his elderly brother, there were no men at home. Now the Kurds were shrieking so loudly that we could hear them with horror in the hospital. They wanted to get the two old men and molest all the women that night. They screamed fanatical curses in all directions.

I had requested two gendarmes from the governor to protect our hospital. They must have come with other gendarmes into this quarter of the city. I asked them to see to it that order prevailed. They did so and drove away the bloodthirsty, sensation-seeking mob.

The next morning, I found old man Shiko dead in front of his house. He had sacrificed himself for his family in the hope that the mob would leave the women and children alone. A day later, I pulled his elderly brother from his narrow hiding place.

When peace had returned to the city and our district, I could, for the first time, return to my family in the vineyard. Fortunately, my family had not heard about the events in the city. Early the next morning, before I had returned to the city, a shootout began in a neighboring vineyard. Riders from the city had arrived and were hunting down Armenians, who had found refuge in the neighboring vineyard. I heard afterwards that they were looking for Armenians who had fled from Karaköprü. They were shot down. Imagine the fear of those Armenians who were in my vineyard. A considerable number had sought and found protection with my family. They implored me, above all, not to abandon them now. But my presence was urgently required in the city. How would they get along in the hospital, and what would happen there if it became known that I was not on the premises?

We had just noticed the gendarmes after they had killed the refugees and we were preparing to return to the city. So for the time being, my people in the vineyard had nothing to fear. When I arrived at the hospital, I found the remaining inhabitants of the Shiko house there. They explained that they had to stay under the protection of the hospital. I could not send them away, so I distributed them throughout the hospital and in my own apartment.

I visited the Turkish governor that morning. I thanked him for reacting so quickly to my request for protection at the hospital. I asked him for ongoing protection until things returned to normal. I also told him my opinion about the events of the day before. The governor regretted the incident but said that he had succeeded in restoring order, and he could guarantee that such a situation would not occur again.

It was actually a quiet day in the city. The murdering did not start up again. But who could blame the terrified Christians if none of them left their houses that day and the days that followed? In the evening, I took a walk with my wife in the Syrian quarter in order to comfort friends. But we had to step over bodies. The air was already putrid with the smell of death in the streets. Although the Turks called upon the Christians to bury the dead, no one dared leave the house. Finally, the Turks themselves had to gather the bodies. They were dragged face down through the streets and buried in a makeshift grave.

It could be assumed that in the Armenian quarter, there were still some wounded who did not dare leave their houses. On the third day, wounded Armenian women appeared in our clinic. The first of the wounded men came several days later.

On the days of the massacre, the master tailor Hagop fell into the hands of the Young Turk Ahmed Bey. Hagop begged at his feet for mercy. Bey drew his revolver and shot him down with the words: "That is mercy for you, you Armenian dog."

Our pharmacy assistant, who had gone to the post office shortly before the outbreak of the storm on August 19, had not returned. We had to assume that he was a victim, but he appeared the next day. The Turk who had hidden him in his house brought him to us.

None of the Armenians in our house could be persuaded in the next few days to leave, even though the government had announced that nothing would happen to the Armenians. I, therefore, had to do the necessary shopping or hire Mohammedans to do it.

Now, one has to know that in Urfa, as almost everywhere else in the Turkish Empire, the trades were almost exclusively in the hands of the Armenians. In order to ensure that there was bread for the next few days, the government, only after great effort, was able to get the Armenian bakers to leave their houses and hiding places. For the next few weeks, a gendarme kept guard to protect the Armenian bakers. Armenians in other trades that were not absolutely necessary were not seen for weeks on the street.

8. Deportees from the North

Urfa was the transit point to the Mesopotamian steppe for hundreds of thousands of those trains of deportees who came from the northern *vilayets*[25] of Sivas, Erzurum, and Mamuret ul-Aziz. These trains arrived in Urfa ever sadder and more miserable. There were no longer any men among the deportees, and only women and children from four to twelve years old were on the trains. The reports of those who could steal away from the camps and flee to us in the Armenian quarter were such that the tongue has no words; the appalling atrociousness is unspeakable. Thousands had started out together; but of those thousands, only small groups arrived in Urfa. That was the case for all the trains. And every deportee caravan arrived with reports of experiences that overwhelmed the senses in their monstrosity.

These occurrences had to diminish the Urfa Armenians' hope of remaining unharmed. They held clandestine meetings in their houses by night in order to advise each other on their bleak situation. Like the drowning man hanging on to a weak reed, those fearful ones entertained an illusory hope of rescue: The army of the Entente! The Entente, the Armenians thought, was the only force that could rescue them. They debated what they could do but never came to a conclusion. What could they do? Self-defense was out of the question. The blood of the youth had been washed away. Especially on August 19, more than one hundred men had been taken away in addition to both destroyed labor battalions. Now and again, an outside deserter showed up. The countrymen always helped the deserters to resist an evacuation if one should occur.

In order to illustrate the nature of the deportations, I would like to report on the experiences of some of our female workers as they reported them to me. I am convinced of the complete authenticity of their statements.

1. Vartar Kazanjian from Adıyaman reported: "We had found out that all our men had already been led off and killed, as we women and children received the order to emigrate. A large crowd of women then went to the governor to ask him not to send them away but to kill them on the spot. We wanted to request this kind of death as an act of mercy; but even this mercy was not granted, and we had to emigrate.

"One can reach the Euphrates River from our city Adıyaman in ten hours. Our human caravan took ten *days* to travel that distance because we were led back and forth so many times. Many of our young women and girls disappeared on the way to the Euphrates River. The first two nights they left us alone, but then they forced us every night to give them young girls, who came back the next morning dishonored. Once we attempted to send the debauchees young women instead of girls. The next morning, the mothers who perpetrated this deceit were shot down.

"In order to rescue the twelve-year-old daughter of my sister, I blackened her face to render her unrecognizable; then I gave her a baby to carry on her arm. We were able to deceive the gendarmes and Kurds who surrounded us because they thought the daughter of my sister was a young woman. As we arrived in Urfa, she already had the third baby on her arm; the others had succumbed to hunger and suffering.

"We had to wait for four days at the Euphrates River. We were robbed there and dishonored. Whoever had no money was thrown in the river. One woman from whom they had hoped to extort money was bound with a rope and thrown into the water. After a while she was pulled out and asked if she cared to part with her money? But she had none. She was tied again and thrown in the water. This time she succeeded in loosening the rope and drowning in the rapids of her own free will. Finally, the caravans ran out of food. One could get something to eat from the Kurds only at exorbitant prices. The way from Samsat to Urfa can be covered in ten hours; we took eight days. We left Adıyaman with 2,000 people and arrived in Urfa with only 400. These 400 were almost all sick or about to die from hunger.

"I had relatives in Urfa, and I wanted to flee to them. So I waited for the right moment to slip away from the caravans. I was able to do that. On the way, a Turk grabbed me, and he wanted to drag me into a nearby cave. In my fear, I took my last bundle of money and gave it to the debauchee and told him it contained fifty pieces of gold. He was so astonished that he let me go, and I fled back to the caravans. I had actually only given him fifty quarter *mejidiyehs*.[26] The next day I had to bury the dead, and I succeeded in slipping away to the German mission hospital.

"But when the people were evacuated from the hospital, I had to march again. Until Akçakalé, all the women and children evacuated from mission houses were treated well. Typhus was soon for many a merciful redeemer. Those who did not fall victim to typhus had to continue the march. Those who got sick along the way stayed behind; no one took care of them.

"Then I had to join the march to Rakka. The journey was gruesome. There was nothing to eat or to drink. Only after many days did we see Rakka beckoning from the distance. We hoped that we would be thrown into the river. Just before the city, the news came that we could return to Urfa; the sultan had pardoned us. A last hope spurred on our death-weary hearts. But only a few made it back to Akçakale. I became ill there. The others made it back to the vicinity of Urfa; but as the city became visible in the distance, they had to return to Rakka. It was horrible. As I awoke from my illness, I found myself in the house of Arabs. I was very well cared for; and when I could take a few steps again, the Arab brought me on a donkey to the hospital in Urfa."

2. *Almast Tamassian reported:* "At the time of the massacres of 1915, my parents had to emigrate from Divriği to Sivas. We were allowed to live there under the protection of the American missionary, Miss [Alice C.] Bewer.[27] My mother placed great value on education, and all seven of her children were sent to the mission school. I was trained as a teacher by the Americans in Harput. My only brother was a pharmacist. Our large family had to make the terrible deportation march together with thousands of fellow Armenians. The first few days of the journey went well; we were escorted by American missionaries. They were then sent back by the government. As soon as the Americans left us, our suffering began. First, they took away our men. They were tortured terribly before our eyes and then—often very slowly—killed. Thousands of women and children were thrown in the Kızıl.[28] Then, we were sent into the mountains where one could hardly go by foot. We were never again sent through a village. For days at a time, we received neither bread nor water. We had the largest loss of life at the Euphrates River near Samsat. More than 10,000 were thrown into the rapids. After the river, we had to wait a week. The money we had was stolen, and our girls were dishonored. The most devout soul was in despair. As long as one had some

money, one could preserve a little honor; but when the money was gone, that was not possible anymore.

"Because it was impossible to change clothes or wash, the dirt and stench gained the upper hand. Many of us had knife and sword wounds, which could not be cared for. Some of these unfortunate people had worms crawling over their bodies. One could hardly look at them. But we were so possessed by our stupefaction that nothing more made an impression on us.

"When we were finally driven on, we had to walk over dead, decomposing bodies. Finally, we were led onto a mountain where a large crowd of Kurds surrounded us. They stole all our clothing. My sister could not scale the mountain; she was completely exhausted and near death. She asked me to beat her to death with a club so she would not fall into the hands of the tormentors again. She took her last money from her hair and gave it to our mother. But a Kurd saw it, and, in the next moment, tore it away from her. It was really our last money. We had to leave behind the sister, never to see her again. After we left the mountain, my brother's wife gave birth. We could not find one scrap of clothing to swaddle the newborn; we had nothing on ourselves. As we continued, we came to a well that was full of decomposing human corpses. When we came to the next well shaft, they threw us in; but there were already many bodies in the depths and not much water, so not all who were thrown in died. They threw stones on us from above, and those who were hit were released by death. Unfortunately, no stone hit me. One of my sisters also survived in this hell. We spent the night in the terrible fetid air. We wished a thousand times that we were dead. When no one came the next morning to perform the work of mercy of throwing stones down the well shaft, we debated what to do. We found some money among the dead for our possible rescue and the next chapter of the ordeal. We knew that the money was most often hidden in the hair. We collected a few Turkish pounds, which we jingled the next time a Kurdish head looked down from above. The Kurd understood. He pulled us out and took the money as payment; we preliminarily escaped hell. How greedily did we breathe in the pure air!

For three days, we wandered lost in the mountains. One night I lost my sister. I do not know what happened to her. Now, I was completely alone. To whom could I turn? Finally, I saw a shepherd and asked him to show me the way to the next city. He said that there were no nearby cities, but not far away was the deportee road. He pointed it out to me. I soon made my way back to the deportees. There were groups of my countrymen who had come together to a place called Mohammedi Khan.[29] None of my relatives was there. A gentleman Mohammedan took me from there to Urfa. His name was Mohammed Halil, and he was one of the richest men in the city. But I was very sick when I arrived. Since I was not getting better, he sent me to the mission hospital. There was no space there, and I ended up in the courtyard of the Syrian Church, where others as miserable as I was eagerly awaited death. Finally, a woman said to me that I should go to the Künzlers because they helped all Armenians. I set off for their house, which was only fifteen minutes away; but in my great weakness, I needed three full hours to get there. I arrived at the house in a fever and received clothing, protection, help, and medicine. That was the end of my great suffering. I recovered slowly. And when Mr. Künzler opened an orphanage after the armistice, I was the teacher for what little remained of my people."

3. *The experiences of V[Y]ekhsa Bedrossian.* "It was July 10, 1915, when I had to leave my home in Harput with about 2,000 men, women, and children. My husband lived in America. I was able to take some money, clothes, and a bed on a donkey. My two daughters, ten and twelve years old, had to go with us. The first few days went by without incident from the Turks living nearby or the gendarmes escorting us. We stopped near Malatya. As deportee groups from Erzurum and Sivas joined us, we continued, not as we had hoped to Malatya, but south over the steep Taurus Mountains. We often had to climb on all fours over the cliffs. Many children and elderly people did not survive the hardships. There was no thought of burying those who had fallen. They lay where they fell, a welcome prey for wild animals. We had long since given up our baggage

because we had been forced to send back the donkey we had taken with us. In the high valley between Malatya and Adıyaman, the surrounding Kurds robbed us. They took our men from us. They were taken off to the side and killed. We were so far gone that we would have gladly died if we could only know what would happen to our children. On the way to Samsat, most of the young women and girls disappeared. Each Kurd in the vicinity took what he wanted from them.

"Beyond the river, on Urfa territory, our suffering reached a low point. No one received water without paying for it. We were driven from the wells with rifle butts. At a large spring where we took a break for a few days, we were completely robbed of money and jewelry. The robbers stole many kerosene canisters—the well-known boxes for transporting kerosene in the Orient—full of gold and jewelry. When there was nothing left to steal, we were driven into a stone desert. A large number of Kurds surrounded us. They took away our clothes and removed any of our possessions that might be of value. In the course of this clothing removal, it was discovered that there were some adolescent boys disguised as girls. They were hacked to pieces on the spot. Now the Kurds drove us—a large naked crowd of about 2,000 girls and women—onto a narrow place, and the nightmare began. We were shot at from all sides. An awful stampede started. Whoever was standing on the edge was shot down, and whoever was in the middle was suffocated. I only escaped death because I was able to stand on the dead bodies. With excruciating effort, I was able to pull both my daughters onto the raised mound. Their bodies were completely blue. There were only a few hundred of us left alive when the Kurds left us. Gendarmes, who could have driven us on, were nowhere to be seen; so we just sat there on the ground, each of us longing for our last hour. The next day, we had to move on because the smell of decaying flesh was too terrible. My two children cried day and night with little voices: 'Mother, bread, mother, bread!' ['*Mayrik hats, mayrik hats!*']. When some Kurdish horsemen came our way, I asked them to take my daughters with them. Thank God, they did! They took them along. I do not know what happened to them; I never saw them again. I could not cry any more when they left, my stream of tears had run dry. I only wished that I would die soon. I could not be very far from death. I had not, it seemed to me, eaten for weeks. Now and again I went a few steps farther with some other women like me who were looking for death. Finally, we entered a Kurdish village in order to ask for water. Although we were completely naked, the village Kurds first demanded money. After they saw that we had nothing for them, they drove us from the water. I wanted to drink from a puddle; but as soon as I tried, I received a blow on my arm from a sword. We continued without having been able to drink. The Mesopotamian August sun burned our naked bodies. To shield ourselves from the midday sun, we dug holes with our bare hands in the plowed earth and covered ourselves with dirt. When it got cold at night, we also used the dirt in these holes to protect ourselves against the cold. With large burns on our bodies, we finally reached a Christian village near Urfa. There, we received bread, water, and some clothing. I was given a short child's shirt, with which, after sixteen days of nakedness, I could cover only my most necessary nakedness. About 200 women slowly assembled in this village, the survivors from the 6,000 people who had started together on the journey from Malatya.

"Our stay in the village did not last long. The gendarmes came and drove us into a crowd again. That day we arrived in a deportee camp in Urfa. The next day people from Harput came to the camp. They had come in earlier transports to Urfa. They wanted to see who the newcomers were. Like many of us, I had become unrecognizable to them. Among those seeking us out were people from Harput to whom I identified myself. I was advised to flee; but that was only possible with a bribe. I borrowed a gold pound from a woman, and I gave it to the guard that night and was free. But where could I go? I would have gladly gone to the German hospital but could not find it. A Turk seized me and dragged me to his house. I soon became very ill, but this Turk himself took me to the mission hospital. I was able to recover there. I only escaped evacuation with the

Urfa population because on the day when the police picked up all the Armenians from the hospital, I had a high temperature. I later became the cook in Mr. Künzler's house.

"I still have the child's shirt with which I covered my naked body and will keep it as a relic to show my husband when I can see him again."[30]

9. The Calm before the Storm

After August 19, many people sought shelter in the houses of Europeans in Urfa. It was impossible to grant the many pleas to be taken in. When the time came for the evacuation, the government would hardly be stopped at the doors of the Europeans. But the pleas to be taken in were granted anyway, as much as places could be made for them. All of those taken in had to provide their own food.

In Urfa there was a carpet factory that belonged to the Deutsche Orient-Handels-und Industrie-Gesellschaft.[31] After the Armenian massacres in 1895, Dr. Lepsius moved the factory from Friesdorf in the Harz Mountains to Urfa and built it up over the years. Hundreds of widows from those times were able to provide a living for their children in this carpet factory. The factory had to close down at the beginning of the war because exports were no longer possible. There was lots of space in the rooms of this factory, where more than 1,000 people could stay. Many also brought things of value with them without registering them when they arrived. Among those staying in the factory were a number of men who knew what was in store for them.

During a visit I made to the governor in Urfa in mid-September, he told me that the Armenians did not want to go to work any more. It had been confirmed that many had barricaded their houses. The Armenians could, of course, not expect mercy any more with such a confrontational attitude.

During sick calls in Turkish homes, I often saw how tense the situation had become. More than one Turk said to me that he would slaughter the Armenians without mercy.

The deportations from the north continued. Once, several hundred naked women arrived in Urfa. There were no more men left at all among the deportees.

If one had to travel through the country during these times, then one ran across human cadavers lying around everywhere. If the dead were hastily buried, this was done so poorly that the wild animals had no problem pulling out the bodies again. One always ran across blood-stained places where people had been killed. I had never seen such misery and distress in this land of chronic need. And yet, the worst had not yet begun for Urfa. It was clear to everyone that the worst was yet to come along with the numbing feeling of not being able to escape what was about to happen.

There were no more Armenians in the bazaar in the city markets or wherever trade and commerce occurred. Who could know when the bomb would explode? In order to put up resistance, the Armenians needed, above all, weapons and ammunition. There was a more or less good weapon in every home. But there were only a few modern rifles. Now a cold-blooded, brave Armenian who eventually was to become the soul of the resistance used the quiet before the storm to go to the provincial capital of Aleppo, buy ammunition, and bring it to Urfa. He disguised himself as a Turkish officer and outfitted some friends with Turkish military uniforms. He gave them Mohammedan names and transported them through the country with ammunition bought in Aleppo. Most of the time they went through villages and avoided the small towns. The caravans arrived in Urfa at sunset. Anyone who saw the caravans did not think twice about them because such troops were constantly traveling through the country in those wartime days. The leader, Mgrdich,[32] could only use the time shortly after sunset, when the population was not in the streets but at home eating dinner.

During this time the blacksmiths, of all the tradesmen, had a lot of work to do; their job was the manufacturing of hand grenades.

10. Deathly Fear

The first shots rang out in the Armenian quarter on the night of September 29. The next morning I heard it said that in a house where people had been carousing, some drunks had fired their weapons for fun.

The police came at noon to investigate the shooting. The Armenians had requested the investigation because it was clear that the behavior of their irresponsible countrymen represented a renewed danger for the already extremely harried Armenian people, and that one had to deal decisively with such irresponsible individuals. The police found the house from which the shots had originated sealed. When they tried to enter it over a low, flat roof, they were greeted with gunfire and had to retreat. They now, of course, had to call for reinforcements; and what would normally have been a harmless incident became a top state priority of the Turkish officials.

It was noon when I planned to travel by carriage into the city in order to take the sick American missionary Rev. [Francis H.] Leslie[33] out of the confines of the city. A guard who was already standing in front of his door prevented everyone, including me, from entering. I could not remove the sick man. When the police arrived with reinforcements, they were greeted anew with gunfire which was well-aimed and mostly fatal. The police had great losses and retreated. Every Muslim who showed his face in the Armenian quarter was shot down. The Turks erected barricades in the streets at night and separated the Armenian quarter from the Turkish. The Armenians occupied all the important houses on the periphery of their quarter. From there, every Turk, Kurd, or Arab who showed his face was a welcome target.

At first the agitated Turks could do nothing against the Armenians. But it must have inflamed fanaticism among the Mohammedans that no *mullah*[34] could ascend his minaret to call the Mohammedans to prayer, as was the custom, because a well-aimed Armenian bullet would have snuffed out his life. Most of the time the Armenians acted defensively. Some days there was a heavy exchange of gunfire, especially at night. A panic suddenly broke out in the Muslim quarter on the third day, just as I was on my way to make a house call on a sick Mohammedan. "The gâvurs are coming, the gâvurs are coming," the inhabitants shouted in the streets. The shopkeepers quickly shut their shops and fled to their houses. Others appeared with weapons on the street, but nothing happened. Apparently, someone had seen some armed Armenians on the street.

There were no soldiers in those days in Urfa. The gendarmes were preoccupied with plundering and bullying the deportees marching outside the city; therefore, the government telegraphed to Aleppo for help. A general[36] was sent with a division of troops, and the Kurds from the surrounding area were also mobilized against the insubordinate Armenians. When a large crowd of these mounted Kurds tried to enter Urfa, they were fired at by Armenians in broad daylight. By making a great detour, they finally entered the city. They had to gallop through a short stretch of field that lay in the line of fire. We saw the skirmish from my house. One of the horsemen fell from his horse, hit by a good shot. An hour later, the wounded man was brought to our house on a donkey. The Kurdish officials could do nothing against the entrenched Armenians. Anyone who showed his face would fall victim to the gunfire of the watchful Armenians. Even the Turkish infantry, which arrived on the third day of the occupation, could not make headway against the entrenched Armenians. First, the heavy artillery had to be brought in.

11. Occupation of the German Industrial Grounds

The previously mentioned carpet factory with its warehouse and workshops for spinning, dyeing, and hand weaving was between the two enemy camps. The large buildings towered over the whole Muslim quarter; therefore the occupation of this building complex had to be of great value for both the combatant parties. It is also significant that the Armenians first thought about occupying the factory, from whose roofs one could easily sweep the whole Muslim quarter. In addition, there were about a thousand countrymen in the rooms. The director of the firm, Mr. [Franz] Eckart,[35] was told what the Armenians wanted to do. What should he do to stop it? Should he just let the occupation occur? Would that not mean the ruin of the company? One must after all assume that the Turks would finally overwhelm the Armenians. The expected bombardment would also be disastrous for the building. Another thing to fear would be plundering; naturally, there would be no distinction made between German and Armenian property. So with a heavy heart, Mr. Eckart decided to ask the Turkish government to occupy the factory plant before the Armenians came to do the same.

Instead of immediately occupying the building, the Turkish general waited until the next morning. The Armenians who had found refuge in the factory rooms were informed by the younger brother of Mr. Eckart of the plans to turn the building over to the Turks. This news created outrage in their ranks. Most were not ready to surrender without resistance to the Turks. Therefore, a large number broke out through a window the next night and fled into the Armenian quarter. I never understood why Armenians, after they found out that the Turks would occupy the building, did not decide to occupy it themselves.

The next morning the Turkish general took over the German building. About 400 people, mostly women and children, were presented as factory workers. The general ordered their transfer to the German orphanage on the outskirts of the city. However, seven men, also employees of the German factory and the German orphanage, were put in jail. Mr. Eckart was assured that nothing would happen to them. Although Mr. Eckart asked to take them into his private home, the Turkish general refused the request. He had other things in store for them. Besides, they had to be interrogated to see whether they really were not involved as Mr. Eckart maintained.

The same day, the expected ordnance arrived in Urfa. The Turks wanted to bring it in by daylight, but the Armenians were vigilant. Since the street was about 500 meters from the line of fire, the Turks were forced to stop the transport of their cannons halfway to the destination. The troops beat a hasty retreat. Only with the onset of night were they able to bring the murderous devices into the city. A terrible battle began. Some courageous and technically informed Armenians broke out in order to steal the locking pieces for the ordnance. They were not able to do so. Despite a half hour of heavy shooting about 300 meters from our house, no one seemed to have been killed in this skirmish. The Turkish bullets mostly struck the erect Muslim gravestones that lined the entire street.

12. The American Mission Station

At the highest point of the Armenian quarter was the American Mission Institute, which consisted of several connected buildings. From the beginning of the occupation, there was heavy gunfire from these buildings. It was therefore, without a doubt, occupied and controlled by the Armenians. The director of the institute, the American Mr. Leslie, was also present. In addition, there were so-called "belligerents," or European civil detainees, who, one had to assume, had fled into the American house from the beginning. The situation of these Europeans and Americans was certainly not enviable, especially now that the bombardment was about to begin. Mr. Leslie succeeded in sending the governor a letter by throwing it into the Mohammedan quarter; and from there, it found its way to the governor. In this letter, [Mr.] Leslie, together with the belligerents, asked to be freed. The general called me after receiving the letter. He said that since I was Mr. Leslie's friend, then I should try to free him and the civil detainees. For this purpose, he gave an order that no one who left the quarter from the American [Mission] Institute was to be shot at.

I suggested that the general give me permission to enter the Armenian quarter and bring out the people. But this somewhat hasty and imprudent suggestion was not accepted. The general thought that since I was Swiss, he did not want to assume the responsibility for such an attempt. I then suggested that I be allowed to send Mr. Leslie a letter, and that was granted. I wrote right away and asked my friend to leave the American house with the belligerents and to go to a certain street.

I went behind the barricades with this letter. I shouted an Armenian name long and loudly. Finally, an answer came from the house. Who was I? I identified myself: "Jakob Effendi" I asked the person who had answered to come so I could hand him a letter. He need not be afraid, nothing would happen to him. But the Armenians asked me to come into the quarter because nothing would happen to me. Finally, an adolescent boy looked out of the door and asked me again to come. I told him to go to a certain house into which I would throw a letter weighted with a stone, and he was to take it to the American missionary, Mr. Leslie.

When Mr. Leslie did not appear in the course of three hours, I went back to the barricade and shouted again. It took a long time again. Finally, I heard that Mr. Leslie's answer could be read on his house.

Under police protection, I climbed the hill from where I could see the American building with binoculars. On the wall in large letters stood the message: "We want to come, but they won't let us."

That evening the American Institute was bombarded with cannon fire from three sides.

13. Collapse of the Resistance

After being bombarded for several days, the various barricaded houses on the periphery were to be stormed. Since a large number of wounded would be expected, as the chairman of the German mission hospital I received the order to remove all the patients and to keep all the beds free for the wounded. A few days before, the Turks had expelled the sick Armenians from the municipal hospital because it was no longer appropriate to do something good for the countrymen of the insurgents. Many of the expelled patients were sent to me. I acquiesced to a Turkish demand, moved into the large house belonging to Shiko, and relocated all my patients there. From the carpet factory building, I took all the beds I needed from those that had belonged to the Armenians who had been driven out.

The first wave of the attack did not lead to taking the occupied houses. The attackers had to retreat with great losses. Some Syrian Christians from a labor battalion were sent out with axes to break down the doors and died in the attack. After the first attack, a large number of wounded Turks came into our hospital for treatment. One of the wounded said that twenty-three of his comrades had stormed an Armenian house; and after just a few minutes, with nothing to show for their efforts, they had to retreat. In addition to several dead, all but five were wounded. The hand grenades thrown by the Armenians had taken a heavy toll.

The Armenians had enough food to hold out for months. Although the Turks had shut off the water from the city from the beginning, that did not matter because almost every house had a well in addition to a running water conduit. The nine-centimeter grenades did not inflict great damage on the massive stone buildings. Larger caliber artillery was not available. The incendiary grenades caused little damage to the houses because there was so little wooden material. If a single house or a room actually burned, that represented no great advance.

There is no doubt that by simply sticking together, the Armenians could have held off the Turks for months. But the old nemesis of the Armenians, their dissension, was fatal for them and a help for the Turks. Read the history of this, indeed, highly intelligent people. They were never unified. The watchword for the Swiss, "All for One, One for All," is one they do not know.

We already mentioned the leader Mgrdich, who was still the soul of the resistance. On the fifteenth day of the occupation, when Mgrdich was struck by a piece of shrapnel from a grenade during a consultation in the church, a great crowd of men, women, and children, favored surrender. The Armenian Protestant pastor, a man who had studied theology in America, indeed tried to negotiate with the Turks. He sent a few women with a white flag to the general who demanded unconditional surrender. The Armenians could no longer hope for mercy. The men were facing certain death; and the banishment of the women and children was just as certain. Why not wage a defense to the death? A large number of the women and young girls wanted nothing to do with surrender and preferred to die fighting than to lose their honor and die of hunger; but they could not prevent the surrender on the sixteenth day. The pastor urged the fearful ones not to surrender. He accompanied this with the assertion that the Russians were already in Diyarbakır, only two days journey from Urfa.

14. The Surrender

On the morning of October 16, the Armenians surrendered to the Turks. Women and children, according to the order, were supposed to assemble in certain streets and not carry anything in their hands. Those who had something in their hands would be immediately shot, according to the order from the general. The men were to assemble in other locations with their hands held high during their surrender. I hoped that Mr. Leslie and his charges would be among the first ones to appear, and I went to the police in order, if possible, to see them and talk to them. On the way there, I ran into a long, long line of women and children. It was an abominable, gruesome, and despairing sight to have to see all these horrific, despairing, and familiar faces and to read the hopelessness in their expressions. They were, more than ever before, the victims of death. They wrung their hands and cried to me: "O, brother Jakob, save us, save us!" But what could I do for them? Nothing. I was near despair myself that there was no way to bring about their rescue. The women and children were preliminarily herded into three large buildings. They were to wait there until further notice. The men were divided into two groups. Those who looked like they might be of some significance were put in jail, and those who did not look like they were revolutionaries were brought to the Mosque courtyards where they were closely guarded.

I met Mr. Leslie, the belligerents, and his Armenian employees at the police station. Thanks to the good relationship I always had with the police, I was allowed to speak briefly with Mr. Leslie. He gave me some money that he had with him. No sooner had I put it in my pocket than a policeman appeared and demanded to see the contents of my pockets, which I immediately showed him. He thought that Mr. Leslie had given me a revolver. Since I noticed that I was not welcome there, I left. There was a large crowd in front of the government building. A Russian with a long, white, flowing beard had just been brought in. He was a detainee who lived in the Armenian quarter where he had been found. He could neither walk nor speak and was brought in on a donkey. He lay stretched out on the platform of the police building. The gendarmes kicked him. I saw at first glance that he was severely ill and had no idea of what was happening around him. I stepped between him and the gendarmes, and they left him alone. My request to the police commissioner to transfer the sick to the hospital was granted; the dying man did not make it. I tried to make my way farther into the city because I had patients to visit in the Mohammedan district. The agitation in the streets was enormous, and the scenes were terrible. Well-known Armenians were being brought in from all directions. They were escorted by soldiers who sustained wild curses and stones from the mob. I thought it advisable to turn back and return to the hospital. A seventeen-year-old girl had just been brought in by Turkish soldiers. She had been shot in the abdomen because she had refused to surrender. Why the soldiers dragged her to us instead of just killing her, I was not able to understand. Apparently, she had impressed them with her courage and her beauty. Luckily she died quickly and was spared any further evil.

As evening approached and Mr. Leslie had not returned from the police, I went there with some food. It was as I suspected; he was in jail. Through my efforts, I succeeded in getting him released and took him home with the guarantee that I would not let him escape. On the way home, we crossed over a mosque square, which was sealed off by soldiers. They ordered us to leave immediately. We had hardly reached my house, which was 200 meters away, when a group of Armenians was shot on the mosque square. Shots rang from other directions too.

It was clear that the slaughter of the Armenians of Urfa had begun.

15. Hagob

The human slaughter lasted for a few days. It was carried out in the hours before sunset. The dead were usually put in mass graves. In a little valley on the way to our vineyard, a number of people had been killed and the bodies covered with a little earth. In the spring, when there was a heavy rainfall, a number of the half-decomposed bodies were washed out. Later, human bones were carried away by the water and scattered farther down the valley.

One day during the slaughter, someone knocked at my door at ten at night. I was already in bed. In the dark of night, I could discern an unclothed human form through the glass window in the house door. I opened the door. A man covered with blood was standing before me: "O, Jakob Effendi, for God's sake, give me a little place where I can die." It was Hagob, the hospital porter, shivering from the cold. His whole face was contorted. I did not need to ask him what had happened. There was no doubt that he was one of those who had been led to their deaths on that evening near our house. Through a turn of fate ordained by God, he had escaped death. He had been left for dead, but he was only severely wounded and unconscious. What should I do now? At the moment I really did not know. That same day the Turkish general had threatened me, saying that if I took in Armenians in the future, he would treat me like one of them. The poor fellow was brought into a little room and covered. Then I hurried into the bedroom where my wife was anxiously awaiting me. You can believe me when I say that in those days, when bullets were flying through the air and death was lurking in every corner, the women were in constant fear if their husbands even took a step out the door.

But this time because I was so perplexed, it was my wife who got me back on track. "The poor fellow is wounded, and a doctor in wartime is required to treat friend and foe alike. And this man is even a friend. It is simply your duty to take him to the hospital." The good woman was right. So I got dressed and took the poor man to the hospital, which was not near our house. We stitched his many wounds, and he recovered.

16. Turkish Promises

We Europeans brought some food every day to the women whom the Turks had brought into the three Khan buildings,[37] as well as to the men in jail. We also brought food to the seven men who had been led away from the carpet factory and thrown in jail under orders of the general. In the course of the surrender, these seven men were brought to the so-called Petroleum Khan, which was outside the city. We were also able to send them food there. We could see the people. One morning I brought them the food myself. This gave me the opportunity to see them all and speak with them.

They looked terrible, hardly recognizable. They said that they had been repeatedly bastinadoed. The pastor, the father of our orphans, showed me his swollen arm, which had a large abscess. That was how the Turkish general treated the people whom he had promised the German industrial director would be left alone! On the way back I called on the general, and I asked him to give me the father of our orphans so that I could take him to the hospital where he had to be operated on. After all, he had promised to spare these people.

But he lit into me: "What, you dared to talk with these traitors? Who gave you permission to do so? If you do that again, I will give you the same treatment. I will now issue an order that will make a new visit impossible for you."

These words from a man, whose willfulness held the whole population of Urfa hostage, did not sound hopeful. It was the last morning that the seven men saw. That afternoon they were shot according to martial law on a hill before the city. The general did not even think it worth the effort to inform Mr. [Franz] Eckart, who found out about the execution after the fact from a Turkish doctor associated with the house of the German Mr. Eckart. The doctor had acted as coroner; and from his descriptions of the victims, [Mr. Eckart] was able to conclude that they were his seven employees, about whom he had had no misgivings because he had trusted the word of the Turkish general.

17. The Death of Mr. Leslie

The American missionary Francis H. Leslie was my best friend. He had been on Turkish soil for just three years. We understood each other in everything very well. With my experience and knowledge, I could often support him. As I lay deathly ill in the spring with spotted fever, he was a true help to my wife. On his own, when our Armenian doctor was not able to master my situation, he called the famous mission doctor, Dr. [Fred] Shepard,[38] from Ayntab to my sick bed. We only differed on one point, namely politics. I was a friend of the Germans, while he was a friend of the Entente. But that never came between us. Why should it?

Because his wife was in her first confinement, he had sent her in the spring to Ayntab where there was a female mission doctor. He thereby had to live through all the terrible events in Urfa alone. He only had Armenian help at his side when he worked.

In June about 500 civil detainees came to Urfa. The American consul in Aleppo entrusted the care for all these people to Mr. Leslie. It was a tremendous job! Although he was assigned two helpers, it was just too much for the greatly overburdened man. At the beginning of July, I brought him the consulate shield and flag, which the American consul in Aleppo had sent by me. In a letter to Mr. Leslie, he was informed that he had been named an American consular agent. The Sublime Porte had already given the government in Urfa the necessary instructions. Mr. Leslie was supposed to hoist the flag on the next Sunday.

Early that Sunday morning, the stars and stripes were waving over the American building, and the consular shield hung over the door. But the moment of glory was short-lived. Around noon the police appeared and ordered Mr. Leslie to immediately take down the flag because he did not have permission to hoist it. There was nothing left to do but comply.

In those days a captured American, the mission's Dr. [Floyd O.] Smith[39] from Diyarbakır, was led through Urfa. Apparently, this gentleman had made himself unwelcome by his public protest against the deportation of Armenians from Diyarbakır, which is why the Turks transported him to Beirut on the coast. Mr. Leslie was able to speak with the prisoner for a moment in front of the police.

After he had been thoroughly shaken in May, Mr. Leslie had no peace. In March 1915 two Americans showed up in Urfa. At the request of the American consul in Aleppo, Mr. Leslie had sent the consul a postcard with secret writing indicating the arrival and further destination of the guests. In May the consul wrote back that he had only received a copy of the postcard and that the post office had kept the original.

At the beginning of August, the American vice consul arrived in Urfa. I hoped that Mr. Leslie would now have it easier. But right after the massacre on August 19, the vice consul took off for Aleppo, leaving the whole burden of work to Mr. Leslie again.

In September Mr. Leslie began to show signs of persecution mania. I strongly urged him to travel to Aintab to see his newborn offspring and the young mother. With great effort, I persuaded him to give up his work for the detainees. I only had a one-hour consultation per day in the orphanage, and, at his request, I took the contents of the orphanage cashbox home with me because I thought it would be safer. I had to promise my friend to accompany him to Aintab because he feared that he would be killed by the Turks. In fact, I was not available; but I thought that once we had left Urfa, the poor fellow would calm down and I could return quickly to Urfa and let him continue alone. As has been reported, I wanted to take the sick man out on September 30; unfortunately, I was prevented because of the guards standing at the gates.

I went once again by foot to the hill where the American Mission Institute was located, walked around, and found him. I asked him to come this time, but Mr. Leslie did not want to hear about leaving.

"Don't you hear it? It's starting, now it is either live or die with them. How can I, how may I leave my orphans now? Would you do that now? No, you wouldn't. How can you ask me to do that? I will live or die with them."

I could certainly understand him, but he was sick. I had to leave empty-handed. I did not see the courageous man for sixteen days.

The American consul in Aleppo telegraphed me to ask if I wanted to take over the work for the belligerents. I would be provided the necessary assistance, but I did not need long to think because it was impossible. It was enough that Mr. Leslie had already succumbed to this work. How could Mr. [Samuel] Edelmann, the vice consul who was in Urfa at the beginning of August, leave the city again? Was it not his duty to stay and do this work himself? What did he have to do in Aleppo, where there already was a consul? I accused them, with or without reason, of cowardice. The situation had become too hot for him, and he had beaten a retreat to Aleppo, where he was safer than in the witches' cauldron in Urfa. So I telegraphed him laconically: "Impossible."

It was understandable that the sixteen-day occupation had worn down Mr. Leslie's nerves. When I saw him again with the police, I was shocked by his insane glance, although I had anticipated as much. A few days after the surrender of the Armenians, [Mr.] Leslie was my guest, as I reported. I used every art of persuasion I knew, giving him a thousand reasons, to try and drive out his fear that the Turks were going to hang him. Indeed, I should have sent him right away to Aintab. Even this was not possible because he was, in fact, a prisoner of the Turks. He had to appear every day in front of the court-martial. If he was relatively calm in the morning, he came back each time completely broken.

It was in the afternoon when I was called to appear before the court-martial. My presence was required during the surrender of the Armenian property in Mr. Leslie's hands. The Turks took possession of about 2,000 gold pounds and pieces of jewelry of about the same value. During the transfer, I saw an officer, who was helping to count the gold push, an antique gold piece under the rug where we were sitting. No sooner were we through with counting when the general came in, and that gold piece was conspicuously gleaming under the table. Now it also had to go into the sack, which was then ceremoniously sealed.

When I arrived home that evening with [Mr.] Leslie, I mobilized all my talents of persuasion to prop up the broken man. The surrender of all that priceless Armenian property that had been entrusted to him was what was depressing him to that day.

At the end of October [1915], Mr. Leslie asked me one evening for strychnine because he would not let the Turks hang him. During a long discussion with him, I reminded him about his young wife and child and reproached him for the thoughts that were incompatible with his vocation as a missionary; I succeeded somewhat in pacifying him. In addition, there were no grounds for him to be upset about the prospect of being hanged. I was always informed about the progress of the court-martial proceeding against Mr. Leslie because I had a friend in the court-martial. He had told me that they had nothing against Mr. Leslie.

On October 30, Mr. Leslie was at the court-martial as usual. He had been badgered for several days because of a strongbox key that he was supposed to have surrendered to the Turks because it was Armenian property. On being asked if he was in possession of the key, he answered unclearly that he could no longer remember. He gave them all the keys he had, but none of them fit. Since the strongbox belonged to the wealthiest Armenian salesman in Urfa the government was eager to find out how much was money was in it. That was the cause of the ceaseless badgering.

It just so happened that on this morning, a gallows had been erected on the horse market where a number of Armenians were to be hanged in the afternoon. Mr. Leslie had to pass by these gallows on his way back to my house. The sight of them was apparently the last straw for him. Before he had reached my house, my nine-year-old son saw him fall down on the street. He called his mother immediately, and she rushed to the scene. Mr. Leslie still recognized her because he looked at her as if he wanted to say something, but in that moment he lost consciousness. There was a strong smell of phenol in his mouth and his chin was burned with this acid. With the help of a man, my wife brought the unconscious [Mr.] Leslie to the hospital, where we immediately flushed his stomach with a vinegar solution. But the spirit of life did not return, and a half hour later my friend stopped breathing. The police were informed, and they appeared with a member of the court-martial. The following note was found in Mr. Leslie's pocket in English:

"I wish to hereby make known that my friends Mr. Eckart and especially Mr. Künzler have no guilt in my death. I took the poison on my own from the orphanage pharmacy.

Urfa, 30 October 1915.

Francis H. Leslie."

This was the latest and hardest blow for me in those days of suffering. He had been a dear friend to me, a brother in the fullest sense of the word. Now he was a victim of the times, and I had to survive him. My prayers had not been able to reach him. He was too sensitive for this evil land. I had to report his death to his young wife. How would she take the blow, alone now with a three-month-old little daughter?

On the afternoon of October 31, [Mr.] Leslie was to be buried. I had a grave dug for him in the Protestant cemetery. All Europeans, especially the many belligerents, came for the simple ceremony. Just before it was to begin, a policeman came and forbade me to bury the dead man in the cemetery. The cemetery now belonged to the government. My position with officials meant nothing. The general, who was the governor, also added the following remark:

"Who do you think you are? You must obey our orders. Do you think that your presence here can overturn the order?"

I had no choice but to hurriedly dig a new grave in a stone desert outside the city and to put to rest the mortal remains of my friend.

18. Court-Martial Investigations

During this time, I had to participate in a court-martial investigation. When our pharmacist had been taken from the hospital in June and imprisoned, his brother Armenak was supposed to follow him to jail. But because he laid severely ill with a lung disease in the German hospital, his imprisonment was postponed. In the course of the summer, he had recovered. Since the situation had deteriorated on a daily basis for the Armenians, I kept him in the hospital, although he really did not belong there. The extorted testimony of Armenians had now implicated Armenak, so that one morning the police wanted to take him from the hospital. What happened is that in the night before the outbreak of the revolt, this man fled the hospital in order to go to the Armenian quarter and take part in the insurrection. The head nurse had not told me about this flight. I was therefore in the dark, and this incident brought me into more disfavor with the court. But I had been in Turkey too long to let such things bother me much; my skin was thicker than that of my deceased friend [Mr.] Leslie.

Armenak was one of the ones who had not cooperated with the surrender. When Mr. Eckart was at the American [Mission] Institute four days after the surrender, Armenak suddenly came out of hiding, fell at his feet, and begged for help. Mr. Eckart was appalled. A soldier who saw Armenak shot him down before the German's eyes.

The court-martial investigations further revealed that Rev. Karekin [Oskerichian], an Armenian vardapet, was still hiding with the Europeans. Therefore, I was called before the court. I told the court that the Rev. Karekin was not staying with me. The other question was whether he was with the Germans or the Danish woman, Miss Jeppe. I said I did not know. At that point, the German officer Count Wolfskeel,[40] adjutant general in service to the Turks, was supposed to debrief Mr. Eckart, Miss Jeppe, and me at the behest of the generals. He demanded that we swear that we did not know where Rev. Karekin was. We could change the oath into a word of honor, which would mean we did not know where Rev. Karekin was at the time.

A quarter of an hour after the proceeding, Count Wolfskeel traveled to Aleppo and indicated that he was sick. In fact, the situation in Urfa, in which he was involved as a consequence of his duties there, had become uncomfortable for him as he saw how the Armenians were being treated without consideration of guilt or innocence.

The next day Miss Jeppe was subject to a house search anyway. During the house search, the police noticed that all of the people in her house were Armenians. On another day, the president of the court came in person and wrote down all the names of the Armenians who were still in our houses.

19. The Forced Evacuation

The forced evacuation of the women and children was supposed to begin after the men in the mosque courtyard and prisons were all eliminated. Their psychological hardship had, meanwhile, reached a low point. How can that be described in words? My wife, who went into that camp every day, saw the indescribable. I went into the camp daily at first, mostly to collect those who had been wounded during the occupation. Once when I came with bread, the women called to me: "Are you bringing us bread? Us, the children of death? Don't bring us bread; bring poison, lots of it. Oh, don't let us be evacuated; see to it that we die here. You know yourself what it means to be taken to the steppe!"

Other women showed me their bottles of poison and wanted to know how much one could take so that the rest could be taken by as many more women as possible.

And the mothers with their infants! Their milk had long since run out, and there was no other source of nourishment. Few mothers found the courage to throw their children in the stream, so that they could be quickly released from their suffering. They were laid out in the courtyard, row after row. They cried there until they could cry no more. When the crying stopped, they gasped a few more times for air until death released them. Most often in the morning, the previously mentioned stream was filled with the bodies of women and girls who wanted to escape the deportation this way. Finally, the government shut off the water.

And then the transport of those consecrated to death! Is there a way that it can be described? The women do not want to go on the street. Gendarmes drive them on with whips. Outside a woman throws herself on the ground. She does not want to stand up. The gendarme threatens to kill her on the spot. He stabs her with his bayonet; she still does not want to stand. The gendarme stabs her again, not so that she dies, but is only wounded. The blood runs out of her wounds. She finally decides to stand and walk. Another woman has gone insane. She runs with her hair in the wind, sings, and laughs. Another woman tries to slip into a side street. A gendarme notices her and follows her. One shot and she has been released, luckier than her sisters. Many Mohammedans are standing in front of the city. An Armenian woman identifies herself, and Mohammedans take her and disappear with her. There goes the fourteen-year-old daughter of an Armenian merchant. A Turk sees her, now he grabs her, but she resists. She would rather die in the steppe than go into a Muslim house. A gendarme comes by; he does not want to help the Turks, but a piece of gold is shining in the hand of the Turk. The gendarme changes his mind.

The struggling girl disappears with the Turk. She will have a sad fate in the harem.

I have already reported about what happened to all these unfortunate people along the way. There was no doubt that there was a plan and a will that all the people from Urfa should perish in the desert. They were led back and forth so long that there was no one left to transport.

Before the evacuation was over, on the same day and at the same hour, all our charges were picked up. We were hoping that they would leave them to us. The people were first led in front of the house while the house search was conducted again. Since I thought all my charges were outside, I innocently opened up a clothes closet in the presence of the police who were conducting the search, and suddenly a young Armenian woman jumped out. She had to go too, of course.

My nine-year-old son begged the policemen outside for his "grandmother." She should not leave, he thought, and kissed the hand of the police director, who was almost in tears himself. But it was no use; the old woman had to go too. Who was this grandmother? She was a sixty-five-year-old woman, a widow, who had worked in our household for sixteen years. For us she was more than a servant. She was considered by my children as their grandmother and felt herself as such.

The next morning my wife went once more to the commander to try to persuade him at least to let this old woman stay behind. The commander, who had already picked out the prettiest girls from the camps and had given those he did not keep for himself as gifts to other officers, told my wife: "Give me her daughter, and you can keep the old woman." But my wife was not able to do that. The daughter was already in the camp.

As the women were leaving, I comforted them. They were only being taken to the police for identification purposes, and she would be allowed to return tomorrow. But old Mariam, the good "grandmother," said: "My son, I will never return." ["*Oğlum, daha gelmem!*"] She knew the Turks better.

As for the women and children, all of these people from our houses had to march. A number of men, many of whom had been kept by Mr. Eckart, were not killed like the others but were sent to Aleppo where they were made soldiers.

But old Mariam returned in the night after she was evacuated. Together with other women she had been permitted to rent a carriage. The gold helped, and the coachman let them out near the city. Mariam reappeared the next morning with her daughter in my house. But no sooner had they arrived than a policeman came back after them. The women fled out the back door and tried to hide in the hut of a nearby vineyard. Since the policeman had seen them entering our house, he first searched the house, then the gardens nearby, and found them. They did not return this time.

20. The Harassment

The general also paid a visit to our German hospital at that time. He inquired intently after the names and illnesses of individual patients. Apparently, he had heard that the hospital was still full of patients, some of whom were Armenians. He now saw Mohammedan patients who had been wounded in the attack on the Armenian quarter lying in the hospital next to Armenians who had been shot at on August 19. I also had to explain to him how it was that Hagob, who should have been killed, came back to the hospital. The general also visited the auxiliary hospital I had set up. Upon his departure, he thanked me, apparently sincerely, for the great work that I had done for the many patients. His only complaint was that Mohammedans and Armenians were together in both hospitals.

His visit had two bad consequences. That evening the governor sent me an order to evacuate the auxiliary hospital immediately because the government wanted to set up the facility as its own hospital.

It was already night and, therefore, impossible to start the evacuation. I went to the governor and asked for a deferral until the next day, but he did want to hear of it. I promised him that I would give him the key the next morning at seven o'clock. He only accepted my suggestion with reluctance.

Early in the morning, I organized transportation. Several Mohammedan patients could be released, which created some space. I had to temporarily transfer some patients into the cellar, but I kept my promise to turn over the key at seven o'clock.

But the Turks didn't bring in their own patients until a few weeks later, while I had to evacuate overnight.

The second consequence of the general's visit was a tour the next day by the Turkish military doctors in the presence of the city doctor who had the superintendency over our hospital. No sooner had the doctors left the house than the police appeared and took away all the male Armenian patients who were able to walk. Among them was the previously mentioned Hagob, who did not return again because this time the executioner did his work more thoroughly.

21. A Consolation

Since the government recognized after August 19 that it could not do without some Armenians, they made a small, select list. Some bakers and blacksmiths were to be allowed in Urfa. Our Armenian doctor was also allowed to remain—but not until a court-martial investigation had shown that there was nothing suspicious about him or his writings. But all these people who were supposed to be kept in Urfa at first also had to leave after a few days. Apparently, there must have been some order that the Armenians had to be completely evacuated. Our doctor only remained because he lay unconscious with spotted fever.

The plague had already returned at the time of the occupation of Urfa. It cut a great swath through the deportee camp and was the answer of the death-wish prayers for thousands of deportees. Most of those who succumbed to it lost consciousness after the second day; and those, like the marchers, who had no care, died after a few days without regaining consciousness. All of those who fell victim to this helper in a time of need stayed back on the edge of the road until death released them. Our Mariam only had a journey of two days before she got sick and died.

But the plague did not stop at the doors of the Mohammedans. If it was a consolation for the banished ones, it was an implacable enemy for their persecutors in the city and the countryside. There was no house to which the plague did not pay a visit, no house from which those who had succumbed to the disease were not carried out. The number of victims of this disease must have been incredible because it slowly spread throughout the entire Turkish Empire. In the vicinity of Harran,[41] whole villages, except for the children, were wiped out.

22. A Turkish Orphanage

It should be mentioned that a mood of charity also surfaced among the Turks. When countless little children without parents cried and screamed in the camps where the Armenian women and children were herded together, the government decided to erect a Turkish orphanage. About a thousand orphans were taken in. Armenian women were hired as nurses because no Mohammedan woman would stoop to such work. This made it possible for a small number of Armenian women to stay in Urfa. Infants were also picked up, and wet nurses were needed for them. There were enough Urfa women whose infants had died who were able to perform this duty. When the wet nurses were required, the story of the exposure of Moses repeated itself. Mothers lay down their infants so that the children would be picked up. If a Turk took the infant into the orphanage and asked for a wet nurse, the infant's mother stepped forward to offer her service. However, the death rate in this orphanage was very high. From the approximately 1,000 orphans who had been gathered, fewer than 200 were still alive after six months. All the Christian children were given Mohammedan names, and the older children were instructed in the Islamic belief. When a terrible famine broke out in the winter of 1917-1918, a large number of children were released again. Only those who showed any hope of becoming a good

Mohammedan could stay, and they were then placed in the trade school that had existed before the war.

It must have been very difficult for the government when it had to release these ethnic Armenian remnants—there were about twenty left—in December 1918. They all came into our orphanage, the founding of which will be described later.

23. Traitors

Just as there are bad elements among every people, so was the case with the Armenians. There was also a very small group of men and women during those days who, when death was looking for victims, lowered themselves to betray their brothers. Perhaps it is understandable because the greater part of the Urfa population, to the extent that it was Armenian, did not approve of the revolt, but, for better or worse, watched it happen. They wanted to take revenge by betraying their countrymen. With most, however, revenge was less a factor than fear for their own lives. Those Armenians who did not surrender on October 16 and who did not want to look death in the face with a weapon in their hands had to go into hiding. Deep wells, hidden vaults, and street sewers were the typical, often very inaccessible, hiding places.

By pointing out such hiding places, a half dozen men and women rescued their miserable lives. They were the ones who could remain in Urfa, provided they converted to the Muslim belief, which was not difficult for such creatures.

One of these traitors had a very rough time. He maintained that there were Armenians in a well. When he called down to them that nothing would happen if they came up, there was no answer. The police ordered that he be let down into the well. He was lowered down on a rope. When he was at the bottom, he started screaming horribly. He was quickly pulled up again. He was badly hurt with several knife wounds. The well was sealed, and the Armenians hiding there were buried alive. The Turks, incidentally, did that to many wells when they suspected that Armenians were hiding there.

24. Sundry Sanctuaries

The extermination did not go as quickly as had been intended, and it took several weeks before all of Urfa was free of Armenians. It was apparently no easy task to drive out over 15,000 people and either slaughter them or deport them. Only at the end of November did things return to normal. From time to time, one heard a shot when plundering soldiers had again found some Armenians in their hiding places and finished them off.

Many Armenians had friends among the Mohammedans, who were not so hard-hearted that they would have taken part in the obliteration of the Armenians with the same unbelievable cynicism as the government.

Armenian women and children who were not killed were disappearing daily from the deportee camps. They found shelter with such humanitarian-minded Muslim friends. In addition, it became the rule that every Mohammedan took what suited him from the unfortunate women and girls in the camp. Although all these Armenian women had to take a Mohammedan name upon entrance into a Mohammedan house, this did not mean that they had to become Mohammedans. It seemed to the government, which knew about this kind of escape, that too many Armenians were surviving this way, so they put a stop to the practice by announcing that anyone who took in Armenians also ran the risk of deportation. The Christian Syrians and the Catholics of Urfa, who although small in number, would have given Armenian women shelter, understandably accommodated themselves to this Turkish order, especially because they were living as a minority among the Mohammedans.

Only a few high-ranking officials among the Turks followed the order. The majority of the Turkish, Kurdish, and Arab inhabitants in and around the city ignored the wishes of the government. The chief justice of the city was also called upon by the court-martial to give up the Armenian Christians staying with him. For disciplinary reasons, this man was moved from Erzincan to Urfa in July 1915 because he had protested there against the expulsion of the Armenians. During the troubled times in Urfa, he presided over a meeting where he opposed the atrocities against Armenians. He had taken a number of Armenian women into his house. The general called the man to him after this meeting and said to him:

"Who do you think you are that you dare to work against the central government and to publicly call for mild treatment of the Armenians and even to hide Armenian women in your house directly against my orders? If you do not stop, you will see that we have the power to bring you to reason."

The general did not wait for a reply but indicated to the chief justice that he should leave. One must understand that as *kadı*, the chief justice was the second highest official in the city.

No sooner had he gone home than the police appeared with orders from the general and took away the Armenian women. In spite of that, a few days later he took refugees into his house. Among the Mohammedans, I know of no other more noble soul than this kadı. I was personally closer to no other follower of Mohammed than to him. We parted later from each other like the best of friends, like brothers.

For decades, a Franciscan mission also had its headquarters in Urfa. The fathers of French origin left Urfa at the beginning of the war. Those fathers who were Ottoman subjects remained. The latter had dared hide an Armenian Catholic priest,[42] which was dangerous. The fathers were successful in their daring until winter 1916. Then the government succeeded, thanks again to the previously mentioned traitor, in taking the priest prisoner. He was found in the Catholic Church celebrating Mass. All [Franciscan] fathers were taken prisoner as punishment; but because at the time Urfa no longer had a court-martial, they were put in jail in Adana.[43] One died there of spotted fever. They were liberated after the armistice. But the Armenian Catholic priest was hanged in Adana one day before his pardon went into effect.

As has been mentioned, the missionary Miss Jeppe, who worked for the German Orient Mission, had dared to hide seven men.[44] She had more luck than the fathers. In spite of three thorough house searches, the police had not found the seven men. With the constant agitation, the lady had, indeed, taken too much upon herself, and she was prostrated for almost six months with a nervous disorder as a consequence of those terrible days.

On the occasion of the last house search in summer 1916, the police took our Arab servant prisoner in order to force him to testify. They beat him fearfully, but the upright fellow, who was completely informed of what went on in our house, did not betray us. He was also a Mohammedan. All due respect for such loyalty!

25. The Liquidation Commission

At the beginning of December 1915, a Liquidation Commission—the first in Urfa—began its work. It started with the sale of the Armenian property that the plundering soldiers and the mob in the city had left behind. The Armenian sales warehouse, the houses, gardens, and country homes were supposed to be emptied or administered. This work took two years, during which time different commissions ruled one after the other. As soon as one commission had sufficiently enriched itself with Armenian property, it was replaced by one headed by another official who continued to rule, just as greedy for the wealth and possessions of the dead and banished as his predecessors.

The previously mentioned court-martial translator worked as the recording secretary for these commissions. He told me how the sales of supplies from the Armenian warehouses were conducted. Before the auction even began, the best and most valuable items were stowed away in the private homes of the commission members if they were Turks.

An Arab came into the possession of a piece of diamond jewelry, which, without a doubt, had been taken from an Armenian. He showed it to a wealthy Turk. This man offered him a few pounds for it, but the Arab wanted to have the advice of a jeweler. The Turk went directly to the shop of the jeweler and told him about the diamond. He suggested a deal, which the jeweler agreed to. The Turk paid the merchant thirteen pounds and disappeared when the Arab showed up. The jeweler purchased the jewelry from the Arab for thirteen pounds. When the Turk returned to see the jewelry, the merchant took thirteen pounds from the cashbox and gave it back to the Turk with the remark that the sale was not completed. But the Turk sounded the alarm, there was an exchange of words, and the police finally intervened. When they saw the jewelry, they took it from the two disputing parties with the justification that it was Armenian property and therefore belonged to the government.

I later received precise information and established, without a doubt, that the precious jewelry never made it to the commission. It had certainly found a customer before it could be put under "official protection." It may be assumed that police director and the president of the commission shared proceeds from the sale.

26. British Psychosis

The spotted fever outbreak that I have mentioned several times in these pages, most often causes unconsciousness on the second day after the onset of the disease. The psyche of the patient during the course of the illness, which lasts fifteen to seventeen days, is unconsciously but constantly at work. Just as a devout person does not curse under anesthesia or a profane individual curses rather than pray, the same is true during the spotted fever. Whatever lives in the psyche of the person is extraordinarily lively in typhus delirium. If, after the onset of the crisis, the patient slowly regains a normal state of consciousness, he will believe in the actual existence of his fantasies of talking pictures that he experienced in the unconscious state. During my illness, I had seen a peace agreement ceremoniously signed. Afterwards, I could not believe that peace had not been reached. Among my typhus patients, I had a full-blooded Englishman. One morning, as I was making my daily rounds in the hospital, he had just quietly regained consciousness. He asked me with a beaming face: "O dear, do you not hear?" "What is it?" I asked. "All the bells in the whole world are ringing," he answered. Without bothering to ask me again, he called with his still weak voice: "Thank God, the whole world is now English!" The war had also come to an end for him, but the whole world had become English. The great English dream of a world empire had made a public appearance in the sick brain of this honest missionary.

Today, as I write this, the World War is really over. Don't we have to recognize that it almost happened like that sick man imagined? But whether all the world will thank God is still an open question.

27. Doctor without a Degree

The Armenian doctor in our German mission hospital had been sick since November, 1915 so I had to do all the work alone. Indeed, since the beginning of the war, that had been the case because the Armenian doctor was preoccupied daily with military medicine. A Jewish municipal doctor had taken over the superintendency of our hospital at my request. I was able to authorize a salary for him. As long as there was any doctor with a degree in Urfa, I was not allowed to work alone as one, because I did not have the required degree. The Jewish doctor gladly took the money but did not help me. He did let me manage my own affairs, and, given the circumstances, that was also a good thing. He asked me to do my utmost for the patients in the hospital and in the city, as he had complete trust in my knowledge. He was not enthused about the magnitude of the demands that he would have had to take upon himself. During the typhus epidemic, I had worked to do what almost exceeded human capacity. I not only had to care for our twenty-five-bed hospital, which usually had forty patients, but the patients in the city also had to be visited. Days when I made over one hundred visits in the city were no exception. In addition, my wife and son were sick at home with typhus.

If one could not cure the illness with medicine, then a careful observation was indispensable. Great misfortune could often be avoided. There were many patients who, after the disease had taken its course, had to have a dead limb amputated due to the lack of earlier medical observation. With efficient care and correct supervision, something like that never happened. From November 1915 until May 1916, I was a helper and a source of consolation for more than 2,000 patients.

28. The Closing of the German Mission Hospital

In the first days of May 1916, the Jewish municipal doctor, under whose formal protection I performed the work described above, was supposed to be transferred to Mosul. He was still in Urfa, but he had already turned over his office to a newly arrived health inspector, a caustic Turk. I went to him to ask him to take over the superintendency of our hospital, as the previous municipal doctor had done. I did not find him at home and wanted to go back in the afternoon, but he came to me first. Around noon he arrived and asked to see the diploma authorizing me to practice medicine. Since I had none, I had nothing to show him. I asked him to take over the direction of the hospital, since a large city with 60,000 inhabitants could not go without a doctor and hospital. But he did not want to hear about that; instead he paid a visit to the hospital, sealed off the operating room and the pharmacy, and then ordered me to clear out all the patients by the evening.

As deeply as this treatment injured me, especially because I was fully aware that this man would do little or nothing for the poor patients, it was also urgent for me personally to have some peace. Over the long run, my otherwise robust constitution could not bear up under the enormous workload.

In July a German major and a German lieutenant were supposed to come to Urfa. Before they arrived, I went to the governor and offered our hospital for the sick soldiers. If the hospital were commandeered, so much the better; I would receive a compulsory takeover. My offer was accepted, but the pharmacy and the operating rooms were still sealed.

Soon after the arrival of the German major, I was ordered to clear out Dr. [Andreas] Vischer's[45] private house. Dr. Vischer was the head physician of the German clinic, but he was on military leave in his homeland, Switzerland. The Turks wanted to use his house as a hospital. I immediately went to the German major, who had been put up at the Franciscans, and asked him to move into Dr. Vischer's dignified house, which was in a magnificent location and was much healthier than his current apartment. My proposal was accepted. He detailed some soldiers to me to guard the house; and a few hours later, when the Turks came and wanted to move into the house, it was already under military occupation. That was a happy solution for me. Miss Jeppe, the sick Danish missionary who was hiding seven Armenians, lived there and still had to be cared for. A house search had been conducted just a few days before, and the pretty and immaculate residence would now be spared from being turned into a Turkish litter box. What did it matter if the inventory of our head physician was used? What would have happened if the Turks had been able to stay there!

So the major moved in. He was sick with jaundice at the time. Although he had several native military doctors, he preferred to be treated by me. Since he was now my patient, I had to take medicine from the pharmacy now and again. The major continually gave the order to unseal the pharmacy, but it was always sealed again by the health inspector. When the pharmacy was unsealed, I could always take any additional medicine that was needed. I confess that I made liberal use of the opportunities.

The major's case was difficult, but he finally recovered completely. The first thing he did upon release was to call in a sanitation official to unseal the pharmacy and operating room. He said that it would not do to have a hospital without a pharmacy and operating room.

However, when the major was redeployed in August 1917, a new health inspector arrived in Urfa, and he had the pharmacy and operating room sealed again. Since I was present at the time, I discreetly opened the sliding window so that I could later effortlessly get into the pharmacy without having to go through the door to get medicine. Those were certainly unwritten prescriptions to which one had to resort to do business in Turkey; but it did something soothing for the spirit to be able to use those tricks at the right time against Turkish irrationality.

The former Armenian doctor later returned from prison but had to work as an officer. As an officer, he could not treat non-Turkish patients, which also meant he could not be in German service either. But, he wanted to earn money. So I worked with him, and together we set up a clinic, pharmacy, and operating room in Dr. Vischer's house, one step at a time. I had some income from my hospital work; the subsidies from the mission were less. I was, therefore, able to pay our nurses in hard currency. In the two years during which they had only taken care of the Turkish soldiers in the hospital, they had not received any compensation.

I received special thanks for my work from hundreds of patients in the fall of 1917 when a dangerous eye inflammation spread through the country. The Armenian doctor had neither the inclination nor the time to take care of the army of patients who had assembled. So I took over the care of the poor. Since I was considered an assistant, the health inspector could not get around me. I had taken care of the department of ophthalmology by myself while my European superiors were in Urfa, the last time during the era of Dr. Vischer. Therefore, there was no one who was more experienced in this department in Urfa than I.

29. The Last Deportations

The plan to deport and exterminate the Armenians and to destroy a population of millions was no easy task for those Young Turks. The deportations lasted a full year. The last deportees came through Urfa in June 1916. The strangest thing about this march was that, in complete contrast to all the others, it was made up primarily of young men. How had that happened?

The engineers on the Baghdad rail line were working on building the line at a faster pace during the war. It was almost a vital necessity for the Turks and their allies. Now, one can no more build a railroad in Turkey without the Armenians than one can build a railroad in Europe without the Italians. The Armenians were the essential ingredient in performing every great work. Also, the positions for which one needed a confidential agent were almost always filled by Armenians. A Mohammedan accountant would have been out of the question. When these industrious Armenian workers were supposed to be deported in the summer of 1915, the German and Swiss railroad engineers protested with all their might. One gentleman told me that they had to fight for a whole year against the Turkish plan to eliminate these workers. Finally, however, they had to indeed release several thousand in June 1916. Those men were the last to pass through Urfa. They did not have far to go. They met the same fate in Viranşehir as hundreds of thousands of their brothers. They were all finished off with the knife.

In Der Zor, a little town on the Euphrates River, there was a large concentration camp of Armenians remaining from all parts of Armenia and Anatolia. They numbered about 60,000, mostly walking skeletons. Hunger had disfigured their faces; there was very little human left to be discerned. They had to contend with the starving dogs on piles of manure for a crust of bread or something edible. It even happened that they beat each other to death for a cucumber rind or something similar. The governor was of the opinion that these unfortunates, whose camp no one wanted to come near because of the unbearable stench emanating from it, were no longer fit to live because their camp represented a permanent flash point for epidemic diseases. He ordered its elimination on the spot. People were killed in small groups outside the city and then thrown into the rapids of the Euphrates River in order to spare the work of burying them.

After the years of murder and death from hunger, the Armenians who had been hiding in Muslim houses finally began to hope for a little more security in their lives. Was the arm of authority, which had delivered such ghastly blows to its subjects, sluggish? Had a better view returned? At any rate, open season on the Armenians had come to an end, although there were still many rapes, deflowering of virgins, and molestations, especially of boys.

30. The Fate of Garabed Karatashjian

Here is one example. Garabed Karatashjian, a rich merchant from Urfa, came to me when the time of trouble arrived for the Armenians and urgently asked me to take him and his family into my house. I was not pleased that he offered me money, but I could not withstand his heartfelt pleas, so I took him in. He could make a contribution of his own free will to the hospital cashbox, I thought, if he survived the times to come.

When the Armenians were fighting their last battle of desperation in Urfa, Garabed told me that he wanted to leave my house because he would surely be seized there. He could go to the Arabs, where some Armenians had already fled. The hunted Armenians were safest with them. So Garabed left my house and moved in with Kurds he knew and to whom he believed he could entrust his life. But his wife and children stayed with me until they were picked up by the police with all the others in my house. His wife finally ended up with her little son in Der Zor. I often received news from her. One day Garabed showed up again, just at the time that the Turks were looking for every hidden Armenian. I placed him in a hospital bed as a fugitive Mohammedan Kurd. He was safest there for the time being because the other Armenians had been picked up from the hospital a short time before.

After several weeks of breathing hospital air as a healthy man, I asked him to go on his way— back to the Kurds would be the best since they had protected him until then.

He left. He came back to the city after a few months and went to the governor. He told him how he had been living and placed himself in his hands because he had lived in mortal fear every day, and he could not stand this sham existence any longer. The official acquitted him but had him keep his Muslim name for the time being.

Garabed found out from me that his wife and a child were still alive in Der Zor. He wanted to find them, but I advised him strongly against that. I knew that his wife was with decent Mohammedans in a relatively stable situation, working as a servant. But love is stronger than a good argument. Garabed received a military escort on his way. He was happy when he arrived in Der Zor, where he met his death.

His wife and a child returned to Urfa after the armistice. The Mohammedans for whom she had worked as servant had not turned her in.

31. The Kurdish Deportation

Hardly any European daily newspaper reported that the same Young Turks who wanted to exterminate the Armenians also wanted to drive their co-religionists, the Kurds, who lived in what was actually Upper Armenia, from house and home. This occurred with the excuse, as it was in the beginning with the Armenians, that they were an insecure element, therefore there was a danger that they would go over to the Russians. How much the Kurds themselves contributed to this impression was beyond me. I only know that I also saw among the deportees high Kurdish officers who had fought courageously at the beginning of the war against the Russians and who now considered their treatment by the Turks as bitter ingratitude.

In the winter of 1916 the Kurds were forced to evacuate the areas of Jabaghjur, Palu, and Muş, and also from the vilayets of Erzurum and Bitlis. About 300,000 Kurds had to march to the south. At first they were kept in Upper Mesopotamia, especially in the vicinity of Urfa, but also to the west in the vicinity of Ayntab and Maraş. In the summer of 1917 the further deportation to Konya-Hochebene began. The intention of the Young Turks was to keep these Kurdish elements from returning to their ancestral homeland. They should slowly become assimilated into Turkish Inner Anatolia.

The treatment of these Kurds on their deportation marches was very different from that afforded the Armenians. They did not suffer along the way, and no one was allowed to harass them. The most terrible thing was that the deportation took place in the dead of winter. If Kurdish marchers arrived in the evening in a Turkish village, the inhabitants quickly shut their doors out of fear. The unfortunate Kurds had to spend the night in the rain and snow.

The next morning the residents had to dig mass graves for the frozen Kurds. The suffering of those who finally arrived in Mesopotamia was not over. In the cities where they were housed in half-destroyed Armenian buildings and where the government was still trying to ease their suffering by dispensing bread, the situation was bearable. It was very different in the villages, where the local population had only fear of the Kurds and jealously guarded their dwindling supplies. For these unfortunate deportees, famine began.

Since my rescue work with the Armenians was viewed suspiciously and jealousy by the government, and because I was also deeply moved by the dire need of the Kurds—who are brothers in humanity—I went to Aleppo in December 1916. I wanted to interest the consul there in a relief operation. I hoped that such a campaign might have a good effect on the Armenian relief. My request was warmly received by the German as well as the American consuls. On the way back, I went through the villages in the Suruj[46] and Haran plains in order to get an overview of the number of persons in need in those districts. I found out that about 30,000 new refugees per day were arriving from the north.

I had received a positive answer at the end of December from the consuls; and a Gentleman B. from the American consulate soon arrived with 150,000 francs. The German consul also sent me 300 Turkish liras (7,000 francs). They accepted my suggestion to purchase wheat and barley in different areas, and I would then distribute both among those in need.

In January and February I had grain distributed by my associates in many villages. It was no easy task. I rode into the villages several times myself to see that things were being done correctly.

In one village, I discovered that the surplus wheat did not correspond to the agreed upon quality specified in the contract. I asked the recipients to go to another village where we had a full warehouse, but it was four hours away. A great lamentation broke out. Half-naked souls with hollow eyes fell down at my feet and begged me to give them the bad wheat. They would eat it gladly. I had to give in to their pleading. However, I took a sample of the bad wheat with me to the city, where I showed it to the salesman and received a ton of better wheat as compensation.

The surplus wheat that I had bought soon ran out. Meanwhile, spring had arrived, and the prospects for the harvest were good. The Kurds in the villages made it through the winter by eating grass; and when the harvest came, there was work, which they understood better than the Arabs. They could help with the harvest. But there was renewed famine in the winter of 1917-1918. In spite of a good harvest that year, almost all of the deported Kurds were victims of the famine.

Not only Armenians and Kurds, but also the Arabs, were slated for destruction by the Young Turks. They were also supposed to be decimated in terrific bloodbaths, but the plan could not be carried out because the Arabs were difficult to seize. It was also known that they had English support. A constabulary officer told me that after winning the war, the Turks would settle accounts with the Arabs and that he would gladly take part in mowing them down.

32. Rakka

The little town of Rakka on the Euphrates River, south of Urfa and above Der Zor, had become a large camp for the deported Armenians. The poorest in Aleppo had been occasionally helped by Germans employed in the American Consuulate. When these ill-fated men became soliders, I was asked to help them as often as possible.

I went to Rakka for the first time in April 1917. There were still 6,000 Armenians living under abject conditions there. Although they were free, there was no work. Before I distributed the money I had brought, I went to the governor and asked for permission to help the Armenians. He had nothing against that, so I completed my work in two days and went home again as fast as I could.

In August of that year [1917] I went there again. I paid the friendly governor another visit. This time he also had nothing against the work, so I could distribute the alms among the Rakka Armenians whose numbers had been greatly reduced.

After I left the governor, I went to the house of a Protestant pastor deported from Caesarea in Asia Minor. No sooner had I arrived than a certain Ali Effendi dropped by the house of my host. He was introduced to me as an employee of an American licorice company. He was a Muslim Indian who spoke English fluently and who, thanks to his great influence with the Turkish government, was not sent around just anywhere, unlike other British subjects.

Ali Effendi asked me to come with him as his guest. But I had not the slightest interest; and besides, I did not have a reason to tactlessly leave the pastor's house, as poor as it was. That irritated Ali.

He left abruptly. The pastor told me that this man had been involved in the distribution of relief from Aleppo. It was rumored that he had diverted a lot of the money to his Turkish friends whom he befriended and in turn had seen to it that he— a British subject who had worked in this city before the war— could stay there. I would regret my rebuff.

Soon after the departure of Ali, a gendarme entered the room and asked about a stranger who had supposedly come from Urfa. This gentleman was to go immediately to the constabulary commander. The pastor had not been on a false scent concerning the influence of Ali Effendi. It was unclear to me what the commander wanted from me, but I would find out soon enough.

The Turkish gentleman at first received me with the famous Turkish graciousness. Coffee was offered, and then the state of the world discussed. He then asked who I was, where I came from, how many and which languages I spoke, and what I was doing in Rakka. I explained what he certainly knew: I had come from Urfa and had already been here once with the permission of the governor to distribute alms among the suffering Armenians. I had returned today and had already received permission from the governor to do the same again. In answer to his question of whether I had a passport, I replied, no; anyone could travel in the same vilayet without a passport. The gentleman now showed his true colors.

"Listen, since you don't have a passport, I don't know who you are. I have to assume that you are a spy. Without military escort you have traveled through enemy Arab territory. In addition, you speak the languages of our enemies—English, French, and Arabic. You will remain in Rakka until you produce a passport. So that you understand that I am serious, I will send a servant to pick up your horse harness in order to prevent you from leaving."

I was therefore his prisoner. A nice turn of events. But I did not take the story seriously at first. Although it was already nine o'clock at night, I went back to the governor and had him awakened in order to tell him the story. I said I would abide by his decision and asked that he take care that the commander desist from his intention. But he advised me to let the matter take its course for the time being. He could not do anything against the military commander because the country was at war.

So I went back to the house of my friend. There was Ali Effendi, who had listened in on my interview with the commandant and whose guest he appeared to be.

Ali Effendi then explained what was really going on, namely, that I should give him a couple of pieces of gold to pacify the tiger. I refused the request with indignation because that was not what the relief money was for.

I thought about the situation during the night. If I was kept prisoner here for an extended period of time, my wife would become very fearful because I had promised her that after five or six days I intended to be back in Urfa. If I was not back by then, she would fear that I had fallen prey to thieves. A telegram would not necessarily arrive.

The Arab region through which I had to travel was known to be unsafe, and some people had already fallen in the hands of the thieves. On the way to our destination, our situation had been quite uncomfortable for a half hour. We had taken a break next to a little brook. A troop of horsemen appeared at a great distance on the horizon. They were looking to see if an inviting prey was waiting for them. We had no sooner gotten a glimpse of them than one of the troop rode up to us. My coachman wanted to leave immediately. But what would that do? Then the troop would have overtaken and robbed us. I counseled calm. When there was only the deep little brook between us and him, he greeted us. I greeted him in return and enticed him with a fried chicken leg that I threw over the brook. He ate it. Then he asked where we were going and from where we had come. I told him that I was going to Rakka in order to look after the Armenians, who had been so badly treated by the Turks. He then waved to his companions in the distance, cursed the Turks, and taking friendly leave from us, withdrew. The danger was over; all the horsemen soon vanished.

The morning after Ali Effendi asked for gold, I was willing, if he came back, to signal that I would give the commander a few pieces of gold after I had finished my work. I hoped to recover it because I wanted to put the commander out of business by using my influence in Urfa. The German major was still in Urfa, and he would certainly help me recover the extorted money.

Ali Effendi appeared the next morning. He left me and went to the commander. In order to have done things correctly, I should have given Ali the money right away, but I was too inexperienced in this business. Soon enough Ali Effendi reappeared and announced that it was already too late. The commander had telegraphed to Urfa, so I had to await an answer from there.

I distributed my relief funds in two days and was ready to depart again if I only had my horse harness. I now tried another way. I had gotten to know the kadı of Rakka during my journey with the Persian prince. I went to him and asked if he wanted to be my friend and would he try to free me. The kadı asked me for my word of honor. "Did you give the governor money the first time you were here, and if so, how much? Because after you left a rumor made the rounds that you gave him a large sum of money. This time the constabulary commander wanted some too."

That threw light on the matter. The kadı was astounded when I told him that not only had I not bribed the governor, but that he had not asked for one either. The governor was better than the people and the kadı believed him to be.

On the afternoon of the fifth day, the horse harness was returned to me. I set off immediately and crossed the dangerous region during the night.

In the summer of 1917 the governor brought many Armenians—women, men, and children—from Rakka to Urfa to build a road. They had to consider this an improvement of their situation, therefore only those who were willing to take Mohammedan names were brought to Urfa. The majority were women and children. They only received a daily ration of bread as pay. In the winter they could only live in tents. It was cold, and only a few had clothing. In the Suruj area, the completely naked women had to turn around every time a man came by. I was extremely happy to be able to give these naked souls clothes made by our people in Urfa.

33. Sundry Rescue Work

With the cessation of the deadly deportations, the banished women and children slowly started to flow back into the neighboring cities. In the villages where they had found shelter with the Mohammedan inhabitants—and thereby escaped death—bread had already started to become scarce in the fall of 1916. They were also threatened with moral dangers, especially with the Arabs, among whom polygamy is much more prevalent than it is among the Turks and Kurds. Young women and girls older than ten were supposed to convert to the Mohammedan faith in order to be able to marry Arabs. Whoever could, tried to avoid such a marriage. They hoped to be safer in the cities, which was not always the case. As a rule, they had it easier in Arab homes in the villages than if they were taken in by the Turks in the cities. The conduct of Turkish officers in the bartering of Armenian girls was especially unbelievable and unspeakable. And no one has an idea of the unnatural crimes that were perpetrated against hundreds, even thousands, of Armenian boys.

Our main job beginning in July 1916 was to offer protection to the women and children who were resurfacing. Unfortunately, there was no possibility at the time of opening a Christian orphanage again. As long as the government wanted the Armenians dead, they would never allow it. At any rate, such a project could not be initiated by the Europeans, who would no longer be tolerated in Turkey after a victorious war.

So at first we had to limit our efforts to the distribution of small amounts of money for the living expenses of the needy who arrived in Urfa. They had to take care of the rest by themselves. There was no lack of work for the women, if only for low wages. And the children worked with them. The market was full of small boys who sold everything imaginable. The Armenians are a tough and industrious people, which was once again evident in those days.

In order to maintain a check, the children whom I could give monthly support were registered by name, age, and homeland. This was also necessary because children and mothers always tried to register twice in order to receive a double monthly allowance. Who could blame them? What I could give them was little enough.

Many Armenian girls who were threatened with marriage to a Mohammedan fled to my wife. It also happened that the Turkish wives themselves helped the girls flee. They did not wish to have second wives who were also Christians in their houses. When those girls were under the protection of my wife, they were not given up again. It did not take long to find out where such children had gone. If the previous owner sought out my wife, she just shut the door on him. It did not help to have to keep a watchdog around the house for days at a time. After one to three days, the girls were disguised in Arab or Kurdish clothing and taken by Muslim women friends, who were always with my wife, to Aleppo.

In 1917 carefully hidden from the eyes of the police, she dared to rent two small houses and fill them with orphans. If the police asked me whether I had an orphanage anywhere, I played ignorant; and, for reasons of decorum, they could not ask my wife. It should not be forgotten that because of my work for years as a doctor and helper of the sick, I had friends everywhere in the government and in the police.

I was able to see hundreds of Armenian children and women to safety with about 1.3 million francs which had been entrusted to me from Switzerland, Germany, and America in the course of the years.

I mentioned my wife's Mohammedan women friends. Among them were some truly noble souls, such as an Arab woman who supported her blind husband and four children. This good woman could not bear to see Armenian infants lying on the street. She took them in but never had the joy of seeing one survive. She tried three times, but they all died within weeks or months.

Like the kadı, there were many Mohammedans who, out of basic human mercy, rescued Armenians. A Turkish wife had hidden a number of Armenian women in her home and never required them to take Muslim names. Of course, no Mohammedans dared hide men in the city. But in the villages, there were many who also rescued Armenian men. A portion of self-interest also played a role here. A powerful *agha* [a civilian military leader] told me that he was not so stupid as to kill the Armenian men because what would he do without them? They worked for him and saw to it that his wealth increased.

Because he was always working towards easing the plight of the Armenians, the kadı of Urfa had to tolerate a nickname. He was called the "Armenian priest" [*"Ermini Papazı"*].

34. The Sallow Horse

The officials of Urfa were supposed to provide 5 million kilograms [about 11 million pounds] of grain just for the army in their district. After a good, medium-sized harvest in the fall of 1917, that was not too much. The area around Urfa, a prime grain belt, could support such a demand. But the wheat belonged to the large landowners. First the government received its usual tithe of one-tenth to one-eighth from the total harvest without paying for it. The rest had to be paid for. The government set the price; but, in the opinion of the owners, this was much too low. In addition, payment was made in banknotes, which were not worth much. As a consequence, the wealthy farmers buried their wheat. The government sent technical experts who ferreted out some of the underground storage bins in the villages. Now many landowners no longer dared to sell their hidden wheat, and the price climbed fantastically. In the fall of 1917, a *malter*[47] could be purchased from the threshing floor for twelve francs in hard currency. In the course of the winter, the price for the same amount climbed to eighty francs in hard currency, or 400–500 francs in banknotes. Those who bought their supply of wheat in the fall for the whole year, as was usual, had bread in the winter; and those who could not, like the deportees, had to starve. At the time, Kurdish emigrants were still living in the city. The famine exacted a terrible toll on them. For weeks at a time, those who had starved to death had to be gathered from the streets and the Armenian's half-destroyed houses where they were living. There were days when more than seventy dead were buried in makeshift graves. It was awful to have to look at this misery and not be able to help.

A beggar is on a pile of trash struggling with the dogs over a crust of bread. A few hours later, he is released from his troubles by death. A hollow-eyed young girl wanders naked through the streets. By her gestures, it is clear that she has lost her mind. A few days later, she is also released from her suffering by death. From early in the morning to late at night, a long line of beggars walk the streets of the city, knocking on all the doors, all the time saying the same thing: "Have mercy, we are victims; for God's sake, give us a piece of bread!" ["*Heyran, Kurban, Allahın Hatırı icin, bir parca ekmek verin!*"] Late at night the starving people are still in front of the doors. It was hardly dawn, and the same chant could be heard from the mouths of those who had lived through the night. The others lie dead in front of the doors where the night before they had cried for bread for the last time. In the morning, men are hired by the government to gather those who had been released in the night.

It was characteristic for the surviving part of the Armenian people. Relatively few Armenians died during the winter famine in Urfa. They had their industriousness to thank for that. They wanted and could work. Once they were driven from their homeland, most of the deported Kurds could not work and were threatened with death, even without famine. They did not understand how to make themselves indispensable like the Armenians.

The kadı had preached to the Turks, in vain at the time, that they should take abandoned Kurdish children and women into their homes, as they had done with many Armenians. But, as the kadı told me, it was understandable that no one listened to him. He had tried himself and had taken in two Kurdish women who turned out to be thieves and filthy besides. There was nothing that could be done with these people. It was another thing entirely if an Armenian woman was taken in. Wherever she was, there was order and cleanliness, and her patrons were well taken care of and waited upon. The little Armenian boys also wanted to work and knew how to make themselves indispensable.

The chief staff surgeon in the Turkish hospital took the sermon of the kadı to heart. The nurses there, as was the case almost everywhere in the Turkish Empire, were almost all Armenian women. One day the doctor let go all these Armenian women and hired Kurdish women. He also tried to do the same in our hospitals, where the nurses were at that time subordinate to him although we had hired the nurses and not him. But I stepped in and prevented the expulsion.

What happened to those Kurdish nurses? They only received a small piece of dark [black] bread as a wage for caring for the sick soldiers, too little to live on, and too much to die from. They understood nothing about medical care. It soon stank throughout the hospitals. What the Kurdish women understood well was how to clothe their relatives with hospital laundry. For the soldiers, as well as the hospital, it was a stroke of fortune that the chief staff surgeon soon left Urfa; so the rehired Armenian nurses could reestablish order.

35. Elias, the Coachman

In the days when the Urfa women were waiting to be deported, the coachman Elias, an Albanian Mohammedan, took in a woman known to be an Armenian. Since he was single, she talked him into marrying her, saying her husband had fallen in the war. Elias agreed because, as a Mohammedan, he would only have been able to buy a woman for a lot of money. This way he had a wife for nothing. He also took in both her children and treated them very well. He had his marriage legalized by the kadı and lived very happily with the Armenian woman.

But in 1918 her first husband suddenly appeared. At the beginning of the war, he had been taken prisoner by the Russians and had now returned. He found his wife married to Elias. He also saw his children, who recognized him. He very gently asked Elias to give him back his wife, but Elias did not want to. He did not want to give up such a happy life. But the Armenian brought the matter to the kadı. It was clear to him that he had to make a new decision. It was really not that simple. It would have been easier if the marriage had been conducted illegally, like so many others.

The judge called in the men, the woman, and the children. "Elias, it is clear that the woman is yours. If the woman had not said that her first husband had died, you certainly would not have married her; I also would not have trusted you at the time. But look at the children, how they cling to the legitimate father. And the woman only said that her husband was dead out of dire necessity because otherwise she would have been sent to her death. Since she herself, although she loves you too, would prefer to return to her first husband, I counsel you to give her back. God will bless you for the deed."

Elias answered the judge with tears in his eyes: "I have lived a few very happy years with this woman, and I have loved her children as they were my own flesh and blood. Since I am legally married to her, I know that a Christian can never reclaim her; but I agree that it is better that I give her back to her first husband. May he live long in happiness and joy with her."

36. Mardiros

Among my patients whom the police did not take away when they took the rest of the Armenians from the hospital was Mardiros, an Armenian boy. As a ten-year-old, he had come as a patient from the German orphanage in our hospital. He was not able to stand because of an incurable disease. So he stayed in the hospital even when this was used as a Turkish military hospital. At the time, we took care of him as always. He got in no one's way because he had his own little room.

But in the summer of 1918 the previously mentioned Turkish chief staff surgeon came to our hospital. Mardiros, an Armenian, was an abomination to him. He had his assistant tell me that the patient had to be removed from the hospital. But I did nothing. Then he put the patient, who could only move his spindly arms, along with his bed outside the [hospital] door. After he lay there for two days, to the shame of the doctor, I took him myself and found a place in another house for him.

Mardiros grew to be a young man who bore his suffering admirably and even became a kind of blessing for some patients.

Former patients, including some Mohammedans, often came back to visit him.

Because he could not move his neck, he kept a small pocket mirror in his hand so that he could see at a distance who was coming and going into the hospital. Thieves broke into the hospital two times, and he was the one who noticed it and sounded the alarm so that we could drive them away.

Mardiros is a true Armenian. In spite of his inability to move, he earned 2,000 francs in the past few years. He was a broker. He is informed by adolescent boys about everything going on in the market. If something is cheap, he buys it; and when it becomes expensive, he sells it. If someone wants to get something cheap, he only has to tell Mardiros, who only takes a few percent for his brokering. That is how he earned his 2,000 francs. When I had to buy wheat for the poor under a contract with the English in the spring of 1919, the invalid Mardiros got good quality for a good price for me.

37. German-Turkish and Turkish-German

I already said that after Turkey entered the war, Turkish and German victories were celebrated. The city of Urfa had a boys' choir that performed miserably—but all the more enthusiastically for these occasions. Because of the German brotherhood-in-arms the impression was that the music also should also be heard in our German hospital. Above all, of course: "Germany, Germany, above all" ["*Deutschland, Deutschland, über alles*"].

To be truthful, I was not completely comfortable with these ovations. I remember something that happened back in the spring of 1915. My wife was taking a walk in a garden in Urfa. She was generally considered to be a German because the population there took us Swiss for Germans. A Kurdish woman came up to her and, making a fist, said to my wife: "The time will finally come when we can also pay you Germans back for the evil you are doing to us now. We have to give up our sons because of you, and they will never return again!"

In Urfa there were some Turks who wanted to learn German at all costs. I had to teach them at least the rudiments. I saw during this exercise what I already knew: The Turk is not made for serious work. One of them was only slightly inclined and wanted to travel to Germany. He made it to Constantinople. After a few months, he returned to Urfa because the war had ended. Naturally, he had not learned any German.

Pan-Turkism was a more serious movement among the real Turks. Many nationalists of this stamp made no secret of the fact that after the war ended victoriously, they would ensure that no foreigner, including no German, would settle on Turkish soil. One cannot really hold it against the Turks. One is reminded of the remark of a German officer who thought he was cementing the German-Turkish friendship at a merry feast in the land of the crescent moon with the following words: "We have to become the friends of the Turks during the war so that after the war we can make them more subservient to us."

We do not want to maintain that now that the Entente has won the war, they also did not appreciate this usefulness. With all the fine words about the "freeing of the small people," the only thing that counts on both sides is that cold, naked egoism, the idea which is always hidden but all the more deeply seated as it was in the mind of that German officer: subservience.

38. Germans in Urfa

We have often spoken about the Germans in Urfa. It is worth spending a little time saying something more about them. The often mentioned Mr. Franz Eckart, director of the carpet factory[48] and provost of the German orphanage[49] for the Armenian children, was able to perform exemplary deeds during the war. In speeches at the beginning of the war, he advised the Armenians to conduct themselves within the law. Only with political savvy would they be able to navigate the dangerous rapids created by the war. Unfortunately, his pleadings had as little effect as my own earlier mentioned suggestions and requests.

Map of Urfa

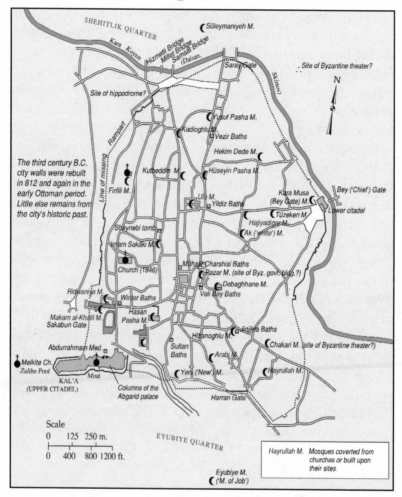

The third century B.C. city walls were rebuilt in 812 and again in the early Ottoman period. Little else remains from the city's historic past.

SHEHITLIK QUARTER

Süleymaniyeh M.

Kara Koyun
Hizmetli Bridge
Millet Bridge
Samsat Bridge
(Daisan)

Saray Gate

Site of Byzantine theater?

N

Site of hippodrome?

Yusuf Pasha M.
Kadioghlu M.
Vezir Baths

Hekim Dede M.

Kutheddin M.
Hüseyin Pasha M.

Firfili M.

Ulu M.
Yildiz Baths

Kara Musa (Bey Gate) M.
Bey ('Chief') Gate

Tüzeken M.
Lower citadel

Hajiyadigar M.
(Ak ('white') M.

Sheynebi tomb

Imam Sakaki M.

Church (1846)

Muhair Charshisi Baths
Pazar M. (site of Byz. govt. bldg.?)
Debaghhane M.
Veli Bey Baths

Ridwaniye M.

Winter Baths

Makam al-Khalil M.
Sakabun Gate

Hasan Pasha M.

Hizanoghlu M.
Jinjina Baths

Chakari M. (site of Byzantine theater?)

Abdurrahman Med.

Melkite Ch.
Zulihe Pool

KAL'A
(UPPER CITADEL)

Moat

Columns of the Abgarid palace

Sultan Baths

Arabi M.

Yeni ('New') M.

Hayrullah M.

Harran Gate

Scale
0   125 250 m.
0   400 800 1200 ft.

EYUBIYE QUARTER

Hayrullah M.   Mosques coverted from churches or built upon their sites.

Eyubiye M.
('M. of Job')

1. The City of Urfa (Edessa) (after A. Gabriel and T. A. Sinclair). Courtesy of Robert H. Hewsen, *Armenia: A Historical Atlas*. Chicago, 2001.

Map of Urfa around 1900. The old city was located within the city walls defined by the six gates. The Samsat Gate led to the "modern quarter" sub-urb in the north, where various mission buildings were built around the turn of the century. The large Armenian Apostolic Church (K) was located south-west of the Ulu Jami (j = mosque). The Armenian quarter, where the Protestant church (P) and the American Mission right next to it are located, extended from the western side of the German «carpet factory» to the south. The Moslem quarter was located to the east of the Armenian quarter. It included the Süryani quarter (at the Franciscan monastery). The houses belonging to the Jews were on the southeast side of the bazaar. (Source: Samuel Guyer, "Reisen in Mesopotamien," in *Dr. A Peters Mitteilungen*. Gotha, 1916.)

In the winter of 1916-1917 Mr. Eckart was able to clothe hundreds of people with the clothing which the evacuated Armenians had left behind in his factory. During the winter famine of 1917-1918, as the provost of the Turkish Military Clothing Institution, he was able to provide many Armenian women with work and thereby rescue them from death by starvation.

However, the Entente-oriented Armenians who later came to Urfa were not fond of Mr. Eckart because he was a German. They even accused him of misappropriation of Armenian property, an accusation that was leveled against all the Europeans and Americans who remained in the country.

Mr. Eckart along with his family were only able to leave Urfa when the Turkish army collapsed. They arrived safe and sound in Constantinople. But some of his children got sick there, so that the journey on to Germany was considerably delayed. As the family was finally boarding, Mr. Eckart was detained at the last moment. He was interned with other Germans on the island of Prinkipo on orders from the Entente commission. His wife and children had to continue without him. In March 1919 [Mr.] Eckart fled from captivity and was shot down on the Turkish-Bulgarian border by a border guard.

His younger brother, Mr. Bruno Eckart, was also in Urfa in the first two years of the war. He knew that three Armenians were hiding in a well in the factory. Although a large number of Turkish soldiers were stationed in the factory for a whole week, he brought them the basic necessities to live. He later helped them to escape to freedom.

It has already been mentioned that a [German] major and a lieutenant had trained Turkish recruits in Urfa for a year. These two gentlemen once treated the population to a little officers' shooting match. Shooting drills were an infrequent occurrence and now, right near the city, a shooting match! There were also nocturnal troop movements with torchlight, which was also a first for Urfa.

The otherwise perpetually dirty streets were cleaned on the orders of the major. If he had remained in Urfa, the city would have taken on the familiar Prussian look, which would not have harmed it.

When these officers had left Urfa, a small German staff sergeant arrived with a motorized platoon of ten German soldiers. They were there to ship wheat from Urfa. At that time, as has been mentioned, the price of wheat was shooting up at a phenomenal rate.

For the children of the Germans and mine, these months when these soldiers were stationed in Urfa were a beautiful time. The field uniforms went in and out of our house. There was much singing; and during the rainy season, when the trucks could not move, our children never lacked for happy playmates.

One winter day, when rain and snow were flailing the windows, a thoroughly wet and frozen German officer entered our house. My wife gave him dry clothing and put him next to the warm stove. The gentleman began mightily puffing on his big pipe. The warmth, the dry clothes, the tidy room, and his pipe helped him forget that he was "way out in Turkey." When I came home at noon, he introduced himself as Dr. Fuhrmann, the chief staff surgeon in Turkish service and a gynecologist from Cologne where he had been head of the women's hospital before the war. We were happy that the winter weather did not allow our guest to depart soon.

In the summer of 1918 the last German soldier came to Urfa. I was in the clinic. An Armenian woman told me that a soldier was waiting for me in the mill, and he wanted urgently to speak to me. The mill was behind the clinic. Whom did I meet there? Standing there was a completely bedraggled motorized soldier who had been stationed in Urfa earlier. [Eugen] Huber from the Black Forest had deserted to Urfa. He wanted me to take him in. For the time being, I sent him to my vineyard where my wife and children were because I had to go back to work. Not more than two hours later my wife appeared in a state of excitement! It was impossible for us to take in a deserter! That would cause us big problems. I had to send him away immediately! But the situation was not so dangerous. I had a free hand as a Swiss. After consultation with another German guest,

[Gustav] Bredemann, PhD, we decided to keep Huber in the vineyard for the time being. He could first recuperate there; he was completely run down. Fourteen days of recuperation lifted the spirits of the despondent fellow, who, like so many others, had had more than enough of the war. I then persuaded him to return to his platoon. Huber left with a letter from me to the chief staff surgeon in Aleppo, the previously mentioned guest. The chief staff surgeon kept him for a few days, and then the deserter returned to his platoon where he could reintegrate without punishment. Unfortunately, he was back a few days later with malaria, and he succumbed in a short time. Now he was free from military service forever.

The chief staff surgeon wanted to recommend me for the Cross of Merit for our accommodation of these runaway soldiers and the friendliness we had displayed to the other German soldiers. But I asked him to refrain because we had only done our simple duty, which we had also done for the enemies of Germany.

Finally, another officer should be mentioned here. He carried no sword by his side and wore no uniform. We called him the "locust general." He and his very dear wife were guests in our house for a long time. This gentleman, the previously mentioned Dr. Bredemann, had performed a very beneficial service in Mesopotamia. He had exterminated the enemies of mankind in the millions. Since I had been in the Orient, I had seen these enemies kill people repeatedly by causing incalculable damage in the wheat fields. But since this "general" had systematically been hunting them down, the "locust plague" had subsided substantially. With one more year of his rational battle, the locust would have ceased to exist as a great plague in Mesopotamia. But this "general" also had to retreat, and he returned to his German homeland. What the Turkish government had not been able to accomplish in decades of work and the expenditure of millions for locust extermination, three Germans who were active in Anatolia, Syria, and Mesopotamia did in three years.[50]

39. The Banknote

Turkey first introduced banknotes during the Turkish-Russian war of 1877. But the Ottoman people had no faith in the value of this paper currency. The exchange rate dropped steadily until it was worth only a sixth of gold's value. Then came the national bankruptcy. The government declared all banknotes worthless, and the country returned to the beloved gold specie. There were merchants who papered their walls with the banknotes.

The World War breathed new life into the banknote. As a consequence of stricter regulations, the paper currency looked good in the beginning; that was in April 1916. All gold coins were supposed to be surrendered to the state, but no one did that. Gold disappeared immediately from circulation. In Urfa, a rich Turk who did not want to take banknotes in payment was banished to Konya. Those who rejected the notes in other towns were also banished. It did not help to increase the value of the currency because the police suddenly broke into the shops, opened the safes, and exchanged the gold they found for banknotes. Gold coins continued to circulate in secret. In the final analysis, the government got the short end of the stick. After only a few months, the banknotes dropped in value, and gold continued to be circulated. However, the banks were not permitted to make payments or conduct business in gold. The longer the war lasted, the more the banknotes dropped in value.

The closer one came to the border, the cheaper were the banknotes. In Constantinople, the value was constantly higher than in the provinces. Even among the provinces, the value varied. Huge sums could be moved around this way. A salesman bought banknotes in Aleppo for gold, received six banknotes for one piece of gold, and turned around and sold three or four banknotes in Constantinople for a gold pound. Even after the armistice and the British occupation in Mosul and Aleppo, Turkish currency was worth much less in Mosul than in Aleppo. A Jewish salesman bought banknotes in Mosul for 120,000 francs, paid 1,200 francs for a seat on an airplane bound for Aleppo, where he sold his banknotes and cleared a profit of 150,000 francs.

It was strange that the value of Turkish currency increased in value in Urfa after the British occupation had begun. The future will show whether the merchants will paper their rooms in banknotes again. During the war, the Arabs were not in this position because they had no rooms that needed papering.

I wanted to buy a liter of buttermilk from an Arab and told him that I would give him 200 banknotes for it. He pointed to his broad coat and said: "If you fill my coat with those notes, I will not give you any milk; but if you give me just one *metalik*,[51] you can have all the milk you want."

The German officers in Turkey, especially those on the Palestinian front, soon saw that they could not buy anything with banknotes. As a consequence Turkish gold and silver pieces were minted in Berlin and sent in the millions to Turkey. How that gold could be used in Germany today![52]

40. The Food Prices

Mesopotamia was one of the regions where food was still cheap during the second year of the war. In the fall of 1915 a *kilé*[53] of wheat cost only 10 francs. In the spring of 1918 the same amount cost 3,200 francs if one paid in banknotes; 650 francs if one paid in gold. On my journey to Baghdad I paid one *metalik* for four eggs. But last year in January one had to pay 2.25 francs for one. Meat, which still costs sixty pfennig for one *okka*,[54] ended up costing sixteen francs. Cooking butter, which cost three francs for an okka in peacetime, reached a price of fifty francs. One paid unbelievable prices for petroleum. A tin container that held eighteen liters usually cost five francs, but then one had to pay 2,000 francs. The cost of all imported items rose, on the average, much more than on domestic goods. It is therefore understandable that imports were suspended. Only when Baghdad had fallen could one obtain smuggled goods in Urfa again, albeit at unaffordable prices. Thin cotton material, such as that used to shroud the dead, was especially expensive. The demand had risen because the plague claimed so many victims. Many people had to bury their dead without a shroud.

41. Dawn

The small remnant of deported Armenians had a long wait for better times. As long as the war continued, there was no hope of returning home or even of moving about freely where they were. But everything has its time, and the war also had to come to an end.

In Urfa we often wondered what was holding the Turkish fronts together. Urfa was crawling with deserters who were repeatedly discovered and returned but always found their way back again. We were, therefore, by no means surprised in September 1918 when we heard about the fall of Nablus and Nazareth in Palestine; Damascus had to follow soon. I was in Aleppo at the time. I hurried back to Urfa because the English might arrive in Aleppo at any time. The reports that I brought to Urfa would send the Germans there on their way. Dr. Bredemann and his wife left immediately for Aleppo, and from there they made their way to Constantinople.

After the armistice, an anti-German sentiment developed among the Turks in Urfa. I had already heard that the Turks wanted to requisition the carpet factory and our hospital. I was administering both institutions at the time. Mr. Eckart had transferred the former to me upon his departure, and the latter had reverted to me just before the armistice. The Turks wanted to relocate the trade school from the American Mission Institute to the factory because the Institute would also revert to me after the armistice because I was the representative of the American organization.

Fortunately, the Turks thought better of the matter at the last minute. They preferred to have their school in a building from which they could not be expelled so soon. I registered our hospital as a Swiss institution because the title deed was made out to a Swiss. I thereby cleared the new obstacles and came into possession of all the buildings. The Turkish mob roundly cursed the Germans. The better elements, of course, could not change from friends to foes overnight.

No sooner had the Entente entered Constantinople than another wind blew into the provinces. Orders were given in effect to liberate all Armenians who were in Mohammedan houses, even those women who were married to Mohammedans.

Now all those Armenian soldiers who had stood their ground as true Ottomans since the outbreak of the war were also free. There were about 200 from Urfa who had survived the war. They stayed behind at first in Aleppo because Urfa was too unsafe for them. Only when the British had occupied Urfa did they all dare to return to the birthplace of Abraham, where they found none of their relatives or their goods and property.

It was very good that I was again in possession of the American Mission Institute building. Although it was turned over to me completely empty, it could immediately be set up as an orphanage. I was able to repair the damage that was caused by the bombardment in 1916.

However, the Turks were not in a hurry to give up the Armenians in their houses. Only if they were sick and ailing were they sent out to the street. Those came to us, and we put them all in the orphanage. Others who had heard that they were free fled to us, and we saw everything imaginable. If an Armenian woman had entered a Turkish house as a girl, it was understandable that, when she came to us, she carried all her jewelry and often very beautiful clothes. Close behind her came a Turk who had given her those things as gifts and demanded them back. Or, a woman fled to us, leaving behind her infant with the Turks. Then the father came with the children and asked that we see to it that the runaway mother continued to nurse the child. The mother would resist because she knew that the child would ultimately belong to the Turks. I soon saw that I could not run an orphanage in which I did not live without official protection; so I asked the governor for a gendarme to keep away the often very covetous Mohammedans.

Sometimes picking up the Armenians from the Turkish houses proved to be very difficult. The Armenian nation could not be rebuilt with the sick. Therefore, we wanted to retrieve as many healthy people from the Turkish houses as possible. As soon as we learned the names of Armenian children and or women and the house where they lived, we could inform the police and ask that those in question be brought to us. That is what happened most of the time. Now it was not always clear to us if the person in question really wished to leave the Turkish house. With children the process did not last long. They could put up resistance or scream: "I am not a gâvur, I am a Mohammedan." But they were simply taken by the police. After a few days, most of those children were happy and glad to be in the orphanage. It was another matter with an Armenian woman who wanted to remain with a Mohammedan. She would try to flee from the orphanage. One must not forget that many of them did not have a bad situation in the Muslim homes, where they had generous amounts of food, good clothing, and beds. When the Armenians were picked up, their best clothes were taken away from them.

There were shortages in the orphanage, not only of food but also of clothes and beds. We often had only one bed for every three or four persons. With the conclusion of the armistice, our sources of funds dried up because banks no longer paid out money. Therefore, I preliminarily took over the considerable cash reserves of the carpet factory and went to the British in Aleppo to ask them for money; but they kept me waiting. They had to first find out who I was.

In one of the wealthiest Turkish homes, there was a cultured and very pretty Armenian girl who had married a deaf-mute Turk. An investigation of this girl was initiated from Switzerland. We knew that she had a sad situation, and we did not want to leave her to that fate. Although we repeatedly informed the police, she was not brought to us. Thanks to his wealth, the Turk was more powerful than the police.

One day a well-bred Turkish woman, the wife of a high official, appeared before me. She pleaded with us tearfully to have the police pick up a certain Armenian woman from Sivas. Her husband was entirely neglecting her and devoting himself only to this Armenian woman. The Turkish woman had borne her husband three lively children. But the man, who was otherwise good, was completely in the clutches of the "strumpet." She fell down at my feet and asked me to get this "strumpet" out of her life. But the Armenian woman, whom we knew, could not be so bad; unlike many others she very obviously preferred to remain with the Turk instead of going on the street. The Turks whose Armenian women came to us sometimes tried to accuse the women of theft. One was supposed to have stolen 1,000 piasters[55] and another more than 2,000 piasters from their houses. The Turks hoped that by making the accusation they could take possession of the women again. In reality, the women were no thieves. Armenian loyalty is proverbial in the Orient. Just because of that fact, they were coveted, and the Turks tried everything to get them back again.

The following strange event will illustrate how seriously the government took the liberation of the Armenian women. An order was given that no more harm could be done to Armenian women, and that they were all to be freed. A Turk who had made no sexual advances on a girl who worked as his servant for three years molested her after the order. She succeeded in escaping and accused the Turk of rape. On the order of the governor, the Turk had to pay the girl 100 gold pounds (2,300 francs).

I had no more money for our daily increasing crowd of children and women in the orphanage. The English had not kept their promise to give me money at Christmas. So, at the end of February, I sent my wife to Aleppo to vigorously remind the English of their promise. Finally, she succeeded in getting help.

I had often asked myself why the English had kept me waiting so long while large sums had been dispensed for the suffering Armenians in Aleppo. I had strongly suspected that slander was the reason. In fact, around Christmas the Armenian assistant doctor who had worked in our hospital fled from Urfa, where he had no longer felt secure, to Aleppo. This gentleman must have slandered me to the English. Like many

Armenians he had taken it very badly that I made no secret of my sympathic attitude toward the Germans during the war. A friend of the Germans was nothing but an enemy of the Armenians, regardless of what he did for those unfortunate people! The doctor had not mentioned that I also had taken in four Frenchmen and an Englishman who had been detained in Urfa. This Armenian psychology is only too understandable if one knows that the Turks had always maintained that the German Kaiser [Wilhelm II] had ordered the deportation of the Armenian people.

In March 1919 an American commission appeared in Urfa to investigate the suffering of the Armenians and the previous relief organizations. These gentlemen came to our house. I was permitted to show them my accounting ledgers and was gratified that they highly praised my work. They considered it necessary to note that from their point of view, of all the relief workers in the empire, none had used the money so diligently for the intended purpose than I had. As soon as these gentlemen reached Aleppo, the English sent money without my having to be asked again. Now those in the relevant positions knew with whom they were dealing.

42. The Destroyed Quarter

The Armenian quarter of the city had been totally looted in November 1915. Many houses had been burned out and had collapsed. Since most of the roofs were made of clay and gravel, they had to be maintained after the onset of the rainy season. Those roofs that were not maintained deteriorated quickly, and many collapsed during the first winter. Only parts of the walls were standing. Those houses that were somewhat intact received new inhabitants, namely the Kurds who came to Urfa as immigrants. They had no interest in caring for the houses and considered it self-evident that they would soon return to their homeland. So they stole every piece of wood and iron that they could find. Every beam was ripped out. If the house collapsed, why did that concern them? That led to the collapse of almost the entire quarter. There were barely fifty houses left from the 2,300 that had been somewhat livable. Most of the surviving houses were those on the border of the Turkish quarter which had been occupied by local Turks right after the bombardment.

The good kadı helped the Armenians as much as he could. He had suggested a general restitution of Armenian property, to the extent that it still existed, to the remaining Armenians; but the governor resisted. So the kadı could only settle matters and help on a case-by-case basis when this was legally possible. In the absence of other relatives, when some Armenians now tried to take possession of a house or garden belonging to an uncle who had disappeared, that was legitimate. The governor wanted, under no circumstances, to simply turn over all the property to the Armenian National Committee for restitution to those entitled to it.

There was soon a lack of space in our orphanage, so I asked for the restitution of the Armenian monastery, which had been used until recently as a Turkish poor house. I hoped to be able to move into the monastery, which was outside the city, soon. Just a few months before I had been there and was happy to see that the windows and doors were still in place. But when the Armenians whom I had represented and I went to take possession of the monastery, I was outraged. All windows and doors were gone; all woodwork over the crossbars had been removed, and, as a consequence, much of the masonry had collapsed. Instead of being able to move into this house immediately, I now had to carry out the most urgent repairs. For the time being, because of wood and glass shortages, windows and doors could not be installed; but because spring was coming, one could quarter the children there. At my request, the Americans wanted to send glass and wood from America, not only for this house but for the whole quarter. We therefore hoped to finish repairs by the next winter.

In March 1919 we occupied the monastery[56] with Armenian children. It had been determined that we could not put women and children together in the large orphanage. Because of their years of living in Muslim houses, the people had become so spoiled that a separation was absolutely necessary. Among the women who had been released, some were expecting.

In addition to a substantial amount of money, we mainly needed personnel. I was not only supposed to oversee all these human beings who had been gathered together but also to put them to work. The Franciscans in Urfa took my request for help seriously. We were able to transfer one hundred women and some children to the Franciscans, who found useful work in handicrafts for them right away.

The weaving mill was soon busy with workers. This trade had previously been done by men in Urfa; but in the last years of the emergency, women had also learned it. The bootmaker also started up shop quickly. The Franciscans also set up boot-making as well as cabinetmaking shops.

We used the Protestant church,[57] which was returned to us without windows or doors, as a school. Almast, whose deportation story I have already told, was the head teacher. It was hard work to reintegrate all of the wild children into school life and an ordered existence. They had learned idleness from the Turks and were as good at it as their masters. Three to four years in Muslim houses had taken their toll on the sensitive and impressionable Armenians, and I fear this negative influence will persist for a long time.

43. Bells and Other Sounds

The Protestant church was somewhat intact after the bombardment. Only the little belfry and its bell had been shot out. One of the domes was also damaged by a bomb. But the hole had been repaired by the Turks when they used the church as barracks for their recruits. Everything that could be removed had been removed, including windows and doors. The bell had lain in the mud for four years because it was too heavy to carry away. Only the clapper and the iron parts of the bell frame had been stolen. The great Armenian cathedral[58] had fared worse. Some corners of the building were completely shot away during the bombardment; of course, nothing that could be removed was left in the church. All the woodwork, floors paved with stone slabs, and stone blocks on the large flat roofs had been carried off. It will not be possible for the Urfa Armenians remaining today to restore the cathedral, and I fear that this historic site will only survive as a ruin.

Since we were able to hold services beginning in February 1919 in the Protestant church, I was eager for the voice of the bell to ring out over the city once again. Syrians and Catholics, who had smaller bells, had not dared to ring them since the fall of 1915 out of fear of the Turks.

I had a wooden bell frame built and lifted the bell into it. On the first Sunday in March the voice of the bell was scheduled to be heard again. We informed all the Armenian houses and the Christians still living in Muslim houses. That Sunday we were a congregation of about 2,000 strong. I rejoiced like a child when the moment came and the bell announced to all the evil spirits that had plagued the Christian people: The Armenians are resurrected; they are alive and have gathered in God's house!

At the request of the Armenian National Committee, the privilege of being able to ring the bell for the first time was to be auctioned off. The highest bidder, the son of the pharmacist who gladly paid 200 francs, climbed the roof and struck the bell with a large iron hammer.

When the first sounds of the bell rang out over the city, tears welled up in the eyes of the congregation: tears of joy and of pain. There was no one who was not deeply moved.

What could the curses uttered by ill-meaning Mohammedans have done at that moment? The Christians of Urfa will also live! And God willing, soon living without fear of the sword of Mohammed, which is my hope for the sake of the Orient in the true sense of their Lord and master.

Two days later was the Armenian national holiday. The Armenians demanded to celebrate it in the church. It was a memorable day. Everyone rejoiced as the telegrams from the Armenian delegation in Paris[59] were read. One began imagining that a free Armenia had been created: "Armenia is arisen!" ["*Hayastan eghav, Hayastan eghav!*"] The hunted and the tormented cried out together in longing hope and indescribable jubilation. "Glory to God" ["*Park'Astutso!*"] rang out again and again through the large room. I rejoiced with them and was moved, although I thought the jubilation was premature. It was understandable that even the slightest prospect for salvation from the merciless rule of the sword of the Young Turks would have to fill every inhumanely tormented heart with joy. Although I was not an Armenian, I shared their sadness over the past twenty years, so shouldn't I be permitted to rejoice with them too?

The next day Armenians from Aleppo came to Urfa. The news they brought with them curdled the blood in every Armenian heart which had burst with joy the day before. A few days earlier, in front of the eyes of the British occupiers, about 100 Armenians were slaughtered by the Turks. Had the murdering not yet come to an end? If a massacre in front of the English was possible there, what could happen in Urfa where no British had been stationed yet?

On the next Sunday I had to take pains to pacify the congregation. If I had spoken on the national holiday about the dawn and the sun that were rising for the Armenian people, I would have had to say that, as in nature after the storm when the sun breaks through with glorious splendor, very often clouds assemble again in front of the sun. But the sun is finally victorious and drives away the clouds. And it would do so this time too. The clouds come and want to make us believe that there is no sun, but the sun is there and we may and wish to rejoice! "Armenia will arise!" "*Park'Astutso!*"

44. Death of the Traitor

The first British officer arrived in Urfa on December 31, 1918. He was put up in a Turkish home, and not, as was the custom before the war, in one of our European homes. I visited him and offered him my house. Since he wanted to meet with the leaders of the Armenians, this was reason enough for him to move into my house. The Armenians would not have entered a Turkish house. He accepted my invitation.

The Armenians who were considered leaders in Urfa were quickly counted: Pastor Ephraim [Jernazian], who has often been mentioned, and the pharmacist Karekin [Effendi Turyekian],[60] who was in Aleppo during the massacre and later came to Urfa. In Urfa, he was thrown into jail and forced to take a Mohammedan name before receiving his freedom again. The third was Minas Effendi, who was a Turkish drill officer throughout the entire war. Although he was from out of town and was not one of the Urfa Armenians, he had played a role in the city since the armistice.

The British officer called upon the leaders to demand the return of the property stolen from them by the Turks. In addition, they should not allow the Turks, even if it was the government itself, to carry off any more stones from the deteriorated Armenian quarter.

The British officer, a colonel, read the Armenians a memorandum for the Turkish governor. It called upon him to be helpful in all ways to the rest of the Armenians, to take care that their property be returned, and to make sure that Armenians in Muslim houses be liberated. The governor could expect that any threats against the Armenians would be severely punished.

The leaders should not just take note of the memorandum; the officer urged them at the same time to watch over the governor to see that he also followed these orders. Asked why the English had not occupied Urfa, the colonel answered that first there had to be a significant reason to do so.

On the third day the colonel left Urfa. It was clear that the English were looking for an excuse to come to Urfa. This excuse would be found quickly. On the morning of January 7, 1919, a murdered man was found in the half-collapsed Armenian church. It was Muhammed Sükri, one of the Armenian traitors whom we have already mentioned. The Turks immediately initiated a police investigation. In the course of the investigation a half dozen Armenians, among them Minas Effendi, were put in prison. The Armenians tried to pin the blame on the

Turks, and the Turks believed that only the Armenians could have murdered the man. The story created a storm and so stirred up emotions that I considered it advisable to send a short report to the British stationed at the time sixty kilometers from Urfa.

Some days later the British colonel reappeared and came directly to my house. He had not received my report but had received Armenian news instead. I gave him a copy of my report. He barely perused it and said:

"So that is what happened? This sounds much different than the Armenian report."

It was clear to the colonel that the incident had been provoked by the Armenians. Only Armenians, not Turks, could have killed the traitor of their people (which by the way was not such a bad thing.)

The English occupation desired by the Armenians did not happen. They blamed me for the delay in the occupation. I was certain that were I to call the English to Urfa, it could only be for a reason which could later be justified.

45. Ali Ihsan Paşa

In January Turkish troops came from Nisibin[61] to Urfa. According to the armistice treaty, these troops were to be demobilized and part of them sent back to the Anatolian interior. Among the troops was Ali Ihsan Pasa, the. high commander of the former Mosul front.

Apparently, he wanted to show the officials of Urfa how one could shoot with modern artillery. One evening he fired off thirty rounds on the nearby mountain. It was a fearsome thunder. One could observe the impacts of the shells and see their terrible violence.

The shooting created great agitation among the Urfa population. The next morning Armenians and Turks reported the incident to the English. I also believed that I should do the same because it was really not the time for such shootings.

Ali Ihsan Pasa set out the next morning with his troops, going to the north; the shooting was the occasion for his captivity. On the orders of the British, he was taken prisoner by the central government in the vicinity of Diyarbakır.

46. The Arrival of the British

Since the February massacre in Aleppo, evil rumors directed against the Armenians had been making the rounds. That agitated them daily. The relief work we were doing contributed inadvertently to the rumors. We could well imagine that this work would especially aggravate the Turks' ill will because it meant taking away the remaining Armenian laborers who had been exploited as slaves. And now these slaves were to be taken away from them!

It did not therefore surprise us one morning when a Christian woman came and told my wife that in the Turkish club patronized by the wealthiest and most respectable Mohammedans in the city, it had been decided to kill Karekin the pharmacist and me. If we were both eliminated, one could keep the Armenian slaves. No one would dare again to take Armenian women from Turkish houses.

I first had to laugh when I heard of this intention. Regarding my person, I was immune to a certain extent from murder attempts because all classes of the population, Mohammedans as well as Christians, were dependent upon me. If the club had also debated about the safety of my person, this could amount to a mild warning.

Two days later the pharmacist was awakened in the night by knocking. The caller was supposedly in urgent need of medicine. Karekin dressed quickly and started down the stairs to the house door. He had already descended a few steps when he began to doubt whether he should go or not. He stood there for a moment. Five pistol shots rang out in front of the house. Now it was clear, the boys at the door wanted to scare the gâvur— if not worse.

The next morning Karekin was at work as usual in his pharmacy, which was located apart from the house. His younger brother came and announced that there were five fresh bullet holes in the house door and that one could see where they all had impacted the wall across from the door. Now we knew that the bullets were intended for the Armenian. If he had not hesitated for a moment on the stairs, he would probably not be alive. It was a miracle that he had escaped assassination.

I was called in to assess the situation. I now saw that I had to summon the British to Urfa; and it looked to me as if they had been waiting for the call. I came home, had my horse saddled, sat down at my typewriter, and wrote simply, "We require representatives of the British immediately because the lives of Armenians are in danger." The Arab with whom I sent this message covered the sixty kilometers with my honest mare in four hours.

The next morning a British colonel arrived with soldiers and three automobiles, and he came to me. The officer inspected the scene of the shooting at the pharmacist's house. The next morning soldiers along with the officer disappeared again. No sooner did the Turks get wind of their departure than jubilation broke out among the malicious elements. They trumpeted throughout the city that the British were afraid of the Turks and had therefore retreated. Now one could take one's time to eliminate the Armenians.

Now the Armenians who had breathed easier when the English had arrived and had dropped in to thank me came pale with fear and accused me of letting the British go again. But I knew something else: They should just stay calm; the next morning they would have something to laugh about.

But it took three days before the big moment arrived.

On the third day I was at work in the clinic. At about ten, a Turkish policeman showed up again and announced that I should come immediately to the governor. But I wanted to finish my work first. During the war I was called by the police so often that I was not in a hurry to respond to them this time. But the policeman insisted. He told me in confidence that foreign-

ers had arrived, and that the governor wanted me as a translator. It then occurred to me that it could be the English. So I
changed my clothes and followed the police. An automobile
stood in front of the *saray*.[62] I entered the reception hall. Next
to the governor sat two English officers who gave a friendly
greeting. A memorable conversation lasting only a few minutes
followed. It ran as follows:

"Do you speak English?" one of the British officers, a lieutenant colonel, asked me.

"Yes, a little," I answered.

"Good, then I would like it if you would act as translator
between me and the Turkish governor because I do not have
an interpreter with me. Ask the Turk whether he had news of
my arrival."

The governor: "Certainly, I received your telegram."

The Englishman: "Why didn't you accommodate me?"

The Turkish answer already sounded meek: "It did not say
in the telegram that you would wait for me."

The Englishman: "Damn you! As a friend of the British and
as governor of Urfa, you did not do your duty and accommodate me."

This English answer, which I confess I translated in a somewhat milder form, still made a strong impression on the Turk.

But the English officer did not wait for an answer and continued: "What have you done to prepare for the lodging for my
officers and my 800 men?"

The governor: "I did not want in any way to anticipate your
decision. There will be enough space. The house of a Swiss is
empty, and there is an empty barracks available for the soldiers."

"Show them to me," he said to the Turkish policemen. To the
governor, he said, "You stay here. After I have seen them, I will
give you my orders."

With these blunt words, the officer stood up. He asked me
to come with him. We got into the automobile; the Turkish
policemen ran behind us; and the barracks were inspected. The
officer wrinkled his nose. He could not house any soldiers in
these barracks. He then asked me for advice.

It was clear to me that since the governor had offered the house of the Swiss [Dr. Vischer], the British would certainly take it. In a mood of justifiable retribution, I answered:

"Take the Turkish Hospital: It is empty and has a great location and plenty of room."

We got back into the automobile and drove to the Turkish hospital. After a short inspection, the officer sent back his first order to the governor. It was: "My troops will occupy the Turkish hospital immediately; transfer it immediately".

"Where is the house of the Swiss?"

Since it was nearby, we went there by foot to look at it too. The officer made an immediate decision here also. There was not a more beautiful house in Urfa. It was nearly very empty because I had only set up a clinic, pharmacy, and operating room. Now that the British were in the country, I could transplant them into our hospital again without having to ask the Turks. The seals had been broken anyway, so I only needed to unlock the doors.

Meanwhile, the British troops had arrived, and they were all Indians. A large train of baggage arrived, and some armored vehicles with a few Tommies.[63]

It was a blessing for Urfa and the rest of the Armenian people in the city! The entry of the British was also a great cause for celebration for the other Christians in the city. The chronic fear of death with which they had lived for so long had come to an end! That was on March 24, 1919. The Syrians and Catholics came and thanked me.

It is to the credit of the British occupation that three high Turkish officials of Urfa were discharged: the governor, the police director, and the municipal president.

The governor was taken prisoner and sent to Constantinople, accused of atrocities against the Armenians. This gentleman had been governor in the city of Baiburt when the deportations began. In addition to all the Armenian men, he had had all the women and children slaughtered in front of the city. After this deed, he was transferred to the city of Arğana Maaden[64] to replace a less willing governor who had been punished. The new gentleman also had all the Armenians, including women and children butchered in front of the city. This useful official was then sent to Urfa. The British were able to let the Turks themselves take care of him.

Since the kadı had told me about the terrible deeds of this governor, I had often asked myself whether he had not acted better than all the other governors who had deported the women and children. Hadn't the women in some locations begged the governors to kill them on the spot instead of deporting them? How unbelievably terrible it was for those most unfortunates along the way! A life of shame, slavery, or death by famine was their certain, appalling fate. But if all the governors had acted as this one had, then from the one and a half million Armenians who had to leave their homes, only 200,000–300,000 would still be alive.

It was in May when panic broke out once again among the Christians in the city of Urfa. Many hurriedly shut down their stands in the market and fled to their homes. An agitated woman came to the clinic and accused the government of distributing rifles to the Mohammedans. I reluctantly sent the woman away. I did not believe her. But she did not go away until I told her:

"I am no longer responsible for such things; go to the British!" The woman went; and in order to be admitted more expeditiously, she said she had been sent by me.

The next morning I was summoned, along with all the Christian notables, before the British commander. We were supposed to explain the cause of the panic. But I had already forgotten about the Armenian woman who had come to me the day before (the woman to whom I had said: "Go to the British.") The commander took us to the Turkish governor, whom he had already ordered to initiate an investigation. The governor had gotten to the bottom of the matter. The Turkish government had transferred rifles from a house outside the city. Nervous eyes must have seen this and created a panic.

47. A Last Unsuccessful Harassment

At about the same time the English arrived, a Turkish health inspector came to Urfa. Since the Armenian doctor had fled to Aleppo in December 1918, the city had had no doctor with a degree other than a Turk who was most often seen careening drunk in the streets in the early morning hours. He had one virtue in that he made no problems for me. He was never called by a patient. So I was able to fully exercise my capabilities in my medical practice. It was a mountain of work that I had to master. Most of the Armenians who came from the Muslim houses needed medical care. Great numbers of Mohammedans also came. In the first five months of 1919, I treated no fewer than 2,000 patients in the clinic. At the same time, there still 200 patients in the hospital and the need for more than 100 operations, among them some very difficult ones. The government also sent me to patients. On top of that, I had to work as the doctor in the Turkish business school. And when the several hundred-man cavalry was without a doctor, I had to assist them too.

The friendly reader should not take this exposition as self-praise for doing what I could with the help of God. I only want to show what I was required to do.

I expected that the new health inspector would make problems for me because I had no diploma. It could not have escaped him that I had taken care of the medical needs in Urfa in the past months, and he would, at any rate, be thankful.

Assuming that I would be pressured again, I turned to the Indian doctor who had arrived with the occupation troops. He granted my request to take over supervision of our Swiss hospital. He spent some time working in the hospital, and we worked well together.

A few days later I received a written request from the Turkish health inspector. If what he had heard was true—that I did not possess a medical degree—I had to close the pharmacy and clinic immediately. But the British commanding officer to whom I showed the letter told me that I should just continue to do my work and not answer the letter. Two weeks later a Kurd died from blood poisoning in our hospital. I had operated on him in the presence of the Indian doctor ten days before.

Two days later I received a subpoena from the examining magistrate. The Turkish board of health had sued me. The accusation was that a Kurd had died from negligence during surgery in our hospital; legal proceedings were necessary because the surgeon did not have a medical degree. I expected to have it easy because I could rely on the Indian doctor's testimony. On the basis of my testimony the examining magistrate referred the case to the English commander, who answered via the Indian doctor. The doctor said that Künzler had conducted the operation in his presence, and the patient had died from blood poisoning. It must be said that it is indicative of the health inspector that he had not examined the dead man. He had sued me on the basis of hearsay.

48. Arrival of the Aid Expedition

Only a few days after the British arrived, four American members of a Red Cross expedition (three women and a gentleman) arrived in Urfa. We were able to transfer to them the American Mission Institute which had 500 orphans and widows. The expedition brought with it needed items, including new energy, money, clothes, and even a truck. The rescue work achieved a new and utterly necessary momentum. The industrial employment program we had started was extended and multiplied; and the schools were better equipped and expanded.

My wife and I breathed easier. The load which we had carried alone since 1916 was taken from our shoulders.

The British took over the relief organization for the many Armenians who were re-emerging daily. With our assistance, they distributed bread to the starving and some money for bare necessities.

We had known for months that Dr. Vischer, the most loved and urgently needed doctor in Urfa would return with his wife. Month after month went by, but he did not appear. Passport and travel problems repeatedly delayed their departure from

Switzerland. As soon as he arrived in Urfa, I wanted to go back to Switzerland to breathe a little air at home again.

The joyful hour of his arrival finally came. The courageous couple had left their children in Basel so that the doctor's wife could devote all of her energy to the relief organization. Now the work in our hospital should be able to set out in full sail again and also in compliance with the requirements of Turkish law. A general feeling of joy about the doctor's arrival was expressed in the city and the country among Christians and Mohammedans. But my joy and that of my wife was the greatest because the hour of our salvation had arrived.

49. An Airplane over Urfa

In May 1919 a large field of stones outside of the city had to be cleared. The British transferred the commissioning of this work to my wife. She hired hundreds of Armenian women and was able to give them a wage. The area was intended to be the first airplane runway in Urfa.

Two weeks later the great moment occurred, the arrival of the airplane. It flew proudly over old Edessa. Everyone went outside or climbed onto roofs and stared. The Mohammedans gave praise to Allah. When the airplane fired off a salvo, all of those who had a bad conscience trembled a little. The Christians gave a great sigh of relief.

50. Concerns about Bills

The concerns about bills associated with our work should not go unmentioned. They were an unnecessary drain on my intellectual energy. As the reader will have noticed, my work had become quite multifaceted. The long columns of numbers marching through my ledgers in the course of the war showed that millions had passed through my hands. The hospital, American Mission Institute, and relief organizations to help the Armenians, Kurds, and internees from the spring of 1916 to the end of 1918 all required accounting activity. On top of that, there was my own large household which had steadily assumed the dimensions of a sheikh's house, where many came, especially hungry human beings, to get something to eat.

Since I was busy during the day, there was no time to do the accounting. It always had to be done at night when the body is already very tired. It was understandable then if the invoices did not add up sometimes. When I woke up at night and the sleep fled from my eyes, I got up and began to count. These were the hours when some of the ambiguities were resolved. Most of the time there was too little money in the cashbox, which was understandable because I had many small expenditures. I have often envied the officials of the Turkish Hospital, which has an operation not much larger than ours but with a special administrator, secretary, and cashier.

All expenses were deducted from my umbrella account. Since the end of 1917 I had known that there was one entry too many in the account. I had not succeeded in finding it in spite of repeated attempts. An entry in the income account must have been forgotten. I requested statements of accounts from Switzerland, America, and Germany. But I did not receive confirmations from most of them. Just before my journey to Switzerland, a Basel bank sent me a general statement that had not been sent to me since 1916. While checking this statement—it was in the night again, my family had all gone to bed—I discovered an entry which had not been registered in my ledgers. Suddenly there was too little money in the cashbox, and a significant sum was missing! What was I to do? For two years my salary had been insufficient because of rising costs.

Since 1917 my wife had put aside the small sum that she received for her work with the relief organization, keeping it carefully out of my sight. She said to herself that when the war is over and we go to Switzerland, we will have put aside a little nest egg. I had often explained to her that she had to put this money into the household because my salary was not enough to support the family. In addition she had sold some things from our home and also put that money aside. Now it was clear to me that the hole in the account had to be filled with the money that the good woman had set aside. But how and when

I was to request it was a matter of diplomacy. One can appreciate how I felt during the next few days. It was not easy for me. Luckily I was caught up in the daily work; but in the evening I had to ask for the money. My wife listened to my opening speech. She understood that she had to hand over the money she had saved, but it was not easy for her. She brought it to me and remarked laconically: "Do you want to sell my dress, too? You can have it!"

Who could hold it against her if she was bitter? But we have a proven method in our marriage that always makes forgiveness easier. We never went to sleep without praying together because one can not sulk and pray at the same time. "It is proved!" ["*Probatum est!*"]

51. Insightful Mohammedans

We human beings are often moved in our thoughts by the question, "why?" The answer "because" is missing just as often. If one thinks about the unspeakable suffering borne by the Armenian people, one asks: Why? As if we might be able to get a satisfactory answer. I want to tell the following story because it contains the answer to my questions.

A few days before my departure for Europe, two Turks from the city came to me. They were craftsmen, and, from what I could see, simple men. They asked me the following question:

"Do you think that the English who are now in Urfa would protect us from attacks by the Turkish government if we became Christians tomorrow?"

I had to answer that I did not know, and that I would find out. But I asked them why they wanted to become Christians.

"You are the one who took away the Armenian women we married. These women taught us a family life that we never knew before. They read to us from the Bible and did our housework. And we were astonished; they became so dear to us that it is impossible for us to leave them. We would rather part from our old belief. And you should know that we are not alone in this view and in this situation. There are about fifty other men who sent us here who are ready to become Christians in order to [hold on to] their new lives with Christian women. Since the Turkish government would throw us in jail as soon as we converted, we wanted to know if the English would intervene to free us."

Two days later these men received their answer. Unfortunately, I had to tell them that the British commander had declared that the British would not get involved in such things. As they were departing, I was compelled to tell the sorrowful men that the Armenians could have escaped the horrible deportations and death by converting to the Mohammedan belief, but they had preferred death and the rest of the unspeakable treatment: "If you would draw upon such strength, you would also suffer; but in your suffering you would be rewarded with victory!"

52. Departure

The description of my experiences during the World War would be incomplete if I were to omit my departure from Urfa; yet my pen resists doing that. Since in all of my reports I have to adhere to the facts, then I must also mention the departure—the more so because it was the occasion of some disturbing hours for us.

The work of the reconstituted Armenian National Committee in the capital consisted of finding work for the soldiers returning home and seeing to it that the widows and orphans could reclaim their property as much as possible. In December 1918 a member of this committee came to Urfa in order to establish an organization there, too. Armenian women complained about me to this man. They had been sent money from a relative named Khachaturian in Germany. I had given them the money. Since the bank transferred the money to me in banknotes, I did not want to pay out in gold. At a time when there were no banknotes in Turkey, I had sent money to Khachaturian's account in gold currency.

I want to say here that I was not the only one who was defamed about financial matters by the Armenians. All the Americans still in the country at the beginning of the war can tell similar stories. At a time when banknotes did not exist, they were given money that was then deposited in a bank. When the banknotes were introduced, the bank could no longer pay out in gold, which had to be turned over to the government. But the banknotes depreciated every day. If the Armenians now came and demanded their money, they wanted it all in gold. But it could only be paid out with the best of intentions in the "shabby" banknotes. The Armenian National Committee member from Aleppo took me to task. But he was a reasonable man and understood the matter completely. The money matter with that woman had another side. I have to go back a bit.

A few days before the war broke out, an Armenian named Khachaturian came to Urfa from Germany. He wanted to pick up his mother and take her to Germany, where his brother had a good position as a dentist. Now he could not leave Urfa because of the war. When the situation for the Armenians looked really hopeless in the spring of 1915, Khachaturian asked me to hire him in the hospital as an attendant. Since he had often been in my house and was familiar to the Germans, I granted him his request.

When all the Armenians were removed from our hospital in October 1915, Khachaturian had to go too. He was not killed but put in the barracks in Aleppo. He wrote me a postcard from there, saying that he had left 135 gold pounds with our doctor and asked me to wire it to him if possible. He wanted the gold to buy his freedom from military service.

But the doctor was already lying unconscious with spotted fever. It would have been impossible to ask him about the money; it would not have helped. A few days before, when I was taking some prescriptions from a drawer that had always been open, I discovered a little bag with 135 pieces of gold. The name "Khachaturian" was written in ink on the bag.

It was clear to me that this money belonged to my friend. How he had been able to put this money in the drawer, I do not know; but the deportation had come so quickly that perhaps he had put it in the drawer himself in the haste. I telegraphed him to go to my bank, and I telegraphed the bank to pay Khachaturian 135 Turkish pounds in person. But Khachaturian did not pick up this money. Two weeks later I found out why: he had died of spotted fever. The money stayed in the bank. I wrote to Germany in an effort to find the brother of the deceased man.

In February 1916 my bank told me that it had finally tracked down the brother because he had heard that the money was in the bank. He did not appear to expect as much as I had transferred. According to the instructions the bank had received, Khachaturian was to come himself to pick up the money, but the bank was also told that he was still sick. (At the time he had been long dead).

Soon afterwards, one of the doctor's relatives came to Urfa. The relative had set his brother, a cunning lawyer, on me. When I asked him what he wanted he said to me:

"You ought to know that my brother loaned this Khachaturian who died in Aleppo sixty pieces of gold just before he died, so that he could buy his freedom. Khachaturian's money is now in the bank, and I want you to order this bank to pay my brother the sixty pounds."

I asked the lawyer to show me the bank receipt. He said he planned to bring it the next day, but he began at the same time to threaten me. If I did not pay this money to his brother, the lawyer said he would go before the government and sue me. Because it was Armenian property, Khachaturian's money really belonged to the government.

I asked: "Why are you threatening me? Have I denied you the payment? I want to see the receipt first. By the way, you can sue me before the government because if the government gets the money, I won't lose anything. My only desire is that the money ends up in the hands of the lawful heir."

After these words, the lawyer stormed out with a curse. The next morning he brought me a receipt without a date or stamp. It was obvious that this receipt had first seen the light of day the night before. But I also was not idle. That evening I telegraphed the bank to wire the German consul 135 Turkish liras. Then I told the lawyer to go with his receipt to the consul in Aleppo, where the money had arrived by then. Black with rage he left. It may be remarked that no one went to the consul on this matter, which was the best proof that only weasels were after this Armenian property.

In the days before my departure, a Syrian woman came to my wife and told her that a rumor was making the rounds that the Armenian doctor, who had returned to Urfa soon after the arrival of the British, planned to sue me. I had also noticed for some days that the Armenian National Committee was planning something against me. Therefore, I asked this committee to come to me so that I could see what the problem was. But no one came. In addition, I heard that someone wanted to arrest me on the day of my departure or at least prevent me from departing.

My somewhat impulsive wife wrote a letter to the Armenian doctor immediately after the woman left. The gist of the letter was that she had heard that he wanted to sue me. This must certainly be a joke, because what could he, her husband's colleague for many years, suddenly have against him. She asked him to tell her immediately whether it was true or not so that she and her husband could know what, if anything, there was to these rumors.

The doctor answered on the back of the letter without bothering to address her: "You shall answer to the law; I want nothing to do with you!"

Now we knew that the unbelievable was true. Since I had no desire to be detained in the last days before my departure, I turned to the British. We asked them to ensure that if there were to be suits against us that these should be filed now. The commander ordered the Turkish governor to issue a communiqué saying that Künzler wanted to leave the country shortly and that whoever had demands on him must submit them immediately. No such suits would be acknowledged on the day of his departure, the commander said. That day the police commissar called me to him. It was fortunately the last time. He showed me a letter that the Armenian doctor had submitted to the governor. I read it through. It said the following:

"Künzler used my illness in 1915 to *steal* from a locked drawer 145 gold pieces, which had been entrusted to me by a certain Khachaturian with the remark that should he die, I could keep the money for myself . . ."

As I read this document, I was flabbergasted. Was it really possible? And a charge like this from a friend who had studied with German assistance, and, on top of everything, knew very well what had been done with this money. Had he become mentally ill? Indeed, there was no other visible excuse for his behavior.

Since the British presence in Urfa, the capitulations suspended by the Turks had been reinstated. That meant that as a foreigner in such a case, I could not be condemned by a Turk. In addition, the commander had ordered that all complaints against me should be submitted. So I told the commander that I had been summoned by the police because of an Armenian suit. I searched through my file of correspondence for all documents relating to the case and presented them to the commander.

A day before my departure, when Dr. Vischer was already in Urfa, the matter came before the commander for a decision. We and the Armenians were all present.

The commander turned to them with the following words:

"You have charged Mr. Künzler with theft. We are very displeased that you did not bring this charge directly to us when we were the ones who called Mr. Künzler to Urfa because of your people.

"Concerning the substance of your charge, we have the entire documentation of Mr. Künzler in front of us, and I can only say that Mr. Künzler conducted himself completely correctly. He sent the money at the time to Germany without knowing that it was a gift to you. If you wish to pursue the matter, then you must address the brother of Khachaturian in Germany. I require you to apologize to Mr. Künzler in my presence and to drop these charges."

The Armenian answered that he knew what had been done with the money but that Künzler had no right to send that money to Germany where, because of the exchange rate, had drastically fallen in value.

He then put the suit in his pocket. When after a few minutes he showed no intention of apologizing, I got up and thanked the commander with the remark that we did not want to take anymore of his time.

On the day of my departure, I received a subpoena to appear before the Turkish court that morning to answer to the charge of theft. Now I had my laugh; now it was too late. The date of departure had arrived; therefore I had nothing more to do with the Turks, and they had nothing more to do with me.

One can understand that this matter caused us a lot of aggravation. The thoughts and endeavors of the human heart are already wicked in youth. The Armenians always want to blame everything on ingratitude. But the matter here was not a deed committed by the people, even if the Armenian National Committee was involved. Because there were two other Armenians under the influence of this man, they made unbelievable demands which had no basis in fact and were rejected by the English.

What hurt more than the actions of the doctor, with whom I had worked for many years, was that the often mentioned Pastor Ephraim did not come to bid me farewell even though I had placed him in a comfortable position in the orphanage. I had loved him as if he were a brother, and I had experienced much joy as well as discomfort on account of his marriage. That was the proof that he also had taken the side of the slanderers.

When I was finally ready to leave Urfa that afternoon, the courtyard of our house was full of loving people—crying, sobbing, and bidding us farewell. I must confess that I didn't calm down until I was on the ship in Beirut. Who could know whether the influence of the ill-meaning Armenians might have made possible some act of violence against me as long as I was on Turkish soil?

53. *Closing Words*

My departure from my place of activity for many years was accompanied by a discordant note. Since I must assume that these comments will make some readers who are already unsympathetic to the Armenians even less sympathetic, I would like to give my view of that people, who, like no other in the world, have had to endure so much that is horrible and unspeakable and whose numbers have been so terribly decimated. Forgive me for doing so, and remember that I worked and lived among that people for twenty years. If my knowledge of the Armenians cannot be called exhaustive, no one will say that I have no right to express my opinion.

For six centuries a freedom-loving and extremely intelligent people lived under a life-destroying Muslim regime of violence. This people experienced periodically recurring mass slaughter. Such a situation and suffering certainly cannot only contribute to the character of a people. One need only look once at the people who marched at the head of civilization and who had to march through the World War. Did the war ennoble their character? No one will seriously maintain that. This war lasted "only" five years. Can we expect that the Armenians should be better than we westerners? They, who had to guard against cunning, perfidy, and raw violence?

The business practices of the Armenians are cited as a bad example in Europe. Now, it is true that the wool cannot be pulled over the eyes of an Armenian so easily. This is much easier to do, as a rule, with the Mohammedans. But hardly anyone knows the business practices of the Armenians better than the Turk. With whom would the rich Turk prefer to do business? With the Armenians! There are countless examples that show that Turks of means really only let the Armenians handle their money. No one understands like the Armenians how to adapt to difficult circumstances in everything and everywhere to extract a profit. Just as building a railroad in old Europe is impossible without Italian workers, there is no commerce in the Orient without the Armenians. But only a small fraction of Armenians are merchants. Eighty to ninety percent of the total population are farmers, and a significant number are craftsmen. The most industrious workers on the Baghdad rail line were Armenians. The positions of trust in the rail construction were occupied by the Armenians. The main cashier and the chief accountant for the Baghdad line were Armenians. It was inconceivable, if not impossible, for a company contracted to build the Baghdad rail line would appoint a Turk or other Mohammedan to a high or important position involving trust.

If the old Orient is finally to undergo a revival, and if new life is to bloom from the ruins of the Orient with new works of culture and cultural values, then it will absolutely need the energy of the Armenian people. Without them the Orient will remain a desert.

Max Eyth[65] wrote in *Behind Plough and Vice* [*Hinter Pflug und Schraubstock*] that there are things that the Orient and the Occident do not understand about each other. Two such examples occur to me if I may be permitted to reflect.

The first concerns truth and lies. With everything that one hears in the Orient, one must first ask: Is it also true? The most beautiful flowers bloom from the well-known oriental fantasy, and the strangest thing is that they are believed no where else more than in the Orient itself. The abbot of a Protestant parish told me eighteen years ago:

"No one can force me to tell the truth before a Turkish government, and God would also not ask me to do that. There, where only the lie is the norm, truth cannot appear."

Now that I have lived almost twenty years in this (I almost said "deceitful") country, I think about that statement much more mildly than I did at the time. It is a commonplace wisdom that truth in deeds and statements only bring the people, the Armenians as well as the Turks, misery and suffering. Here is one example from many:

A young Armenian, Bedros by name, went to Russia to look for his missing father. To travel to Russia legally, the way a westerner would, was completely impossible for an Armenian. So he traveled with a counterfeit passport. He found his father and returned with him to Turkey. The old man was an upright fellow who hated lies. But without the counterfeit passport, he could not have made the journey. With such a passport he was able to cross the border. To make it back to his hometown, another trick was needed or else something bad would happen. In order for the old man to move about in the city, he had to tell the Turkish soldiers on duty at the gate that he came from the next town, Severek. No one doubted him; but the old Armenian could not lie and he confessed that he came from Russia. He was immediately thrown into jail. In jail, he was questioned further and said that his son had brought him out of Russia. In answer to the next question, where was his son; he gave the name of a village and told the soldiers that his son came to the city at night. Then the son was also picked up and thrown in jail. They both languished there for six months.

Should we be the first to throw stones at oriental Christians who want to help as best they can in a country full of injustice? They are born in a swamp and must spend their lives there.

Accuracy in information and statements is not an oriental trait. It is very seldom that one finds a person in the Orient with an acute power of observation. In business life, that is a serious deficit. The European businessman easily makes moral accusations against the Oriental because there is a deficit in training in common sense. I maintain that there is no Turk who would accuse an Armenian of that. The Turk does not expect exactness from an Armenian because he does not know it himself. Here is another example:

One of my Turkish friends is a wholesale merchant. An Armenian administers a branch of his business branch in Diyarbakır. I asked the Turk whether he was afraid that the Armenian would deceive him. "No," he said, "I don't have to worry there. If the 50,000 francs that are in my business were in the hands of a fellow Mohammedan, I would have cause to worry; but nothing will happen to my money in the hands of an Armenian. The Armenian is too calculating for that. He knows that if my business incurs losses, I will remove him from his position."

Then I responded: "How can you know, for instance, that when he purchases an item for you for five francs that he doesn't book it for 5.50 francs? What assurance do you have?"

My friend just laughed and said these telling words: "Yes, he is capable of that. But he would not be so stupid as to hurt himself. Our business can absorb such small matters; it earns enough for us both." That is the Orient!

I fully excuse the discomfort I experienced at the hands of a few Armenians during the last days of my stay in Urfa. The Armenian people have an only too understandable weakness, which also manifests itself to me in a disagreeable way. It is a deep-seated feeling of revenge for the unspeakably disgraceful injustice which they have suffered, and that has given birth to something that will always harm their people.

It would be advisable to recommend to every Armenian heart to banish the attitude of revenge. Now, if God is willing, a free Armenia is being created. It is doubly important that the people lose this attitude that mars their national character. If that does not happen, then new misfortune will follow out of necessity because it cannot be assumed that only Armenians will live in the new Armenia. A large number of the previously despised Kurds and Turks will have to live there for years. If the Armenians allow themselves to be guided by the deep-seated emotions of revenge and retaliation, then the Mohammedans will revolt against the Armenians. A free Armenia must not forget that all around her country live many Mohammedans. Armenians are just a few people to whom something terrible could happen again.

Despite all the unpleasantness I have experienced at the hands of individual Armenians, my wife and I want to continue to work, as we have until now, for this unfortunate people and to do our part so that after all of their terrible suffering, they will become a happy people.

I have a strong desire to leave out the political situation if only for the reason that I am somewhat pessimistic when I look into the future. I will keep the hope that good times will blossom for the unfortunate remnant so that it can forget everything that it has borne since 1915.

Last Experiences in Turkey

[*Der Orient*, 1925/7: Chapters 54–58; 1925/8
Chapters 59–64]

[54.] Back in Urfa

In July 1920 I had to travel to Urfa again. On the way there, I had to look into the condition of the Swiss Armenian relief work, whose station in Sivas had been moved to Samsun on the Black Sea for reasons that were unclear. The Orient Express had just been started up again, and I took this train with a Mr. W., a co-worker.

In Chapter 26 we mentioned the statement of the sick Englishman: "Thank God, the whole world is now English." I have to think of these words again because I was only issued a passport visa after I had received the consent of the British commander-in-chief in Constantinople, who first "permitted" us "Swiss" to proceed to Constantinople.

Since it is not my purpose to give a travelogue, I will refrain from describing the journey to Constantinople and Samsun.

The route from Samsun on the Black Sea led all the way across Anatolia to the Urfa region which was now on the Syrian border and was still at war with France. I arrived at the end of August, four months after the French troops, who had occupied the city in October 1919, were forced by hunger to retreat to Jerablus. But no troops arrived in Jerablus. Three hundred men were massacred three hours from Urfa, and 100 survivors were taken as prisoners to Urfa. The head of the French commander was paraded around on a stick to the unspeakable jubilation of the Muslim population. In those hours in the city, the Armenian population of 3,000, which had reassembled since 1918, was once again filled with a deathly fear that the whipped-up fanaticism of the Turks would be directed against them.

During the ninety-day occupation, which had preceded the retreat of the French, the Armenians had maintained a neutral position. Thanks to that circumstance, the Armenians were not turned upon now.

Dr. Vischer and his wife, who had to endure the occupation, traveled back home in May, leaving the hospital in charge of Armenian doctors and under the supervision of an American woman, Miss [Caroline Mary] Holmes.[66] It was high time that I arrived because the American lady, who saw that the provisional government was averse to the hospital, was about to close it down.[67]

Our Armenian nurses were overjoyed when I once again took over the hospital's rudder, which I had been able to hold firmly through all the years of the war. There was an immediate harmony and a collaboration that benefited many patients. There was no lack of work. The bellicose skirmishes between the French and the Turks in the nearby war zone took care of that. We also had to provide medical care for the 800 Armenian orphans of the American Near East Relief.

[55.] The Spies

I left my wife and children in Switzerland; but my wife was supposed to follow me, traveling via Beirut and Aleppo to Urfa. The area between Aleppo and Urfa was the war zone. Only the American relief organization had permission from the warring parties to travel by automobile from time to time to Urfa. My wife was supposed to come to Urfa by automobile. I succeeded in sending a letter to her in Aleppo, telling her that we could do our work in peace and that there was plenty to do.

When the automobile arrived in Urfa, the police immediately conducted a thorough search of it. They were looking especially for letters. The Turks found a letter from me stuck in a book.

No sooner had she arrived in Urfa than my wife took over the refurbishing of the Turkish hospital. Most of the necessities were missing, but she had the necessary linen made by the Armenians. Within a few weeks, the hospital made a different impression, and the patients felt better there again.

One month after her arrival, we suddenly found ourselves threatened with danger. The court-martial of Urfa had the letter mentioned above translated. If there was nothing in the letter that could be construed as espionage, it was enough that the letter had not arrived with the Turkish post from Aleppo. Perhaps the fact that no other letters had been found when the automobile was searched created the suspicion that my wife had hidden the letter. In addition, the fact that I had arrived in Urfa via *Samsun* and she via *Aleppo* left at least the impression of "suspicion of espionage." Therefore, the court decided to send us into the interior of the country. The Catholic priests and nuns, who were mostly French, had returned to Urfa after the armistice and had also been sent previously to the interior for a few weeks, albeit not on orders of the court-martial.

Thanks to the fact that I was Swiss and that we were both performing very necessary work, the decision of the court was not immediately implemented. The matter was presented to the commanding officer in Diyarbakır who found it unnecessary to transfer us but ordered that we be put under observation. We were then closely watched for three weeks. In the main, we went about our work in peace in the two hospitals. During this time, we were not bothered with visitors because it was an open secret that we were being "watched." The first visit that we had after three weeks was from an officer from the court-martial and his very modern wife, who was the *first* "Turkish woman without a veil" to walk around in Urfa. We quickly became friends. Every week we spent an evening together in our house. We conversed very comfortably with them. The gentleman let it be known that he was the one who had prevented our transfer. He also made no bones about the very precarious financial situation of his family; their salaries had not been paid in months. One can understand that I reciprocated at once with a significant act of friendship and helped this Turkish family in an emergency. They had two children. One good turn deserves another.

[56.] Agitation for the Armenians

My return to Urfa was an occasion of joy, especially for the Christian population as well as many Mohammedans. Twenty years of work for the population had not been in vain. Among those welcoming me back was the Protestant pastor, and I asked him later about the reason for his peculiar behavior when I departed in 1919. I found out what I already knew: The whole campaign was the result of hatred against everything German or pro-German. The pastor had tried to speak on my behalf to the Armenian committee, but he was prevented from doing so by a threat of expulsion if he did. Everyone set their hopes on the Entente at the time.

One who did not visit me was the doctor who had behaved badly to me, as mentioned in Chapter 52. Soon after my arrival, he was sent to the front as a soldier; he defected and was sentenced to death by an Urfa court-martial. Since he was incommunicado, his property was confiscated. He is still alive today. It goes without saying that I forgave him everything and wrote off his behavior as war debt, which should be amortized, forgiven, and forgotten everywhere in the world.

While I was making the rounds in the hospital, I saw a photograph with Armenians, all of whom I knew. There was a pile of Armenian skulls and other dead men's bones piled up in front of the group. The Armenians who had returned to Urfa after the arrival of the British had gathered these bones as the meager remains of their countrymen. The above-mentioned doctor held a sign in the picture with the words: "Turkish Civilization 1915." These photos shocked me, and I asked that they be destroyed immediately. Whether it was done I do not know because there could have been other copies.

In the spring the police conducted a search for papers in a Syrian house. A similar photograph was discovered. As a consequence, the men in the picture, to the extent that they could be found, were seized, taken to Diyarbakır, and thrown in jail. They were freed again in December 1922. Fortunately, most of the men in the picture had already fled from Urfa again. Among the six who were grabbed, unfortunately, was the already mentioned pastor. That meant that the parish was without a pastor, and I had to be once again the comforter from the pulpit—as I had often been during the war.

[57.] The Emigration

The Franklin-Bouillon Agreement[68] put an end to the hostilities between the Turks and the French. On the other side of the Euphrates, the Baghdad line became the border between Syria and Turkey. That meant that Urfa was Turkish; therefore all Christians in the city, especially Armenians, looked to Syria. But the peace brought no freedom of movement. No Christian was permitted to emigrate or even enter a Turkish village on business. For that reason, staying in the country was hell, and everyone wanted to flee across the nearby border. A booming transportation business sprang up. For ten gold pounds Mohammedans brought Christians under cover of night across the border. Sometimes such groups were caught and punished with imprisonment. However, the number of Armenians in the city became fewer and fewer. Finally, the only people who remained were people who could not afford to pay for transportation. Orphans cared for by the Americans and a group of poor people.

Throughout Turkey in 1919, the Americans had gathered a host of 10,000 [Armenian] orphans, all children who had been taken into Turkish, Kurdish, and Arab houses during their deportation. Since the ever-stronger, growing Kemal government made problems and controlled the Americans in many locations, I asked them to help support the many Muslim orphans in Turkey even though they could not control their money. The aid society decided to evacuate their Armenian orphans to a non-Turkish country. Lebanon was a possible destination for southeast Anatolia. The Angoran [now Ankara] government was basically glad about the prospect. In every city where there were orphans, permission had to be asked from the relevant local government. This procedure complicated the evacuation somewhat. However, in the course of eight months (from April to November), 10,000 orphans were evacuated from the southeastern area to Lebanon. Our language capabilities and familiarity with local customs better suited my wife and me than any of the American relief organization workers, who were usually in the country for a few years. The work of evacuating about 8,000 children from the regions of Urfa, Mardin, Diyarbakır, Harput, Kemaliyeh, Arabkir, and Malatya was transferred to us. The task was such a joy for us that we consider it one of the most beautiful phases of our life. Therefore, I would like to pause here for readers in order to show them a few pictures of this evacuation.

[58.] Brew-i-Davo

I went as the leader with our first group of children. The Kurds, through whose territory we had to pass from Urfa to Jerablus, had not seen any Christians in their territory for more than two years. I knew how important it was that all of the Kurds in the territory be informed about what would be happening now. To see whole groups of such children travelling through their territory once again would reawaken their desire to steal some of these children. If they knew that I was at the head of the evacuation, I hoped that their Kurdish honor would stop them from harassing us.

A Kurdish village lay before us. Two carriages had not followed my orders to stay together. They had gone before us and arrived ahead of us. Before the population could see the whole group, they were in the village. "It's a dispatch of gâvurs" ["Va'a sevkiyat-i-gâvurs"], cried the Kurds who stopped the carriage and began a serious plundering. When I arrived in the village square with the main group, I was immediately recognized as I called out to the plunderers: "It's Jakob Effendi" ["Va'a Yacub Effendi"], or "Stop the plundering." The girls threw down the stolen goods and, in spite of my call to wait, they ran off to the other side of the village. I was therefore immediately recognized. I called together the whole village, explained to them that these children had permission from the

Turks to emigrate, and told them that this group was just the first of many others to follow. I told them that I hoped that because I was their friend that, for my sake, they would see to it that nothing happened to any of the children. They excused themselves and swore that no child would come to harm. I was completely reassured that in this village nothing would happen to my charges during the evacuation; and if I were not with the group, nothing bad would happen. That proved to be the case. A thousand came through in the summer months, and nothing happened to any of them.

Another Kurdish village, Siftek, already belonged to Syria, and there was nothing that could threaten our children there. But the population was astounded when they saw the wandering group scooping water from their well. More than one asked in astonishment: *"Va'a dji'e?"* ["What is that?"] I arrived at the well a few minutes later with a group on foot. No sooner was I there than I was recognized and greeted heartily.

One man called out as loudly as he could to the tent dwellers in the distance: "Mohammed, Mahmud, Khallo, come quickly, look who has come: Brew-i-Davo—the brother of David." I was, therefore, the brother of Davo, but who Davo was, I no longer remembered. The Kurds did not believe that I no longer knew who Davo was. In fact, I had carried him in my arms because he had lain sick in our hospital in Urfa for six months. He had often told them that a brother could not be better to him! I asked when that was, and they said that it was about twelve years ago. It was no wonder that I could no longer remember. Meanwhile, Mohamed, Mahmud, and Khallo had arrived, but not Davo; he had just gone to another village. When I went by the well a few days later, there was Davo. When he saw me, he came up to me to give me a kiss. He recognized me because I had hardly changed.

He was a complete stranger to me because twelve years ago, when he was lying sick in the hospital, he was only a twelve-year-old boy. He was a grown man: big and strong with a big mustachio and a bare, hair-covered chest. He showed me his young wife and a child just taking its first steps. Pointing to me, he said that I was his brother [*brew*]. He heartily took leave of his brew whom he would have preferred to take home in order to give him a meal.

[59.] The Confession

I had just left the city of Diyarbakır Eben and was on my way with a group of orphans to Jerablus. The police wanted to conduct a roll call in front of the gate. The names on the passports were read off. It turned out that there were four boys whose names were not read. But four other boys' names were read, and no one answered. Was that not curious? When I started out with this group in Mardin, no roll call had been made. The names were called out once again with the same result. The names of four of boys who were present were not called; and the names of four boys whose names were called were not present.

"Ah, ah!" a little boy about ten years old said, "but they told me when we were leaving Mardin that my name on the journey was going to be Nerses and not Levon." That was also the case with the other three. They had received made-up names. They now all confessed that Miss F., an American woman who directed the orphanage in Mardin, had told them that they were to have new names until they reached the border but they had forgotten these names. I had to laugh about this confession— but not for long. The police declared that the four boys whose names weren't on the roll would be kept there. I drove back to the city to the chief of police, but he also refused to release the children. I went in vain to the vali to ask for their release. So I continued on, discontented with the stupid turn of events; but the boys later found a way over the border.

[60.] The Whirlwind

I was no more than a quarter of an hour from the city gate, sitting in my carriage, and looking through the children's passports again when suddenly a whirlwind descended on us and blew all the papers from the carriage. I had to close my eyes for a few seconds because of the terrible dust. When the storm was over and I could open my eyes again, I looked for the passports in vain. Where in the world could they have flown away? I saw the tempest in the distance, but no papers. I ran after the cloud of dust, hoping that I would find all the missing passports. And about a few hundred meters away, between some boulders, I found five pages with twenty-two names each, but a page with twenty-two other names was missing. Wherever I looked, it was on the way to never-never land. The cloud of dust was already far, far away, and running after it was impossible. So I drove on without the missing page, knowing what would probably happen and what difficulties I was going to have before I reached the Syrian border beyond Suruj. The next police roadblock would be in Severek. And now came the problem. The police wanted to take the roll call before we entered the little town because I said that we could not stay there overnight for lack of space. I immediately explained the problem with the passports. Whether they believed me or not, the children whose names were missing had to stay behind. There was nothing that could be done. I went into Severek to find the *mutessarif*.[69] Since it was Friday, I had to visit him at home, which was very awkward because the Turkish prefer that strangers come to an official place of business rather than to their homes. The gentleman was friendly, listened to me, but told me, regretfully, that the children had to stay there. Finally, he relented and let me go with all the children to a spring about six kilometers from the city because it was the only nearby place where I could set up camp and get enough water for the people and grass for the animals. The following night we were watched by the police to ensure that no one tried to run away. The next day the police commissioner came and conducted a roll call again and demanded afterwards that all children whose names were not on the list be returned to Severek. I put them in three carriages and drove with them to the governor, asking him to let us take the children with us to Urfa because we had a large house there, and there was no facility in Severek to accommodate them. At eleven o'clock, we were able to return to the children and continue. The next evening we arrived at our orphanage, and we were barely in the courtyard when three policemen arrived with the police chief and requested a count. They telegraphed to the government in Mardin and asked about the number of children who had left there. When the whole matter had been clarified three days later, we were allowed to continue.

[61.] The Corral

From Harput, where there were about 5,000 children to evacuate, we had to try to transport them in the largest possible groups. This always required many preparations of a bureaucratic nature and arrangements that pertained to the journey itself. It was mostly fifty groups of 300–400 children who traveled together. During the three months that I needed for the evacuation, I succeeded twice in transporting about 700 children in one day. One group traveled in carriages via Diyarbakır to Jerablus, and one group by mules via Malatya to Karchemis (Jerablus). Those were big days! The faces of the children who went on the journey were beaming. The Israelites could not have been happier when they left Egypt.

In these summer months we did not use hostels for overnight accommodations because they were usually too small. We looked instead for places to camp outside a village, as near as possible to water. When we stopped, we made a wagon train in a broad circle by pulling the tow bar of one wagon up to the rear axle of another wagon. By doing that we made a large circle of twenty to thirty carriages. Then the horses were tied up inside of the circle. In the middle lay the children on wool mattresses. The lead boy assigned to a carriage distributed the food, which was always served cold, to so-called carriage groups of up to fifty—usually fewer. Before they went to sleep, the children sang songs which rang out magnificently in the night. It was important that when such a group finally arrived in Urfa that all the children had a bath and that their dusty laundry was washed. This usually required a stopover of two days. My wife took care of the next leg of the journey. Most of the time she rode the train with the children as far as Jerablus.

[62.] The Greek Orphans from Malatya

The winter of 1920 to 1921 brought untold misery to the Orthodox population of central and western Anatolia. Turkey was at war with the Greeks. There the Turkish government had also decided to deport the Greek Orthodox population. Endless lines of human beings marched from Merzifon, Sivas, and Konya to Harput, Diyarbakır, and Bitlis. Then the winter set in. About ninety percent died along the way. On my first journey to Harput, I saw the bleached bones of thousands of these victims in the Taurus Mountains. However, the Near East Relief, which was working in the country, gathered the children, especially many of those in Malatya. I had to go there too in order to send another 900 on their way. The Americans who had taken in these children were only allowed to give them bread and beds in a rented house. They were not permitted to employ the children. Now Malatya is a place where malaria was rampant. Several children died there every day. During one week when I was there, twenty of these poor creatures died. How could I transport these children, I asked myself. The government here, which was atypically not at all friendly to me, demanded a list of the children who were to go. I divided them into three groups, according to their health. The healthy children were to be sent on mules over the mountains to the south. I hoped that a second, weaker group could be transported by carriage via Diyarbakır. Finally the half-dead children were to be transported by automobile. Because of my ignorance of Greek, I had great difficulties pronouncing some of the strange names. A girl was named Netsemane Karalambos, a boy Karalambos Netsemanos, another girl Nordane Arestaki, a boy Arestaki Nordanos, and so on.

The first group set off happily on mules. Since the expected carriages had arrived and autumn had already begun, I had to decide whether to send the second group on mules also. The terrible thing was that the children in the second group were getting sicker every day, and the children in the third group were getting better. Since I had only one automobile available, I took what was to have been second group. This caused problems with the police who prepared passports according to my lists.

About ten carriages finally arrived. I put the weaker children in them and sent them to Harput. I travelled the next day with the rest, about twelve children, in the automobile to Harput. I took a little boy who was already in the last throes of death on my lap because there was no space anywhere else. After an hour, he died. Since I could not put him down anywhere, his body grew cold on me. After three hours, we arrived in Harput, where I could dispose of the precious little burden.

[63.] From Foe to Friend

In Malatya I had yet another strange experience. The American orphanage there belonged to Mr. [Ernst J.] Christoffel,[70] who maintained a home for the blind until the end of the war. As a German, he also had to leave the country. The Americans moved into the facility and gathered orphans there. After the Americans left, the Turks considered it evident that they were the heirs of the property and seized the German house and property. Knowing this, I tried to persuade the Turks to turn the house with its pretty enameled bed frames into a hospital. Otherwise the beds would have been stolen.

An Armenian was working for the Americans there. He had come back to Malatya just before the war began as an American citizen in order to take his old mother back to America. He had lived for four years hidden in a cave. After the war, he became the male servant of the Americans. The Americans now wanted to station this man with his family in Syria, but the governor would not allow this under any circumstances. I set all the machinery in motion to obtain permission for him to leave, but to no avail. At this point, the health inspector let it be known that the governor also wanted my horse and carriage for his new hospital. So, I went to the saray, where I could talk to

him alone. As we began to talk about the horse and the carriage, I said openly to him that I would gladly do him this favor
but that I expected a favor from him in return—namely, the
release of the above-mentioned Armenian. As soon as I said
that, the gentleman flew into a rage: "What, you want to bribe
me? You damned Americans and Europeans, you slander us to
the whole world, and you are the ones who are bad." He did not
let me speak and sent me away: "Get out of here." I said: "You
don't need to throw me out. I will go on my own." So I left,
hoping I would never see him again because he had behaved so
badly toward me.

During this time, his only daughter became very ill. The
city's three doctors—a Turk, an Armenian, and a banished
Greek—did not know how to treat the child. The city's gendarmerie commander, who had been stationed in Urfa, knew
me well because I had once successfully treated his child in
Urfa. This man asked the governor why he did not call me to
his little daughter's sickbed. The governor explained to the
commander that he had treated me very badly and did not dare
call me now. "But you don't know him, he is not proud. Wait,
I will call him, and I am sure that he will come." That is what
the commander is supposed to have said. That evening as I was
going by the barracks, the commander called to me and
explained the matter. I mentioned the treatment I had received
at the hands of the governor, the kind of treatment that I had
not received in my twenty-two years of dealings with Turkish
officials. That being said, I agreed to see the child if that was
what the governor wanted. The next morning I received a little
letter from the governor who said that he wanted me to come
to see his child. So I went. Before he took me to his child, he
asked my forgiveness; I gave him my hand. Although I did not
have the means to conduct a blood test on the sick child, I
thought I had the right diagnosis and could calm the anxious
father and the even more anxious mother. After two days, the
child's fever subsided, and she recovered. That is what happened, but I did not go back to the saray to say goodbye and
certainly not to plead on behalf of the Armenian. I cannot say

whether it was a consequence of this sickbed visit, but the Armenian was soon released. It was enough that he was free and is back in America today.

[64.] The End of the Urfa Station

In 1922 the gates opened for those Armenians who were still in Turkey. Now they were free to leave the country and indeed it was repeatedly suggested to them that they should emigrate. When they did not want to understand, they were encouraged with rumors of new persecutions. Hundreds had already fled over the border to Syria. The Armenian doctor with whom I had worked since my return in 1920 also fled that September. The budget I submitted in 1922 was not approved by my committee in Switzerland due to the lack of funds. It was left to me to close the hospital. But I could not decide. The doctor also did not want to work for the salary he had been receiving. He had spent large sums to stay out of Turkish military service, and now he had to earn money. I arranged for his salary to be doubled. We had a lot to do. I charged more for the operations than before so that the hospital's cash balance on July 1 was not less than it was on January 1. That was something that had never happened in the history of the hospital. There were no subsidies from outside. I had to go to Harput in the beginning of July to lead the evacuation of the orphans; and almost simultaneously the hospital income dropped. The health inspector in Urfa was always very friendly towards our work. I also saw to that. He also encouraged me to submit my certification from a 1920 exam that showed my practical medical ability to Angora [Ankara]. He believed that I would certainly receive an official license, which would enable me to continue to work without the Armenian doctor. I mentioned that this did not seem to be the right time because I knew that American doctors who did not get their degrees in Turkey had difficulty being licensed to practice in Turkey. But on the insistence of the inspector, I sent in the certification. While I was in Harput the answer came back from Angora *that no foreign doctor who has not studied at a Turkish university will be licensed to practice medicine in Turkey. Also the previous practice of giving examinations to foreigners has been discontinued.*

At that point, the Armenian doctor, who was the official doctor of our hospital, fled. On top of that, all the Armenians left Urfa. At that point, the Americans asked my wife and me to take over the orphanage in Ghazir. I finally decided with a heavy heart to close the Urfa hospital, at least temporarily. I was no longer able to continue as I had, and I did not dare work with a Turkish doctor. So it was that in December of 1922, we left Urfa completely. The first mission workers of Dr. Lepsius had moved to Urfa in 1897, and after twenty-five years we were abandoning the city. Would we be able to put up our tent there again? Or would we always have to stay away from the country where we had given our most vital energy, our greatest love? How much sweat, and how many prayers were dedicated to that country and its people in those twenty-five years!

The Turks and the Armenians: A New Phase

[*Der Orient*, 1928/5]

During the first years of my stay in Turkey, I got to know an Armenian woman who made a strong impression on me. She was—and I say this deliberately—unfortunately, the only woman like this I knew. She had a little dispute with an American woman. She scolded the American woman and said that, she, the Armenian woman, was an *"Ottoman,"* and she would not let an American woman tell her what to do. If I had been a Turk, the remark of the woman would have mightily pleased me. And I dare say today that if there were more such women among the Armenian women, who, because they were members of the Ottoman state, imagined themselves to be *Ottomans*, then we would not have the terrible divide between Turks and Armenians today. When I talk about Armenians here, I mean *the* Armenians who are members of the Turkish (Ottoman) state. However, it is deplorable that this widow is spending her old age as an immigrant in Egypt. Indeed, she was in Constantinople until after the war because her daughter was there. When I spoke to her a year ago, as usual she did not have much use for the Turks and complained that her countrymen, the Armenians, had not treated the Turks properly. This led us to an admission, that this is a complaint made by Armenian immigrants, but still too seldom. The more that confessions like this are made, the sooner a new relationship can occur between the two hostile brothers. What am I saying? Brothers! Turk and Armenians brothers? Yes, brothers, despite the terrible divide that opened up between them around 1860 and despite the terrible events in 1915, 1916, and since then. Haven't they broken bread with each other for almost a thousand years? Were they not always dependent upon each other, and wasn't it great that they understood each other the best even though they practice different religions? Certainly there was often oppression by the Turks throughout the centuries. But most of the time, it did not come from above; it was nurtured by little people who were the inferiors of the resourceful, industrious Armenians. It got really bad for the first time, as history tells us, in the last century. Many nationalities which had previously belonged to the Ottoman state, including Rumania, Serbia, Bulgaria, and Greece, had liberated themselves and became independent. Certainly the independence won by these countries also contributed mightily to a desire that had never been extinguished since it had been conquered by the Ottomans in the eleventh century: a *free* Armenia. Among the non-Mohammedan people, the Armenians were the ones who were most favored by the Turks. If the first little flames had not been fanned from outside, especially by Russia, then the terrible events of 1895, 1909, and 1915 would not have happened. There is, indeed, an ever-dwindling number of Armenians who admit what has been mentioned before: "If we had stayed loyal to the Turks, we would be the darlings of the Turks today! But instead of staying loyal to the Turks, to whom we belonged for hundreds of years, we listened to the Europeans with the awful result of our almost total extinction."

Nothing has caused so much irritation among the people who were involved after the World War than the question of guilt. But nothing contributes more to a reconciliation of those people than answering without prejudice the question of guilt with the absolutely necessary confession. It should also not be so painful for the Armenians to speak about *a joint responsibility* for the great events. But honor always goes to the truth, however bitter that may be. The *Appenzeller* said very fittingly: "It takes two to tangle" ["*Zom Zanke mönd zwee seeh*"]. So both sides are guilty. And that is how the events happened during the World War, when these two people were so much divided from each other. *"The Armenians should put themselves in the shoes of the Turks and ask themselves what would they have done in a fight for life and death if they had known that among their own people there were two million Turks who demanded nothing less than the destruction of the Armenians?"*

But the Turkish side of the previously mentioned confession must also become known. Already during the World War, many Turks said to me that the punishment was too terrible. If we ask today how could it possibly be that from those consecrated to be deported to their death, there are today almost 80,000 women and children who survived and owe their lives to the Mohammedans, Kurds, and Arabs. But thousands also owe their lives to Turks in Anatolia. They could not and did not want to carry out the strict orders of their leaders but sought avenues of escape and took in and hid the outcasts as best they could. This must and should also be *most gratefully* acknowledged by the Armenians. The confession would also lead to a reconciliation. The rescue of thousands by the Muslim population was a deed that shows that there was a conscious admission of the injustice done to the Armenian people. Indeed, in order to initiate a reconciliation or understanding, the leaders, not just the subordinates, must confess. Are there any among them who are prepared to confess? It is difficult from outside Turkey to say what the chances are for this among the leaders of the Turks.

Since the flight of Armenians in great numbers in 1922-1923 under the regime of Mustafa Kemal took place, he cannot belong to that class of leaders who ordered the deportation and extinction of the Armenian people. After the retreat of French troops from Turkish territory, it would have been very easy to give the last merciful blow. He did not do it! But he let them emigrate. *"If you want to go, then you don't want to be Ottomans!"* On a recent journey along the Turkish-Syrian and Persian border, we heard again and again that the Kurds under Turkish rule had been granted an amnesty and that they were allowed to keep their language and their headdress (very important). If this should prove to be true, then one must think about an urgently needed change in Turkish policy, which, although it wants to rebuild the country, always tears it down instead (shutting non-Turkish elements out of the state). Then there would not be much standing in the way of a reconciliation of both elements, the Turks and Armenians.

But I hear Turks say: "Now that they have left, we don't want the Armenians any more as desperately as we need them for the reconstruction of our desolate country. They will always look back to Europe and expect help that is directed against our regime." This leads us to another point, which absolutely must be overcome if an understanding is to be reached. It is the looking to Europe and America and the *trust that the Armenian has had in Europe since 1860*. God helps those who help themselves! Don't look for help from the great powers. One would think that the Armenians had been cured of that. Is that the case? It was 1902: I was on my way from Severek to Harput in a large caravan. There were also five Armenians who all spoke good English. I wondered about that and asked them where they came from and where they were going. They had returned from America, where they had been for the past ten years. They were going back to their homes in Harput. "What?" I asked, "You are returning from a free country, where your lives were safe every day, and are placing yourselves at risk here? Such dumb people!" Their answer was indicative. "That which happened in 1895 will not and cannot be repeated. *The great powers* will never let something like that happen again." Then came 1909 and 1915! The great powers have interceded mightily for you! I asked why they were returning and was silenced with their answer. It was: "The place where the cradle stood!" ["*Beşik Yeri!*"] The Swiss also understand that. The most beautiful work that I did in my life was the evacuation of the 8,000 orphans from Turkey to Syria. But those children were also happy to get out of Turkey. It almost seemed as if they had been brought from the land of Egypt to the land of Canaan so great was their joy. And today? It has been six years. Now I admit that it was not the right thing to do. Remaining in Turkey would certainly have been the right thing to do for both the Turks and Armenians. It may have been a good thing and may yield fruit yet. How are the Armenians faring in Syria, where they emigrated? Above all, they are safe. This is, and remains, a truth that is not to be underestimated. To be safe in life is worth a great deal, and this was not always the case in Turkey. But it is not everything. Having something to eat is almost as important. They have also found that out slowly but surely, although most of them are living very simply. *But it is not the place where the cradle stood!* One can ask: Don't you want to return to your homeland? And they would all say, with many beaming, longing faces: Yes—but. The "but" refers to the question of safety— safety from similar attacks on the individual as well as the people. Isn't that precious little to ask for the people who lost everything they had in Turkey and two-thirds of their population to boot? Yes, it is precious little, and Turkey could and must be able to grant this for its own benefit. But wherever I would ask how the Armenians would imagine this security, I always hear about the same misfortune: "One wants to but cannot trust the Turks; but if a great power would guarantee security, one would go back gladly." Doesn't that sound bleak? Is the Armenian still not cured of this insane idea that there might be something to expect from the great powers! Of course, whoever will not let go of this idea will not fit into the new Turkey. Better stay out and let yourself be eaten up by homesickness.

The Armenians should recollect the time that they really did live "brotherly" with the Turks, and that they, like no others, understood for hundreds of years how to get along with the Turks. If they could do it again today, completely without reliance on the harmful trust in people from *outside*, that would be the man for the new Turkey. One could then, in many real ways, repeat what happened in 1908 when, after the introduction of the new constitution, Turks and Armenians embraced each other. But it is infinitely difficult to forget a deed like that: *Forgetting* the terrible suffering that happened to the people, *trusting* in the possible promise of the Turks. "That something similar will never happen again, that the lives of the Armenians should be as safe as that of any other Ottoman." Certainly the *forgiving* comes before the *forgetting*. And one who is not led by a divine desire will find that difficult.

How often should I forgive my brother; is seven times enough? That is what the disciple asked the Messiah. And we know the answer: Not seven times, but again and again. When forgiveness takes hold, then the forgetting begins; and where the forgetting begins, new trust can begin. And one will be able to do that sooner when one says to oneself: I was also responsible for the misfortune that befell us all.

Who will be the first to extend the hand—the Ottoman Christian or Ottoman Muslim? Both of you do it; forgive each other and come back to each other so that new life can bloom from the ruins and injustices are rectified.

For the Red Crescent

[*Der Christliche Orient*, 1920]

When the war broke out and Turkey was swept up into it, my wife wanted to organize a collection among the women in Urfa for the "Red Crescent." The Red Crescent is a branch of the International Red Cross. The word "cross" is almost hated by the Mohammedan because it is a symbol for Christians. Therefore, the Mohammedans have called their Red Cross institution the Red Crescent. A collection like that among the women was something completely new, unheard of in the world of women in Urfa. It was clear to my wife that she could not reach all the women in the city, so she turned to a few respectable Armenian women. They took care of the collection among the Christian women. However, it was clear to my wife that she also had to go to the Mohammedan women if anything was to be collected from them. Native Christian women would most certainly be driven away from most of the Mohammedan doors.

In order to gain entrance into all Mohammedan houses, my wife had to find a respectable and well-known Turkish woman. She found such a woman in the person of Emine Hanım, whom my wife dutifully accompanied from house to house for four days, from eight in the morning to six at night. It was winter and a bad rainy season to boot. The women were most often wet by midday. In one house, they were given warm stockings to change into while the wet ones dried over the heater.

It became apparent in the first days that Emine Hanım did not know all the Muslim houses; so a woman from the people, an Arab, joined the effort. Then a half mentally ill Kurdish woman, who will be described shortly, joined in. The four women went from house to house and knocked on doors for the Red Crescent. In many houses, they were received with sympathy for their cause. According to oriental custom, my wife had to let herself be praised somewhat because a woman had never dared to do something like that, least of all a stranger who, from their viewpoint, had nothing to do with the Turkish soldiers. Many women said very openly that they would not give anything if my wife did not guarantee that she would make sure that that the money would also be used for the wounded soldiers.

A poor Turkish woman would not be prevented from giving the women coffee and cake. In addition, she made a small contribution for the Red Crescent.

At other locations, much power of persuasion was needed to get something from the women. One had to make such uncomfortable references as: "Don't you have any sons in the war? What would happen if he was wounded and there was not material to dress his wounds?" After hearing such references it could happen that the women would utter terrible imprecations against the war, even against the sultan, Germans, and their enemies. Other women believed that the money was being gathered for the Germans and did not want to help. Or one had to display the contributors' list and say that it would be shown to the governor, and it would look bad if their names were not on it.

Emine Hanım also wanted to show that she was a devout Mohammedan, so she never omitted the midday and afternoon prayers. She might ask for water in one house and do her ritual cleansing; and then in the next house she would say her prayers.

In one house, our contribution team was greeted with terrible imprecations when it became known what they wanted. But my wife never let herself be turned away. This time she said: "You could at least give us a cup of coffee!" ["*Hiç olmaz sa bir kahve verin!*"] They could not refuse that request. When they had drunk coffee, further urgent explanations about the purpose of the visit were given—and even here they received a contribution, albeit a small one.

Often the women were showered with words of praise. Some benefactors already had sons in the war, and tears rolled down their maternal cheeks.

In the one of the wealthiest, if certainly not the most respectable houses, a franc was contributed with great reluctance. But my wife gave it back with the words: "This is too little; you are among the wealthiest families in Urfa, and you can afford a gold piece for the wounded soldiers." The Turkish husband arrived at this point, and he cursed my wife, saying, "Drop dead!" ["*Geberesin!*"] But she answered him: "If you mean dying, then think about the fact that you are an old man and will perhaps go before me. But instead of death, I wish you a long life that you can use to give because there is still time for mercy." Cursing the gâvur mob, he threw two francs at my wife's feet. The Kurdish woman picked them up and kept them because my wife did not want to keep them with the rest of the contributions.

The previously mentioned Kurdish woman, named Subha, was a special moral support on these tours. On account of her sporadic mental illness, she was considered a kind of saint by the Mohammedans, who considered all mentally ill people to be holy. Subha was a widow and had no children of her own, but she took in abandoned children. It was not an infrequent occurrence for small children to be set out in the mosque courtyards. Subha was the mother of these children. She currently had three, among them an infant who she took with her on the contribution tours for the Red Crescent. She let one woman and then another nurse him while she constantly begged for food and clothing for all the children. When someone gave too little on these contribution tours for the Red Crescent, she would hiss in reproach at the person that Allah would punish her for greed. And since the women were especially fearful of Subha, they increased their contributions.

The result of this collection was very satisfying. We were able to purchase bandages and medicine for 1,500 francs and to send them by horseback, at the end of 1914, to the front at the vilayet of Van. We do not know if collections for the Red Crescent were organized among the women in other cities. But my wife was very happy with the experience and observations she made on these contribution tours. She gained a rich insight into the world of the Turkish harem; and for the Mohammedan women, this deed of a Christian woman was not something that they soon forgot.

Notes

[1] World War I, also known as The World World, "The War To End All Wars" broke out in August 1914 and lasted until November 1918. The war resulted in the disintegration of four empires: the Austro-Hungarian, German, Ottoman and Russian, and the birth of several new nation-states. The term Entente (*entente*, French for "agreement") or The Triple Entente refers to the three powers, France, the United Kingdom (including its colonies and dominions) and Russia, who declared war against the Central Powers led by the Austria-Hungarian, German and Ottoman Empires. Joining the Entente later were Iraly (1915) and the United States (1917) and several smaller countries. Russia left the Entente after the outbreak of the Bolshevik Revolution in 1917.

[2] Nicolai Hoff, secretary general of Norway's War Ministry, and Louis Constant Westenenk, assistant resident of the Dutch East Indies, were to assume their duties based on a contract signed in May 1914 with the Ottoman government to serve as inspectors to oversee the implementation of the reforms in the Ottoman Empire. Westenenk and Hoff had barely reached their posts when World War I broke out, and the Turkish government promptly denounced the contracts with them and suspended the program of reforms. For an introductory discussion of the reforms, see W. J. van der Dussen, "The Question of Armenian Reforms in 1913-1914," *Armenian Review* 39, no. 1-153 (Spring 1986): 11-28. On the mission, see L. C. Westenenk, "Diary Concerning the Armenian Mission," *Armenian Review* 39, no. 1-153 (Spring 1986): 29-89.

[3] For an account of the events in Zeytun, where the expulsion of the Armenian people from their ancestral home began, see Dr. Johannes Lepsius, *Todesgang des Armenischen Volkes* [Death Marches of the Armenian People] (Potsdam, 1919). *(JK)*

[4] The term Mohammedan is a centuries' old, western coinage that is considered offensive by Muslims because Mohammed is not God. The term is used throughout the text because it accurately reflects the attitude of the author toward the Turks, their religion, and the time in which it was written.

[5] Argus, "all eyes," is a Greek mythological figure with one hundred eyes.

[6] Capitulations were privileges and favorable grants made by the sultans to the subjects of the Christian nations residing and engaging in trade in the territory of the Ottoman Empire. In practice since the early 1600s, the capitulations were repealed on September 10, 1914, and abolished after the signing of the Treaty of Lausanne [1923] (Article 28).

[7] *Bahşiş, Bak[h]shish*: gift or bonus, also bribe, such as in this context.

[8] The two Persian (Iranian) princes had actually come from Switzerland where they had been exiled by the Tsarist Russian government and lived a lavish lifestyle with a monthly stipend for each of 4,000 francs provided by

the Russian government. One of them was married to a Swiss. Salah el-Dowleh had entered Persia disguised as a dervish (a member of Sufi Muslim ascetic religious fraternity who live in poverty and austerity) during the Constitutional Revolution movement, leading an army of 30,000 that clashed with Ephrem Khan's 3,000-strong contingent and was defeated. See Jakob Künzler, *Dreissig Jahre Dienst am Orient* [Thirty Years in the Service of the East]. (Basel, 1933), 44-45.

[9] The reference is to the descendents of the Qajar dynasty, who ruled Persia from 1781 to 1925. At the time of Künzler's encounter with the two Persian princes, the Constitutionalist Revolution of Iran, also known as the Iranian Constitutionalist Revolution, 1905-1911, had triumphed in Iran, ending the feudalist system and heralding a modern era. It was the first of its kind in the Middle East. However, the remnants of the monarchy loyalists made several attempts to sustain and restore the old regime held by the Qajar. The princes mentioned by Künzler were monarchists who made an attempt, in vain, to overthrow the constitutionalist forces under the command of Eprem Khan. For more on Ephrem Khan, see note 11 below.

[10] The "franc" used throughout the text refers to the Swiss monetary unit.

[11] Eprem Khan [Davtian] (1868-1912) was an Armenian revolutionary leader and national hero of Persia during the Constitutional Revolution of 1906. He was born in Barsum in the historic Armenian province of Gardman in the present-day Republic of Azerbaijan, north of Nagorno-Karabakh. A political activist since his youth, he participated in a number of self-defense operations in Sasun, Mush, Van, and Erzurum in western Armenia. He joined the ranks of the Armenian Revolutionary Federation (ARF) in the early 1890s. Then, arrested by the Imperial Russian authorities, Eprem Khan was exiled to Siberia and later to Sakhalin (1892). Escaping in 1896, he moved to Persia where he played a major role in expanding the network of ARF chapters in Tabriz and Rasht. In 1905-1911, Eprem Khan engaged in revolutionary activities unleashed in Persia. After the fall of the Qajar regime and conquest of Tehran in 1909, he was appointed chief of police forces by the Provisional Government in Persia. He was killed on May 19, 1912, during a confrontation with insurgent tribal forces and was laid to rest in the Armenian Haykazian, later Davtian School and St. Astvatsatsin Armenian Church yard in Tehran. For more on the life and legacy of Eprem Khan, see K. Khudaverdyan, ed., *Haykakan Harts' Hanragitaran* [Armenian Question Encyclopedia] (Erevan, 1996), 127; A. Amurian, *Heghap'okhakan Ep'remi odisakaně* [Revolutionary Eprem's Odyssey] (T'ehran, 1972); A. Amurean, *H. H. Dashnakts'ut'iwn, Ep'rem, Parskakan Sahmanadrut'iwn* [A. R. Federation, Eprem, the Persian Constitution] (T'ehran, 1976); and Ismā'īl Rā'īn, *Yiprim Khañ Sardař* [Eprem Khan: Commander] (T'ehran, 1350/1971).

[12] Major Nefiz Bey was a high-ranking Turkish officer with close links to the political elite of the Young Turks' regime. He had participated in the 1908 assault on Başkala, where he reportedly embraced the Armenians as

"brothers." For more on Nefiz Bey, refer to Vahakn N. Dadrian's introductory essay, "Jakob Künzler: Witness to the Armenian Genocide and Resistance in Urfa," in this book.

[13] Der Zor, also Deir el-Zor, an infamous name in recent modern Armenian history, is synonymous with death. It refers to a desert where tens of thousands were led by the Turks to their death in an "open" cemetery. The remains of the victims of the Armenian Genocide are still being discovered by visitors and researchers there. It is also the name of a town, which after the end of the World War I in 1918, became a center where individuals could search for survivors, especially orphans of the genocide. An Armenian community began to emerge in Der Zor between 1923 and 1924; an Armenian church was built in 1929 and a school in 1936. In 1985, on the occasion of the 70th anniversary of the Armenian Genocide, the plans for the construction of a major Genocide Monument were unveiled by Catholicos Karekin II of the Great See of Cilicia. It was completed and consecrated on May 5, 1991. For a brief history of Armenian Der Zor and the Genocide Monument, see *Ter-Zor Luys Hagaw* [Der Zor Illuminated] (Antelias, 1991).

[14] Garmuj, Garmunj, is an ancient Armenian village northeast of Urfa. Its establishment is attributed to King Abgar V, son of King Arshames. In 1850-1895, the town had 400 households, a school, and a church. For more on the origin and history of Garmuj, see H. S. Ep'rikian, *Patkerazard Bnashkharhik Bararan, hator arajin* [Illustrated Geographical Dictionary, Volume 1] (Venetik-S. Ghazar, 1903-1905), p. 268. For the condition of the village during the World War I, see *Diwts'aznakan Urfan ew ir hayordineră* [Herioc Urfa and Her Armenian Offsprings] (Peyrut', Lebanon: Tparan Atlas, 1955), 659-79.

[15] Rakka or Raqqa, an ancient city dating back to 244 BCE and home to two ancient palaces with a city plan modeled and built after Baghdad under the Abbasid rulers. At one point in history, Rakka was the provincial capital of Jezira, located in the northeast of present-day Syria.

[16] *Bastinado*, from the word baston, and baton in English, is a stick, club, cudgel, or truncheon used to beat the bottoms of the feet, generally as a form of corporal punishment in the Orient.

[17] *Vardapet*, a learned cleric of the Armenian Apostolic Church.

[18] Baron Max von Oppenheim (1860-1946) was a German diplomat, archeologist, and authority on ancient history. While on an engineering survey mission concerning the building of the Baghdad Railway, he discovered the mound now known as Tell Halaf. He authored several publications on its history, relics, and archeological significance.

[19] Vartkes, Vardges, [Hovhannes Serenkiwlian] was born in Karin [Erzurum] in 1871. After completing his studies, he assumed a number of teaching positions in several schools before joining the ranks of

the Armenian Revolutionary Federation. He participated in the Bank Ottoman demonstrations (1896) and was exiled to France. Upon his return, he was subject to a number of arrests and imprisonments. Vartkes was elected a deputy from the neighborhood of Skiwtar to the Ottoman Parliament, where he became a resonant voice against nationalist elements. He perished along with Krikor Zohrab in the early months of the Armenian Genocide. He was killed by Çerkez Ahmed on the order of Reşid Bey between Urfa and Diyarbakır by a bullet to his head. For more details on the life and legacy of Vardges, see *Vardges Serenkiwlian, Heghap'okhakan Alpom, Azatagrakan payk'ari hushamatean* [Vardges Serenkiwlian, Revolutionary Album, The Liberation Struggle Memorial Book] 5, no. 6(54), (1960): 161-90.

[20] Grigor [Krikor] Zohrab (1861-1915) was born in the Beşiktaş neighborhood of Istanbul, and received his elementary education at the Makruyan Grammar School. After the death of his father in 1870, young Grigor's mother remarried, and the family moved to the Ort'agiwgh neighborhood in the city. In 1876 Zohrab was accepted in the Lyceum Kalatasara, established in 1868 under the auspices of the French government and the only higher education institution in Turkey at the time, He studied engineering and business; and in 1880 he entered into law practice at his stepfather's firm while continuing his studies at the law school of Kalatasara. At 17 Zohrab began contributing to the Armenian periodical *Lragir* [Newsletter] and later wrote for *Masis* and *Erkregund* [Globe], where he published his first novel. Zohrab gained prominence as a writer and publicist in 1887-1893. The Turkish Constitution of 1876 was restored on July 1908, the same year that Zohrab was elected to the Ottoman Parliament, earning respect among general public, political, and cultural circles in Turkey. He was also a deputy of the Armenian National Assembly. Krikor Zohrab was one of the several hundred representatives of the Armenian elite—intellectuals, doctors, lawyers, teachers, and writers—who were arrested on the night of the April 24, 1915, and sent to their deaths. He was killed by Çerkez Ahmed who shattered his head with a rock. The Ottoman government spread the news that Zohrab had died of a heart attack, but that was refuted by a German journalist, Von Tyszka. For more details, see *PAAA, R14088* Von Tyszka to Zimmermann, 1 October 1915, enclosure no. 1, quoted in the master's thesis of Uğur Ü. Üngör, Holocaust and Genocide Studies: University of Amsterdam, "A Reign of Terror: CUP Rule in Diyarbakır Province, 1913-1923," June 2005, p. 60. Çerkez Ahmed, an infamous and brutal killer, is known to have boasted by saying: "I served this country. Go and look, I turned the areas around Van into Kaaba soil. You won't find a single Armenian there today. While I am serving this country, bastards like Talat are drinking ice-cold beer in Istanbul, and place me under arrest, no, this is damaging my honour!" Ahmet Refik (Altinay), *Kafkas Yolarında: İki Komite, İki kıtâl* [On the Caucasian Roadways: Two Committees, Two Murderers]. (Istanbul: Temel, 1998 [1919], [n. 187], 175, quoted in Uğur Ü. Üngör, Ibid. cf. 349.

21 Pastor Ephraim K. Jernazian (1890-1971) was born in Marash, received his education at St. Paul's Institute in Tarsus and Marash Theological Seminary. He experienced four consecutive waves of genocides in his life: the "Hamidian massacres" of 1895 in his native Marash, during which two of his brothers were killed; the "Adana massacre" of 1909; the genocide of 1915-1917 while in Urfa as an engineering student and a Protestant minister; and finally, the "covert" wave during the Kemalist revolution in 1921-1923, during which his last remaining brother and two sisters were killed. Moving to the United States after 1923, he served as a pastor and community leader in New York, New England, and California. His memoirs, *Judgment Unto Truth* (New Brunswick: Transaction Publishers, 1990), at once "dramatic and dispassionate, personal and analytical, is a chronicle of his life, [and the] trials and tribulations of his people" through the successive waves of genocides extending over a quarter of a century. As a chief government interpreter at Urfa, Rev. Jernazian enjoyed the trust of and was privy to many secrets that were occasionally confided to him by the highest provincial Ottoman authorities. Rev. Jernazian was not affiliated with any Armenian political party or nationalist group, which grants his memoir great weight and credibility.

22 Diyarbakır, ancient city of Tigranakerta, also Kara Amida of the ancients or the "black city" because of the black basalt walls surrounding it.

23 Karaköprü, also called Şeytan Deresi [Satan's Valley], is located on the outskirts of Urfa.

24 *Gâvur*, non-believers, infidels.

25 *Vilayet*, province.

26 *Mejidiyeh*, silver francs.

27 Alice C. Bewer, was an American missionary appointed for life to the Balkans: Turkey, Syria, and Persia (1907-1914).

28 *Kızıl*, "red," named after Kızıl Mountains; Kızıl Irmak [Red River] or Halys River, the longest river within the territory of Turkey, extending over 1,500 kilometers. Referred to as the Marassantiya River in antiquity by the Hittites, it constituted the natural boundary separating Asia Minor from the rest of Asia.

29 Mohammedi-Khan or Mohammed Khan, a remote desert outpost between Viranşehir, Urfa, and Ras-el-Ain, where convoys of 10,000 women and children from Erzerum, Kharput, Sairt, Diyarbakır, and Mardin were herded and remained for several days.

30 In August of 1919 she wrote to me from Aleppo that her husband had died in America. Our search until now for the two daughters has been in vain. *(JK)*

31 Headquartered in Potsdam. *(JK)*

[32] The reference is to Mgrdich Eot'neghbayrian, the legendary leader of the Urfa resistance. Born in Urfa in 1880, he attended school in his native town and later joined the ranks of the Armenian Revolutionary Federation. In 1910 he formed an armed self-defense militia. With the arrival of the caravans of Armenian deportees in Urfa and sensing the imminent calamity which was to befall the Armenians of Urfa, he proposed to resort to self-defense, which was refused by the Armenian community leaders. To avoid providing Turkish authorities any pretext to persecute the Armenian community of Urfa, he left the town, only to return in August and organize the heroic resistance of Urfa. Injured and concerned about endangering the lives of his comrades, Mgrdich asked to be left alone with his wounded brother, Sargis, to whom he spoke his last words: "My brothers and sisters fight to the last bullet. Death is one and the same everywhere." He refused to surrender to the Turks and took his own life with a bullet. His body was taken to Fahri (Fahreddin) Paşa, who had ordered him caught dead or alive. For more on the life and legacy of this revolutionary figure, see H. Hisayan, *Diwts'aznakan hayordin Mgrdich Eotneghbayrian* [Heroic Son: Mgrdich' Eot'neghbayrian] (Athens, 1937); "Eghisabet' Eot'neghbayriani husherĕ" [The Memoirs of Elizabeth Eotneghbayrian (Mgrdich's wife)], in *Diwtsa'znakan Urfan ew ir hayordinerĕ*, 916-28; V. Aharonian, "Mgrdich' Eot'neghberiani keank'n u heghap'okhakan gortsuneut'iwnĕ" [The Life and Revolutionary Activities of Mgrdich Eotneghbayrian], Ibid., 979-97; and A. S. "Mgrdich Eot'beghbayriani heghap'okhakan gortsuneut'iwnĕ" [Mgrdich Eotneghbayrian's Revolutionary Activities], Ibid., 998-1015. For episodes and reminiscences from his life, also see, Ibid., 1016-27; V. Aharonian, "Eot'nekhpahrants' Mkrtich'e, (hayĕ ew heghap'okhakanĕ), Urfayi 1915t'. goyamarti ghekawar," [Mkrtich Eotneghbayrian: The Armenian and the Revolutionary: Leader of the Battle of Urfa 1915]; *Hayrenik' Amsagir* v. 18, no. 11 (Sept. 1940): 105-10; no. 12 (Oct. 1940): 94-99. v. 19, no. 1 (Nov. 1940): 168-71; no. 5 (Mar. 1941): 116-23; no. 6 (Apr. 1941): 163-68; no. 7 (May 1941): 131-39; no. 8 (Jun. 1941): 79-85; no. 9 (Jul. 1941): 102-06; no. 10 (Aug. 1941): 115-21.

[33] Rev. Francis H. Leslie of Northport, Michigan, a missionary, was appointed American consul agent for the entire district of Urfa. During the massacres and the heroic battle of Urfa, he pleaded with Jesse B. Jackson, the U.S. consul in Aleppo, to send his Vice-Consul Samuel Edelman to help. Suspected of collaborating with the Armenians, Rev. Leslie was constantly interrogated but given permission to stay with the Künzlers. Unable to endure what he had witnessed, and tortured in prison, he "allegedly" committed suicide. Despite the efforts to present the cause of his death as suicide (on the evening of October 30, 1915), including a fabricated suicide note, later it became clear that Rev. Leslie had been poisoned. The news of his death was announced by the American Board of Commissioners for Foreign Missions (ABCFM) and U.S. Ambassador Henry Morgenthau notified the State Department. On the basis of a telegram from the American Consul in Aleppo, the State Department launched a special investiga-

tion to determine who was responsible for his death. Rev. Leslie had been acting as an intermediary for 300 British, French, Italian, and Russian refugees who had been interned in Urfa. See "A Missionary Poisoned: The Rev. F. H. Leslie of Michigan Killed in Urfa," *New York Times*, November 13, 1915. For more details, see, P. Balakian, *The Burning Tigris: The Armenian Genocide and America's Response* (New York, 2003), 254-55, cf. 10-14; Ida Alamuddin, *Papa Kuenzler and the Armenians* (London, 1970), 68-72; E. Jernazian, *Judgment Unto Truth* (New Brunswick and London, 1990), 50-51.

[34] *Mullah*, Muslim clergy. A title commonly given to local Islamic clerics or mosque leaders.

[35] Franz Eckart, a German missionary who was assisted by his wife Emma, arrived in Urfa in 1897 under the auspices of the German Orient-Mission and assumed his position as director of the new German orphanage and a few years later as the manager of a rug factory (Masmana) established by the mission. After a trip back to Germany, Eckart returned to Urfa a changed person "filled with a poisonous, fanatical, German nationalism and hatred" against the Armenians. See Ephraim K. Jernazian, *Judgment Unto Truth*, 67-69, 86-87, and *Diw'ts'aznakan Urfan ew ir hayordinerě*, 503.

[36] The reference throughout the text is to General Fahreddin (or Fahri) Türkkan, the commanding officer of the 12th Turkish Army Corps.

[37] Millet Khan [Han] buildings, Urfa's governor's office, dates back to the Ottoman era and was constructed by Yavuz Sultan Selim at the beginning of the 16th century. With over one hundred rooms, at some point it served as barracks and later as the German orphanage, which accommodated hundreds of boys and girls. Shortly after its establishment, workshops specializing in shoemaking, textile, and carpentery were set up through the efforts of its directors.

[38] Fred Shepard, an American medical missionary, spent thirty years among Armenians, Turks, Kurds, and Arabs in Ayntab prior to 1915. For more on his life and legacy, see Alice Shepard Riggs, *Shepard of Aintab* (New York, 1920; New Jersey, 2001).

[39] Dr. Floyd O. Smith and his wife, American Board missionaries from Diyarbakır, attended many Armenians, particularly those who were cruelly tortured. The Turkish authorities prepared charges against Dr. Smith for using cipher in his private correspondence, and he was ordered to appear before a court-martial in Beirut. About the middle of July 1915, a cable from Dr. Smith reported that he and his family were at the Greek Island of Rhodes, apparently expelled from Turkey. See "The Turkish Atrocities in Armenia," *The New York Times*, September 29, 1915. A statement by Dr. Smith on the destruction of Christians in the Ottoman Empire was made in September 1917. This is one of twenty-one such reports that appear in James Barton's *"Turkish Atrocities": Statements of American Missionaries*

on the Destruction of Christian Communities in the Ottoman Empire 1915-17, [Ara Sarafian, ed.] (Ann Arbor: Gomidas Institute, 1998), 89-93.

[40] Eberhard Count Wolfskeel von Reichenberg witnessed the destruction of Armenians in Zeytun, Musa Dağ, and Urfa. His letters to his wife and father provide us with frank insights into the mind of this German officer during the genocide of Armenians. In all three cities, Eberhard was called in because of Armenian resistance to deportation and destruction. Wolffskeel's "zeal against Armenians was considered beyond the call of duty, and he was recalled to Germany by the German military authorities". For more on Wolfskeel and his activities and views, see Hilmar Kaiser, ed., *Eberhard Count Wolffskeel Von Reichenberg, Zeitoun, Mousa Dagh, Ourfa: Letters on the Armenian Genocid.* (Princeton and London: Gomidas Institute, 2005).

[41] Harran, Haran, Kharan, located 80 kilometers southeast of Urfa in the same-named valley, was allegedly established in 2500 BCE by Sam, one the grandchildren of Canaan, according to Patriarch Michael the Assyrian (1126-1199). For a brief history and origins of Harran see, *Diwts'aznakan Urfan ew ir hayordinerě*, 679-82.

[42] The reference is to Father Vardan Ashjian, born in Mardin in 1873 and consecrated as the head of the Catholic Armenian community of Urfa. With the help of a Turkish military commander, he saved the lives of many Armenian conscripts by appointing them as deacons and other church positions permitted by the law. After the three waves of Urfa massacres, (August 19, September 23, and October 1, 1915), he was ordered exiled to Der Zor, an order which he refused to obey; he took sanctuary with the Franciscan order. Upon his arrest, Father Ashjian was sent to Adana where he appeared before the Turkish Military Tribunal, found guilty, and imprisoned for eighteen months. He was hanged in Adana only one day after the armistice. See *Hovhannes Ark'. Nazliani husherě, A. hator* [Memoirs of Archbishop Hovhannes Nazlian, Volume 1] (Beirut, 1960), 357-58.

[43] The Franciscan brothers, accused of providing sanctuary to Father Ashjian, were also prosecuted and served sentences of various lengths. Father Benedict, who was accused of hiding Father Ashjian, was exiled first to Marash and later to Adana, where he was sentenced to fifteen years imprisonment. Father Thomas of Ba'abda of Lebanon and Brother Rafayel of Mosul were also exiled with Father Benedict on the same charges. After the armistice, all three were allowed to return to their places of service in Kharberd and later Malatya. *Hovhannes Ark'. Nazliani husherě, A. hator*, 358.

[44] In Dr. Andreas Vischer's large, two-story residence, Karen Jeppe received Rev. Karekin, his wife, and three children (Levon, Arshak, and Hripsimé); his adopted son Misak Ter Petrosian and his wife Lucia; Khachatur Oskerichian; Petros Ter-Petrosian; Avetis Sanosian, and Khecho of Garmuj. See *Diwts'aznakan Urfan ew ir hayordinerě*, 522.

[45] Dr. Vischer, son of a prominent Swiss clan from Basel, arrived in Urfa in late 1903 subsequent to the departure of Dr. Hermann Christ.

[46] Suruj, see *Diwts'aznakan Urfan ew ir hayordinerĕ*, 684-85.

[47] *Malter*, an old German measure of capacity in Prussia 659.5 liters.

[48] German rug factory, *Diwts'aznakan Urfan ew ir hayordinerĕ*, 500-02.

[49] Ibid., 495-500.

[50] For those interested in the method of extermination, see the monograph on applied entomology "Die Heuschreckenplage und ihre Bekämpfung," Verlagsbuchhandlung Paul Parey, 1918. *(JK)*

[51] *Metalik*, 5 pfennig (Pf) of hard currency; an old German coin in use since the 9th century until the adoption of the euro by Germany in 2002.

[52] In 1921, when this book was published, inflation began again in Germany, reaching 700% by July 1922. (Translator's note).

[53] *Kilé*, weight measure equivalent to 160 kilograms (about 320 pounds).

[54] *Okka*, weight unit equivalent of 1,225 grams.

[55] Piastres, Piasters, is a monetary unit used in Egypt, Lebanon, Sudan, and Syria.

[56] Monastery of St. Sargis is located in upper Mesopotamia about five miles southwest of Urfa. According to tradition, it was built by Apostle St. Thaddeus. It was a functioning monastery until the 1915 Armenian Genocide, after which it also served as an orphanage. The monastery had a valuable collection of Armenian manuscripts and a school. One of the most revered fathers of the Syriac-speaking and Armenian churches, St. Ephrem the [A]Syrian, Yeprem Asori [the Assyrian], 306-373 ACE is buried there.

[57] The Protestant Church, the Church of the Apostles, was one of seven Protestant Armenian churches established in Cilicia in 1855. It was converted to a mosque and named the Fırfırlı Mosque. For more on the history of the church and the Protestant Armenian community in Urfa and its founding fathers, see Rev. Eghia S. K'asuni, *Lusashawigh: Patmut'iwn hay Awetaranakan sharzhman 1846-1946* [Path of Light: History of the Armenian Evangelical Movement 1846-1946] (Peyrut', 1947), 91-92, 133-34. *Diwts'aznakan Urfan ew ir hayordinerĕ*, 334-39.

[58] St. Astuatsatsin [Holy Mother of God] Cathedral, also known as Ink'-nankar Astuatsatsin [Self-Portrait Holy Mother of God], a fourth-century structure, it was renovated in 1845 under the auspices of Bishop Harut'iwn Gapenchian and benefactor M. Ghazar Dadian. Buried in the church is Patriarch Addai, ordained by St. Thaddeus. For more details see, S. Ep'rikian, *Bnashkharhik Bararan*, 646-47.

[59] The reference is to welcoming news received from the Paris Peace Conference of 1919, organized to negotiate treaties between the Allied and Associated Powers (Entente) and the defeated Central Powers. The conference opened on 18 January 1919 and lasted until 21 January 1920. Avetis Aharonian, heading a delegation, represented the Republic of Armenia at Conference, where he signed the Treaty of Sèvres on behalf of Armenia.

[60] Pharmacist Karekin Effendi Turyekian, born in Harput along with Abraham Attarian served the hospital for several years.

[61] Nisibin, Nusaybin, the ancient city of Nisibis (2 BCE – 1 ACE), near Mardin, the residence of the early Armenian kings, town in southeastern Turkey, near the Syrian border. In early Christian times it was a center of Nestorianism. As recently as this year a mass grave site containing 40 human skulls and numerous bones were accidentally discovered by the villagers of Xirabebab (Kuru) an Armenian village during digging for they departed, created a major controversy on the origins of the mass grave and their fate. For more on this issue see, Irem Günery, "Cutting the Gordions Knot – Are the Questions Since 1915 Going to be Answered," *Turkish Weekly*, 12 February 2007. Elazar Barkan, "Mass Grave Investigation in Mardin Province – Press Release," *Salzburg Seminar*, 27 April 2007. Siamanto, "Mass Graves in Mardin," *PanArmenian.Net*, 12 May 2007.

[62] *Saray*, a palace or royal court; in this context, a provincial governor's building/headquarters.

[63] Tommies or Tommy, is a term used for a private in the army and became commonly used in the British Army since World War I. Also used by the French in reference to the British soldiers. Another version of the name "Tom" has also been used with regard to the paratroopers.

[64] Argana Maden, Arğana Maaden or Maden, town located south of Ergani Maden district well known for its copper mines, where horrible atrocities were committed during the genocide. Most of its residents along with a convoy of 1500 arriving from Harpoot were killed, predominantly men over the age of 11 were "pushed over the edge of the Made cliff into its deep ravine." The destruction of the Maaden Armenians resulted in the destruction of the Maaden economy. For more on this subject see Uğur Ü. Üngör, "A Reign of Terror: CUP Rule in Diyarbekir Province, 1913-1923," Master's thesis 'Holocaust and Genocide Studies,' University of Amsterdam, Department of History, June 2005), 53-57. Mary W. Riggs, "The Treatment of Armenians by Turks in Harpoot" (10 April 1918), in Barton, *Statements* [n. 255], p. 33, inquiry Document no. III. Also, Joseph Pomiankowski, *Der Zusammenbruch des Ottomanischen Reiches: Erinnerungen an die Türkei aus der Zeit des Weltkrieges*. [The Collapse of the Ottoman Empire: Experiences in Turkey during the World War] (Wien: Amalthea-Verlag, 1928), 210.

[65] Eyth, Max. *Hinter pflug und schraubstock* [Behind Plough and Vice]. (Berlin, 1943).

66 Catherine M. Holmes, *Between the Lines in Asia Minor* (New York, 1923).

67 For the complete text, see Andreas Vischer, *Erlebnisse eines Schweizerarztes bei den türkischen Nationalisten* [Experiences of a Swiss Doctor among the Turkish Nationalists] (Basel, 1921). Also *Der Orient,* no. 3/4 (1924).

68 Also known as the Treaty of Ankara or the Accord of Ankara, it was signed on October 20, 1921, between France and Turkish revolutionaries (Turkish Grand National Assembly), marking the end of the Civil War. Among the terms of the agreement, Turkey acknowledged French sovereignty and mandate over Syria.

69 *Mutesserif,* lieutenant governor.

70 Ernst J. Christoffel, *Wie vier deutsche Jungen uns in Malatia am Euphrat besuchten* [How Four German Youth from Malatya Visited the Euphrates] (Malatia: [Blindenheims "Bethesda"], 1912).

Appendix

Letter from Jakob Künzler to Johannes Lepsius

Basel, Schönbeinstrasse 36,
April 26, 1920.
Mr. Dr. Joh. Lepsius
Potsdam

Dear, very esteemed Dr. Lepsius,

I have now written down my "Experiences" [Erlebnisse] and sent them off to the Tempelverlag publishers. Since I have never published a book before, I am turning to you with the request to support me with help and advice. Be so kind and read the document through once. It will contain much which will interest you greatly. How the little work is best published, you will know best whether it should be a brochure or book, what price it should have, whether the publisher should pay the printing, or whether I must carry the costs and afterwards receive the proceeds are all things I do not know. I leave it to you because you are the professional in such matters. I would appreciate it if I could do the corrections of the printing before I return to the Orient. I will leave at the beginning of June. That must be taken into consideration. Or someone else must do the corrections, which, because of the many names, would be very inconvenient.

I hope that you are doing well. Are you coming to Switzerland again? Certainly not before we are back in the field. I am now supposed to set up a Swiss orphanage with my wife in a free Armenia. I suggested that it be combined with husbandry, agriculture, and industry. I am to receive the necessary staff of workers. But I will only direct the main business with my wife, who will do most of the work because I want to devote myself to my medical profession more than ever. But where will a free Armenia be? I hope to meet with Aharonian[1] in the next days and discuss everything with him.

The house of my sister-in-law, Mrs. Maass in Safed, has also been taken away by the English.

I will also keep an eye on your matters in the Orient, and where I can, support them. Of that you may be assured.

We have placed our boy in the educational facility in Schiers, where he will first finish the secondary school, then go to the technical class, and after graduating, he will go to the Politechnikum in Zürich.

You wrote to me that you want to buy the house in Urfa that belongs to me and Dr. Vischer. But this can only occur if you are certain that your work is still possible there. It could be a while before you know that. If a free Armenia is created, we must assume that in Urfa there will be so few Armenians left that such a carpet factory can no longer be operated. The Muslim population is also so decimated that there is not much manpower left for factory work. In addition, you must also consider that resuming carpet manufacture there will consume a great amount of capital. I wish I could view the matter more optimistically!

First, I will go to Urfa, where I will dissolve the station and then go as soon as possible to Armenia. Where that is, is not yet known, as I mentioned. The completion of the peace treaty could shed some light as to where we will settle. Wherever possible, it should be a place where, until now and in the future, no other Evangelical mission does its work.

I will take Krikor Krikorian[2] with me. We will use him in our work.

Heartfelt greetings from my wife and from your devoted

Br[other] Jacob Künzler

Letter from Jakob Künzler, Basel, to Dr. Johannes Lepsius, Potsdam, after he had sent his book manuscript to the Tempelverlag publishers in Potsdam. The original (typewritten) is in the Lepsius Archive in Halle, Nr. 02291. (Transcription including notes by Prof. Hermann Goltz, Halle)

Notes

[1] Avetis Aharonian (1866-1948), educator, writer, ditor, social activist and prominent political figure, attended the Univeristy of Lausanne, Switzerland (1898-1901), where he studied history, philosphy, and audited courses in literature at the University of Sorbonne in Paris. In 1917 he served as the chairman of the Armenian National Council, which proclaimed the independence of the Republic of Armenia (1918-1920). During the short two years of the republic, he served in many capacities among them as the president of the parliament of the Republic of Armenia (1919). Also, as a member and later head of the various national delegations represntign Armenia at international meetings, negotiations and treaties such as Constantinople (1918), Paris Peace Conference (1919-1920), where he signed the Treaty of Sévres (August 10, 1920) on behalf of the Republic of Armenia, which guaranteed the incorporation of the historic Armenian provinces within the boundaries of the new republic, known as "Wilsonian borders" after U.S. president Woodrow Wilson. However, the provisions of the treaty was never materialized and the fate of the territories was determined by the Treaty of Alexandropol followed by the Treaty of Kars (1921), and finally the Treaty of Lausanne (1922-1923).

[2] Son of the Armenian Evangelical Pastor Bedros Krikorian, who was active as an orphanage father in Urfa where he was murdered in 1915. The mother of Krikor Krikorian and one of his sisters were deported. Krikor Krikorian came to Germany before the First World War to study machine building in Breslau. After he had to break off his studies because of the war, he earned his living as a worker (not to be confused with the Pastor Krikorian who was with the German Orient-Mission in Bulgaria). *(G)*

Bibliographies

Selected Bibliography of
Recommended Readings on Urfa

Any attempt to compile a comprehensive bibliography on specific aspects of the Armenian Genocide, specially when addressing a particular geogaphical area, requires extensive, systematic, and methodical research in three areas: the Armenian periodicals published in the Ottoman Empire and elsewhere in 1894-1922; non-Armenian sources, such as missionary reports and memoirs, diplomatic documents, and private correspondences; and Turkish-language documents issued by government entities and private sources. Despite voluminous source materials on the Armenian Genocide, a comprehensive bibliography is yet to be compiled and published. Periodical press materials are among the most neglected.

The pages of the Ottoman Armenian periodical press are replete with reports and articles dedicated to developments in the Armenian communities—from the remotest villages of the Empire to the largest metropolitan centers. Various aspects of life in Urfa—including the massacres, resistance, and presence and activities of the American and German missionaries— have been chronicled in numerous articles in *P'unj* (Bouquet, Constantinople), *Masis* (Constantinople), *Arewelk'* (The East, Constantinople), *Hayrenik'* (Homeland, Constantinople), *Sion* (Zion, Jerusalem), *Tsaghik* (Flower, Constantinople), *Surhandak* (Courrier, Constantinople), and *Biwzandion* (Byzantium, Constantinople). They are recommended for further research.

The list provided below is a selected multilingual bibliography on Urfa in general and the events of 1915 in particular; it also includes works dedicated to Jakob Künzler and his legacy. This project has generated renewed interest in the subject, and we welcome any information and references to materials on the life and legacy of Jakob Künzler, both in Urfa and later in Lebanon.

Primary Sources

Bryce, Viscount. "The Towns of Ourfa and AC." Chap. 17 in *The Treatment of Armenians in the Ottoman Empire, 1915-16: Documents Presented to Viscount Grey of Fallodon, Secretary of State for Foreign Affairs*. London: H.M. Stationery off., Sir J. Causton [printers] 1916.

Great Britain. Foreign Office. *Blue Book: Turkey*. 1896, No. 5. (Correspondence Relating to the Asiatic Provinces of Turkey. Reports by Vice Consul Fitzmaurice, from Birejik, Ourfa, Adiaman and Behesni). London: Harrison and Sons, 1896, 19 pp. (Great Britain. Parliament, *Sessional Papers*, v. 106, 1896).

Great Britain. Foreign Office, F.O. 195/1930, X/L05446, pp. 30-72, or folios 185-206. G. H. Fitzmaurice.

Gust, Wolfgang, ed. *Der Völkermord an den Armeniern 1915/16: Dokumente aus dem Politischen Archiv des deutschen Auswärtigen Amts* [The Armenian Genocide during the First World War 1915/16: Documents from Diplomatic Archives of the German Foreign Office]. Springe, Germany: 2005. See especially *Künzler*: 19, 21, 26, 28, 56f., 72, 176f., 241, 280, 282, 418ff., 433ff., 482. *Urfa: Aufstand*: 56f., 63f., 89, 177, 279, 282, 345, 351f., 364f., 385ff., 406, 410f., 418ff.; *Deportations*: 19, 240f., 282; *Deportierte* 26, 245f., 255, 386f., 478, 526f; *deutsche Anstalten*: 21, 240f., 364f., 433f.; *Internierte der Entente*: 385f.

Sarafian, Ara, comp., and ed. *United States Official Records on the Armenian Genocide 1915-1917*. Princeton and London, 2004.

Books

Armenian Language

Armen, Anuysh. *Ayruats k'aghak'i me patmut'iwně* [The History of a Burned City]. Halep, Syria, 1945.

Arewian, Abraham. *Patmut'iwn Edesioy kam ur k'aghak' K'aghdets'wots'* [History of Edesia {Urfa} or the City of the Calcedonians]. Hedesea {Urfa}, 1881.

_____. *Patmut'iwn Hedeseoy ZhT' dar* [History of Edesia in the 19th Century]. N.p.: 1889.

Avagyan, Eduard. *Urfayi verjin ahazangě* [The Last Ultimatum of Urfa]. Erevan, Armenia, 1990.

Gahuechian, Eghia. *Husher Urfayi 1915 t'.: herosamarti u hetagay iradardzut'iwnneru masin* [Memoirs of Urfa, 1915: On The Heroic Battle and its Subsequent Developments]. Erewan, Armenia, 1995.

Gnachian, M. H. *Heghap'okhut'ean zoherĕ* [The Victims of the Revolution]. Boston, 1935.

Hisayian, H. *Anmah Tiparner, patkerner ew hishatakner Urfayen* [Immortal Figures: Images and Memories of Urfa]. Paris, 1945.

Jernazian, Ephraim K. *Irawunk'ĕ chshmartut'ean: husher ch'ors kotoratsnerē*. [Judgment unto Truth: Memories of Four Massacres]. Post'ĕn, 1990.

Kilejian, Karapet. *Edesioy soskali depk'ĕ* [The Horrible Incident of Edessia]. Bulgaria, 1904.

Lut'er [Aram Sahakian]. *Urfayi herosamartĕ*. [The Heroic Battle of Urfa]. Peyrut, 1933.

Matthew of Edessa, (12th cent). *Patmut'iwn: Zhamanakagrut'yun Matt'eos Urhayets'i*. Translation into Modern Armenian with annotations by Hrach' Bart'ikyan. [History: The Chronicle of Matthew of Urfa]. Erevan, Armenia, 1991.

Nazlian, Hovhannes Archbishop. *Trapizoni T'emin vichakawor Hovhannes Ark'. Nazleani husherĕ. Merdzawor arewelk'i 1914-1928 shrjani k'aghak'akan-kronakan depk'erun masin* [The Memoirs of Archbishop Hovhannes Nazlian, Prelate of the Diocese of Trabzon on the Political-Religious Events of 1914-1928 in that Region]. Peyrut, Lebanon, 1960.

Orberian, Zareh V. *Urfayi verjin orerĕ 1915-in* [The Last Days of Urfa in 1915]. Peyrut, 1961.

Sahakian, Aram. *Diwts'aznakan Urfan ew ir hayordinerĕ* [Heroic Urfa and Her Armenian Offsprings]. Beirut, 1955.

Nerses, Shnorhali, Saint [1102-1173]. *Oghb Edesioy* [Eulogy of Edessa]. Erevan, 1973.

Zuits'erats'i hayaser Eagup K'iwnts'ler ir hayanpast gorts'uneut'ean 40 ameakin arti'w [Swiss Armenophile Jakob Künzler: On the Occasion of the 40th Anniversary of His Legacy]. Beirut'-Halep, 1946.

Other Languages

Alamuddin, Ida. *Papa Kuenzler and the Armenians*. London, 1970.

Alcok, Deborah. *By Far Euphrates: A Tale on Armenia in the 19th Century*. Neerlandia, Altanta, GA, 2002.

Armenien, ArbeitsKreis, ed. *Völkermord und Verdrängung: Der Genozid an den Armeniern die Schweiz und die Shoah* [Mass Murder and Repression: Armenian Genocide, Switzerland and the Shoah]. Zürich, 1998.

Blair, Susan K., ed., Leslie A. David. *The Slaughterhouse Province: An American Diplomat's Report on the Armenian Genocide, 1915-1917.* New Rochelle, NY, 1989.

Bliss, Edwin Munsell. *Turkey and the Armenian Atrocities: A Reign of Terror.* Fresno, 1982. Previously published n.p.: Edgewood Publishing; New York: Hibbard & Young, 1896.

Contenson, L. de. *Chrétiens et Musulmans.* [Christians and Muslims]. Paris, 1901.

Eckart, Bruno. *Meine Erlebnisse in Urfa* [My Experiences in Urfa]. Potsdam-Berlin, 1922; Armenian translation, Erevan, Armenia, 1990.

Feigel, Uwe. *Das evangelische Deutschland und Armenien: die Armenierhilfe deutscher evangelischer Christen seit dem Ende des 19. Jahrhunderts im Kontext der deutsch-türkischen Beziehungen.* [Evangelical Germany and Armenians: The Assistance of German Evangelists to the Armenian Christians since the End of the Nineteenth Century in the Context of the German-Armenian Relations]. Göttingen, Germany, 1989.

Filian, George H. *Armenia and Her People, or the Story of Armenia by an Armenian.* Hartford, CT, 1896.

Greene, Frederick Davis. *Armenian Massacres or the Sword of Mohammed.* Edited by Henry Davenport Northrop. Philadelphia: National Publishing Co., 1896.

Gründer, Horst. *Christliche Mission und deutscher Imperialismus 1884-1914* [The Christian Mission and German Imperialism: 1884-1914]. Paderborn, Germany, 1982.

Harris, J. Rendel and Harris, Helen B., eds. *Letters from the Scenes of the Recent Massacres in Armenia.* London, 1897.

Holmes, Mary Caroline. *Between the Lines in Asia Minor.* New York and London, 1923.

Hovannisian, Richard G. ed. *Armenian Tigranakert/Diarbekir and Edessa/Urfa.* Costa Mesa, CA, 2006.

Jeppe, Karen. *Erlöst vom Mohammedanismus: Schicksale armenischer Christenkinder* [Delivered from Islam: The Fate of the Christian Armenian Children]. Potsdam, 1926.

Jernazian, Ephraim K. *Judgment unto Truth: Witnessing the Armenian Genocide.* New Brunswick, N.J., 1990; Armenian translation, Boston, 1990.

Jorga, Nikolaus. *Geschichte des osmanischen Reiches* [History of the Ottoman Empire]. 5 Vols. Gotha, Germany, 1908-1913.

Kieser, Hans-Lukas, ed. *Der verpasste Friede. Mission, Ethnie und Staat in den Ostprovinzen der Türkei 1839-1938* [The Missed Peace: Mission, Ethnicity and State in Turkey's Eastern Provinces]. Zürich, 2000.

_____. *Die armenische Frage und die Schweiz (1896-1923)* [The Armenian Question and Switzerland: 1896-1923]. Zürich, 1999.

Kieser, Hans-Lukas, and Dominik J Schaller, eds. *Der Völkermord an den Armeniern und die Shoah.* [The Armenian Genocide and the Shoah]. Zürich, 2002.

Matthew of Edessa, 12th cent. *Armenia and the Crusades: tenth to twelfth centuries: the Chronicle of Matthew of Edessa.* Translated from the original Armenian with a commentary and introduction by Ara E. Dostourian. Belmont, MA; Lanham, 1993.

Matthew of Edessa, (12th cent). *Urfalı Mateos vekayi-naṁesi, 952-1136 ve Papaz Grigor'un zeyli, 1136-1162* [The Chronicle of Matthew of Edessa, 952-1136 and Rev. Grigor 1136-1162]. Ankara, 1962. Translated by Hrant D. Andreasian. Ankara, 1962.

Nerses, Shnorhali, Saint, [1102-1173]. *La complainte d'Edesse* [*Oghb Edesioy*]. Translated with an introduction by Isaac Kéchichian. Venise, 1984.

Peabody, Emily C. *Corinna Shattuck: Missionary Heroine.* Chicago: Women's Board of Missions of Interior, 1913.

Edwin Pears, *Turkey and its People.* London, 1912.

Pierce, James Wilson, ed. *The Story of Turkey and Armenia with a Full and Accurate Account of the Recent Massacres Written by an Eye Witness: A Sketch of Clara Barton and the Red Cross.* Baltimore, 1896.

Riggs, Henry H. *Days of Tragedy in Armenia: Personal Experiences in Harpoot, 1915-1917.* Ann Arbor, MI, 1997.

Schäfer, Richard. *Geschichte der Deutschen Orient-Mission* [History of the German Orient Mission]. Potsdam, 1932.

Schenkel, Karl. *Jakob Künzler, der grosse Lebensretter* [Jakob Künzler: The Great Savior of Life]. Bern, 1951.

Segal, Judah B. *Edessa/Urfa: kutsanmış şehir* [Edessa/Urfa: The Blessed City]. Istanbul, 2002.

Sick, Ingeborg Maria. *Karen Jeppe; im Kampf um ein Volk in not. Berechtigte Übersetzung.* [Karen Jeppe: About War and a People in Distress: Authorized Translation]. Translated by Pauline Klaiber-Gottschau. Stuttgart, [1930].

Vischer, Andreas. *Erlebnisse eines Schweizerarztes bei den türkischen Nationalisten* [Experiences of a Swiss Doctor among the Turkish Nationalists]. Basel, 1921.

Vischer-Oeri, Gertrud. *Erinnerungen an Urfa* [Memoirs of Urfa]. Basel, 1967. Hektographiert, Riehenm, Universitatsbibliothek.

_____. *Tagebuch aus Urfa* [Diary from Urfa]. N. p.: 1919/1920.

Articles in Periodicals and Edited Works

London Daily Telegraph, "A Dreadful Massacre," 18 January 1896.

London Daily Telegraph, "The Urfa Massacres: A Fearful Holocaust," 19 May 1896.

Bryce, James, and Toynbee, Arnold. "The Towns of Ourfa and (Aintab)." Chapter XVII in *The Treatment of Armenians in the Ottoman Empire, 1915-1916: Documents Presented to Viscount Grey of Falladon by Viscount Bryce*. London, 1916.

Aharonian, Awetis. "Urfayi herosamartě" [The Heroic Battle of Urfa]. *Hayrenik' Amsagir* [Hairenik Monthly] v. 11, no. 11 (September 1933): 56-61.

Dostourian, Ara E. "The Chronicle of Matthew of Edessa [Matteos Urhayetsi]." in *Armenian Tigranakert/Diarbekir and Edessa/Urfa*. Edited by Richard G. Hovannisian. Costa Mesa, CA, 2006.

Eckart, Bruno. "Meine Erlebnisse in Urfa" [My Experiences in Urfa]. *Der Orient* (1921): 54-58, 119-26, 133-46, 154-60; (1922): 20-34.

Fits'moris, Ch. H. [Fitzmaurice, G. H.]. "Urfayi 1895-i kotoratsě" [The 1895 Urfa Massacre]. *Hayrenik' Amsagir* v. 24, no. 1 (Hun-P'etr. 1946): 65-75. Written on the occasion of the fiftieth anniversary of the 1895 massacre: An official British Report). Translated by A. Partizian.

Gappenchian, A. "Urfayi hayerun herosamartě" [The Heroic Battle of Urfa Armenians]. in *1915-1965 Hushamatean mets egherni* [1915-1965: The Memorial Book of the Great Genocide]. Edited by Gersam Aharonian. Beirut, 1965.

Gawar, K. N. "Urfa." in *Hin karotneru chambov* [Along the Path of the Old Longings]. New Jersey, 1973.

Goltz, Hermann. "Wenn dieser Brief veröffentlicht würde und er in türkische Hande fiele . . ." Vier Schreiben von Jakob Künzler 1915-1920 aus Urfa und Basel Fünf weitere Dokumente aus dem Dr. Johannes-Lepsius-Archiv, Halle ["If this Letter Were Published and Were to Fall into Turkish Hands . . ." Four Writings of Jakob Künzler 1915-1920 from Urfa and Basel. Five Further Documents from the Dr. Johannes-Lepsius Archive in Halle] Chapter III in *Die Armenische Frage und die Schweiz. question armenienne et la Suisse (1896-1923)*. Edited by Hans-Luks Kieser. Zürich, 1999.

Hug, Ralph. "Volk auf der Schlachtbank" [A People on the Slaughtering Block], *Tagblatt*, 30 April 2007.

Jeppe, Karen. "Hilfswerk für die verschleppten Armenische Frauen und Kindern in Syrien und Nordmesopotamien" [Relief Work for the Kidnapped Armenian Women and Children in Syria and Northern Mesopotamia]. *Der Orient*, no. 23 (1923): 19-23.

Kaegi, Walter. "The Muslim Conquests of Edessa and Amida (Diarbekir)," in *Armenian Tigranakert/Diarbekir and Edessa/Urfa*. Edited by Richard G. Hovannisian. Costa Mesa, CA, 2006.

Kieser, Hans-Lukas, ed. "Betroffenheit, Aufbruch und Zeitzeugnis: Basels Verbindungen mit Urfa, 1897-1922." [Shock, Destruction, and Testimony: Basel's Connection with Urfa: 1897-1922] Chapter III in *Die Armenische Frage und die Schweiz (1896-1923)/La question arménienne et la Suisse (1896-1923)*. Zürich, 1999.

_____. "Ottoman Urfa and Its Missionary Witnesses," in *Armenian Tigranakert/Diarbekir and Edessa/Urfa*. Edited by Richard G. Hovannisian. Costa Mesa, CA, 2006.

Kaegi, Walter. "The Muslim Conquests of Edessa and Amida (Diarbekir)," in *Armenian Tigranakert/Diarbekir and Edessa/Urfa*. Edited by Richard G. Hovannisian. Costa Mesa, CA, 2006.

Maranci, Christina. "The Art and Architectuere of Amida (Diarbekir) and Edessa (Urfa)," in *Armenian Tigranakert/Diarbekir and Edessa/Urfa*. Edited by Richard G. Hovannisian. Costa Mesa, CA, 2006.

Naayem, Joseph, O. I. Rev. "The Fate of Urfa," in *Shall This Nation Die?* New York, 1920.

Tachjian, Vahe. "Expulsion of the Armenian Survivors of Diarbekir and Urfa, 1923-1930," in *Armenian Tigranakert/Diarbekir and Edessa/Urfa*. Edited by Richard G. Hovannisian. Costa Mesa, CA, 2006.

Thomson, Robert W. "Early Armenian Christianity and Edessa," in *Armenian Tigranakert/Diarbekir and Edessa/Urfa*. Edited by Richard G. Hovannisian. Costa Mesa, CA, 2006.

Urhayets'i, G. A. "Urfan ew ir erkamseay haykakan ink'nawarut'iwně" [Urfa and Its Two Month-long Armenian Self-Rule], *Hayrenik' Amsagir*, v. 5, no. 11 (September 1927): 139-43; no. 12 (October 1927): 129-35.

Vaux, Bert. "The Armenian Dialects of Dikranagerd/Tigranakert and Urfa," in *Armenian Tigranakert/Diarbekir and Edessa/Urfa*. Edited by Richard G. Hovannisian. Costa Mesa, CA, 2006.

Selected Bibliography of
Works by Jakob Künzler

In addition to his tireless efforts serving the multiethnic community of Urfa as a medical doctor, Jakob Künzler found time
to write on a vast number of topics. His books and scores of
articles cover such wide-ranging topics as health, community
relations, animal care, geography, ethnic groups, biographical
sketches of people and personages, and meteorological data on
Urfa and its environs.

Approximately 160 of Künzler's articles from publications
of the Deutsche Orient-Mission are catalogued in *Deutschland,
Armenien und Türkei 1895–1925* [Germany, Armenia, and
Turkey: 1895-1925], which was published by Herrmann Goltz
and Axel Meissner in 1998. (See especially pages 554–56, 569,
577, 595, 614, 616, and 620.) The articles appeared in *Der
Christliche Orient* [The Christian East], *Mitteilungen aus der
Arbeit* [Information about the Work], *Der Orient* [The East],
and *Orient im Bild* [The East in Pictures]. The catalogue also
includes writings by Künzler's wife Elisabeth and his daughter
Marie in two children's magazines, *Der Stern der Weisen* [The
Star of the Wise] and *Der Kleine Orient* [Asia Minor], as well
as a 1903 yearbook, *Ex Oriente Lux* [Light from the East]. All
issues of these magazines were released on microfiche in 1999
by the K. G. Saur publishing house in Munich, Germany, and
are available in the Lepsius Archive in Halle, Germany.

The selected bibliography of articles by Jakob Künzler,
predominantly compiled by Emanuel Riggenbach, appeared
first as an appendix in Künzler's *Dreissig Jahre Dienst am
Orient* [Thirty Years in the Service of the East]. (Potsdam,
1933), 136-44. Some of the entries are missing page numbers.
Unfortunately, I have not been able to rectify the situation.

In the course of research for this bibliography, this editor
came across a number of articles, apparently written by Künzler, listed in a bibliography in *Zuits'erats'i hayaser Eagop
K'iwnts'ler ir hayanpast gortsuneut'ean 40 ameakin art'iw*

[The Swiss Armenophile Jakob Künzler: On the Occasion of His 40th Anniversary Jubilee], which was published in Beirut in 1946. (See especially pages 130-31.) Unfortunately, the information provided on the sources of the pieces was insufficient; therefore, a decision was made not to include them in this bibliography.

The bibliography is divided into the categories of books and pamphlets, followed by articles. The latter are arranged thematically. It is my hope that this bibliography will provide an incentive for readers to explore other sources, especially German-language writings, to uncover other works by Jakob Künzler and his wife. That will help expand our knowledge of the events in Urfa and the legacy of this exceptional couple.

Books and Pamphlets

Im Lande des Blutes und Tränen. Erlebnisse in Mesopotamien während des Weltkrieges [In the Land of Blood and Tears: Experiences in Mesopotamia During the World War]. Potsdam, 1921. Reprinted with introduction and revisions by Hans-Lukas Kieser. Zürich, 1999, 2004.

Garabed und Djürdji, Vater und Sohn. Lebens-und Sittenbilder aus dem christlichen Mesopotamien [Garabed and Jurji, Father and Son: Photos of Life and Customs from Christian Mesopotamia]. Potsdam, 1925.

Dreissig Jahre Dienst am Orient [Thirty Years in the Service of the East]. Basel, 1933.

Dein Volk ist mein Volk. Das Lebensbild einer Heldin seltener Art, der Dänin Karen Jeppe [Your People Are My People: The Biography of a Heroine of a Rare Kind, the Dane Karen Jeppe]. Basel and Leipzig: H. Majer, 1939.

Köbi, der Lückenbüsser, im Dienst des Lebens, Selbstbiographie des Dr. med. h.c. Jakob Künzler [Köbi, the Stopgap in the Service of Life: Autobiography of Doctor of Medicine h. c. {honorary degree} Jakob Künzler]. Edited by Paul Schütz. Kassel, Germany: Johannes Stauda-Verlag, 1951.

Köbi, Vater der Armenier: Selbstbiographie des Dr. med. h.c. Jakob Künzler [Köbi, Father of the Armenians: Autobiography of Doctor of Medicine h. c. {honorary degree} Jakob Künzler]. Edited by Paul Schütz. Kassel, Germany: Johannes Stauda-Verlag, 1967.

Ohannes: Aus dem Leben unseres Färbers in Ghasir [Ohannes: From the Life of Our Dyer in Ghazir]. Potsdam: Tempel-Verlag, 1926.

Der Raub der Kurdenbraut. Erzählung [The Rape of the Kurdish Bride {narrative}]. Potsdam, 1925.

Seltsame Lebensgeschichte eines syrischen Mönches [The Peculiar Life History of a Syrian Monk]. Potsdam, 1922.

Articles

Abbreviations

Appenzellische Sonntagsblatt	*ASB*
Appenzeller Zeitung	*AZ*
Archiv für Wirtschaftsforschung im Orient	*AWO*
Basler Anzeiger	*BA*
Basler Nachrichten	*BNR*
Pro Juventute	*PJ*
Der Christliche Volksbote aus Basel	*CVB*
Der Christliche Orient	*DCO*
Der Orient	*DO*
Der Schweizerische Sonntagsfreund	*SSF*
Die ärztliche Mission	*DAM*
Jahrbuch der Deutschen Orientmission	*JDO*
Maria Magdalena Christliches Frauenblatt	*MMCF*
Meteorologische Zeitschrift	*MZS*
Mitteilungen über Armenien	*MÜA*
National Zeitung, Basel	*NZB*
Neue Schweizer Zeitung	*NSZ*
Orient in Bildern	*OIB*
Ref. Schweizerische Zeitung	*RSZ*
Syrische Reifeerinerungen, Basler Nachrichten	*SRBN*
Zeitschrift der deutschen Institute für ärztliche Mission	*ZDIAM*

1. From Künzler's Work in the Mission Hospital in Urfa.

"Die Missionsklinik in Urfa" [The Mission Clinic in Urfa]. *DCO* 2 (1901): 8-12.

"Araber im Missionsspital in Urfa" [The Arabs in Urfa Mission Hospital]. *DCO* 2 (1901): 87-91.

"Zu den Anfängen der Klinik in Diarbekir" [About the Beginnings of the Clinic in Diyarbakır]. *DCO* 2 (1901): 192-94.

"Orientalisches aus der ärztlichen Praxis in Urfa" [Oriental Practices by Doctors in Urfa]. *DCO* 3 (1902): 91-95.

"Unsere Patienten" [Our Patients]. *JDO* (1902): 222-26.

"Türken im Missionsspital in Urfa" [Turks in the Urfa Mission Hospital]. *DCO* 4 (1903): 1-5.

"Unsere Klinik in Urfa" [Our Clinic in Urfa]. *DCO* 4 (1903): 129-32.

"Jahresbericht der Missionsklinik in Urfa" [Annual Report of the Mission Clinic in Urfa]. *DCO* 5 (1904): 69-73.

"Klinikbericht" [Report of the Clinic]. *DCO* 5 (1904): 73-75.

"Klinik in Urfa" [Clinic in Urfa]. *DCO* 6 (1905): 36-38, 49-57.

"Freude in Urfa" [Joy in Urfa]. *DCO* 6 (1905): 85-86.

"Der Kurdenarzt" [The Doctor of the Kurds]. *DCO* 6 (1905): 174-76, 189-92.

"Unsere Kranken im Januar" [Our Sick in January]. *DCO* 8 (1907): 52-57.

"Geistliche Krankenverfolgung" [Prosecution of Mentally Ill Patients]. *DCO* 8 (1907): 42-45.

"Raubüberfall in der Missionsklinik in Urfa" [Heist in the Urfa Mission Hospital]. *DCO* 8 (1907): 103.

"Ein Patient im Missionsspital in Urfa" [A Patient in the Mission Hospital in Urfa]. *DCO* 9 (1908): 35-36.

"Missionsklinik und Spital in Urfa" [The Mission Clinic and Hospital in Urfa]. *DCO* 9 (1908): 26-35.

"12 Jahre gefangen" [12 Years in Captivity]. *DCO* 10 (1909): 108-09.

"Urfaspital" [Urfa Hospital]. *CO* 11 (1910): 207-08.

"Camo, der Kurdenarzt" [Camo: The Kurdish Doctor]. *DCO* 12 (1911): 110.

"Ärztliche Mission in Urfa" [Medical Mission in Urfa]. *DCO* 12 (1911): 167.

"Die Ägyptische Augenkrankheit" [The Egyptian Eye Disease]. *DCO* 12 (1911): 153-59; and *ZDIAM* no. 7 (1911).

"Vom Wolf zum Lamm" [From Wolf to Lamb]. *DCO* 13 (1912): 50-51.

"Der Buchstabe tötet" [The Letter Kills]. *DCO* 13 (1912): 69-70.

"Bilder aus der ärztlichen Mission in Urfa" [Images of the Medical Mission in Urfa]. *DCO* 13 (1912): 90-99.

"Das Ferienheim des Urfa Hospitals" [The Vacation Home of the Urfa Hospital]. *DCO* 13 (1911): 170-75.

"Ein Krankentransport in Obermesopotamien" [A Patient Transport in Upper Mesopotamia]. *BNR,* nos. 100-105 (1912).

"Aus der Klinikarbeit" [From the Clinic Work]. *DCO* 14 (1913): 29-30.

"Wer beerdigt ihn?" [Who Buries Him?]. *DCO* 15 (1914): 10-11.

"Das neue Diakonenhaus in Urfa" [The New Deacon's House in Urfa]. *DCO* 15 (1914): 38-40.

"Vom Missionshospital in Urfa" [About the Mission Hospital in Urfa]. *DCO* 16 (1915): 7-8.

"Bericht über den Betrieb unseres Hospitals und der Klinik in Urfa 1915-1916" [Report on the Activities of Our Hospital and Clinic in Urfa: 1915-1916]. *DCO* 17 (1916): 57-61.

"Beobachtungen über Kriegskrankheiten in Mesopotamien" [Observations on the War Diseases in Mesopotamia]. *DAM* 10, no. 2 (1919/1920): 33-45.

"Letzter Bericht über das Spital in Urfa" [Final Report on the Hospital in Urfa]. *MÜA,* no. 23/24 (1923): 267-68.

2. Land and People: Customs and Uses in the Near East

"Ein Nomadenfürst Mesopotamiens: Der Kurde Ibrahim Paşa" [A Nomadic Prince in Mesopotamia: The Kurd Ibrahim Paşa]. *DCO* 2 (1902): 65-70, and *JDO* (1902): 226-33.

"Eine armenische Familie" [An Armenian Family]. *DCO* 4 (1903): 187-89.

"Eine Seele, die suchte und fand" [A Soul: Searched and Found]. *DCO* 4 (1903): 81-85.

"Und fiel unter die Mörder" [And Fell under the Murderers]. *DCO* 5 (1904): 145-48.

"Kurden" [The Kurds]. *DCO* 6 (1905): 142-44, 189-91.

"Die Syrer in Urfa" [The Syrians in Urfa]. *DCO* 7 (1906): 169-73.

"Allerlei aus Syrien und Mesopotamien" [Odds and Ends from Syria and Mesopotamia]. *CVB* 74, no. 52 (1906): 413.

"Eine Hochzeitsreise im Orient" [A Honeymoon in the Orient]. *CVB* 74, no. 19-21 (1906).

"Das Morgenrot einer neuen Zeit" [The Dawn of a New Era]. *DCO* 9 (1908): 173-75.

"Aus Urfa" [From Urfa]. *DCO* 9 (1908): 201.

"Von weit hinten in der Türkei" [From the Depths of Turkey]. *CVB* 76, no. 41 (1908).

"Das Ende des Nomadenfürsten Ibrahim Pascha" [The End of the Nomad Chief Ibrahim Paşa]. *CVB* 76, no. 52 (1908).

"Eine mohamedanische Geschichte" [A Mohammedan Story]. *CVB*, no. 13 (1910).

"Miss Corina Shattuck" [Miss Corinna Schattuck]. *DCO* 11 (1910): 153-55.

"Teuerung in Urfa" [Inflation in Urfa]. *DCO* 11 (1910): 56.

"Sonntag in Mesopotamien" [Sunday in Mesopotamia]. *SSF,* no. 163 (1910): 321.

"Aus Mesopotamien" [From Mespotamia]. *CVB* 78, no. 23 (1910): 180.

"Der wandernde Kurdenscheich als Missionar des Islams" [The Migrating Kurdish Sheikh as Muslim Missionary]. *DCO* 12 (1911): 27-29.

"Aus dem Innern der Türkei" [From the Interior of Turkey]. *DCO* 12 (1911): 35-39, 55-58.

"Die Märtyrer von Osmanie" [The Ottoman Martyrs]. *DCO* 12 (1911): 98-106.

"Chronischer Notstand in Urfa" [Chronic State of Emergency in Urfa]. *DCO* 12 (1911): 108-10.

"Die Ausgabe der Schule in der Mission" [The Expenditures of the School in the Mission]. *DCO* 13 (1912): 65-68.

"Die syrisch-protestantische Schule in Urfa" [The Syrian-Protestant School in Urfa]. *DCO* 13, (1912): 107-10.

"Yester Wartuhi. Ein Bericht aus den Tagen der Christenverfolgung der 90er Jahre" [Esther Wartuhi: A Report from the Days of the Christian Persecutions of the [18]90's]. *DCO* 15 (1914): 40-53.

"Die Erlebnisse des Mardiros während des Weltkrieges" [The Experiences of Mardiros during the World War]. *DCO* 21 (1920): 11-12.

"Jugenderinnerungen aus Teufen" [Youth Memories from Teufen]. *ASB,* nos. 20-23 (1920).

"Sahat, der Waisenjunge" [Sahat, the Orphan Boy]. *MÜA,* no. 17 (1921): 212.

"Deportierte aus dem Norden" [The Deported from the North]. *DCO* no. 7 (1921).

"Etwas von der armenischen Jugend" [A Little on the Armenian Youth]. *PJ* no. 2 (1922): 55-63.

"Arschalus" [Arshaluys]. *MÜA,* no. 20 (1922): 233-34.

Jugenderinnerungen aus Stein" [Youth Memories from Stein]. *ASB,* nos. 41-45 (1925).

"Aus dem Leben des Ohannes" [From the Life of Ohannes]. *RSZ,* nos. 12-18 (1925).

"El-Djim! Geisterspuk aus dem Libanon" [El-Jim! Hauntings from Lebanon]. *OIB* (1927): 54-56.

"Aug um Aug, Zahn um Zahn" [Eye for an Eye, Tooth for a Tooth]. *OIB* (1929).

"Des Armeniers Kosrof schwerste Stunden" [The Armenian Khosrov's Most Difficult Hour]. *OIB* (1929): 49.

"Das armenische Kind" [The Armenian Child]. *OIB* (1929): 87.

"Tina, die Armenierin" [Tina, the Armenian Girl]. *Für Alle-Kalendar,* (1933): 46-48.

3. Geographical, Ethnographic, Political, and Religious Relations in the Near East

"Zum Klima von Obermesopotamien" [On the Climate of the Upper Mesopotamia]. In collaboration with Dr. Hermann Christ, 1901. *MZS,* (1901).

"Haran" [Harran]. *DCO* (1904): 81-85.

"Dunkle Stunden" [Dark Hours]. *DCO* 7 (1906): 17-22.

"Kurden" [The Kurds]. *DCO* 7 (1906): 31-32.

"Klima von Urfa, Obermesopotamien, nach 6-jährigen Beobachtungen" [Urfa Weather: Upper Mesopotamia After 6 Years of Observations]. In collaboration with Dr. Hermann Christ. *MZS* 10 (1906).

"Resultate der meteorologischen Beobachtungen zu Urfa im Jahre 1906" [Results of Meteorological Studies in Urfa in the Year 1906]. In collaboration with Dr. Hermann Christ. *MZ* 5 (1907).

"Tierschutz im Orient" [Animal Protection in the East]. *CVB* 78, no. 16 (1910).

"Das Handwerk in Urfa" [Handicraft in Urfa]. *DCO* 8 (1907): 71-80, 88-93.

"Ibrahim Pascha" [Ibrahim Paşa]. *DCO* 8 (1907): 182-84.

"Eine armenische Geschichte" [An Armenian Story]. *CVB* 75, nos. 40-42 (1907).

"Aus Urfa" [From Urfa]. *DCO* 9 (1908): 12-14.

"Die neue Zeit" [The New Era]. *DCO* 12 (1911): 24-29.

"Nikodamus nächte" [Nicodemian Nights]. *DCO* 12 (1911): 129-35.

"Das Haar des Propheten" [The Hair of the Prophet]. *DCO* 12 (1911): 142-43.

"Aus der Ramasan-Festpredigt" [From the Ramadan Sermon]. *DCO* 12 (1911): 171-73.

"Über den Weinbau und die Aufbereitung der Trauben zu Wein und Traubenkonserven in Nordsyrien und Obermesopotomien" [On the Viticulture and the Preparation of Grapes to Wine and Grape Preserves in Northern Syria and Upper Mesopotamia]. In collaboration with Dr. Gustav Bredemann. *AWO* 4, no. 1/ 2 (1919): 25-54.

"Die Türkei und Armenien" [Turkey and Armenia]. *NSZ* 1, no. 104 (20 December 1919).

"Aufteilung der Türkei" [The Partition of Turkey]. *AZ*, no. 130 (1920).

"Rakka" [Rakka]. *DO*, no. 8 (1921).

"Wo liegt Ghazir?" [Where Lies Ghazir?]. *DO*, no. 6 (1925).

"Der Wolleinkauf am Flusse Chabur und Die neue Türkei" [The Wool Purchase at the River Khabur and the New Turkey]. *BNR*, no. 12 (1926).

"Das Christentum und die neue Türkei" [Christendom and New Turkey]. *DO*, nos. 11-12 (1926).

"Das Europäerchristentum im Urteil des nahen Ostens" [The European Christendom as Judged by the Near East]. *DO*, nos. 11-12 (1926).

"Die Zedern vom Libanon" [The Cedars of Lebanon]. *OIB* (1929): 52-53.

"Die Lage in Syrien" [The Situation in Syria]. *NZB*, no. 446 (1928).

"Bäume voll hängender Trauben" [Trees Full of Hanging Grapes]. *OIB* (1929): 78.

"Jesus-Mohammed" [Jesus-Mohammed]. *OIB* (1929).

"Urfa und die neue Türkei" [Urfa and the New Turkey]. *BNR*, no. 290 (23 October 1930).

4. Travel Descriptions

"Von Basel nach der alten Abrahamsstadt" [From Basel to the Ancient City of Abraham]. *CVB* 68, nos. 7-10 (1900).

"Allerlei Reiseerlebnisse" [Odds and Ends of Travel Experience]. *DCO* 2 (1901): 136-40.

"Von der Schweiz nach Urfa" [From Switzerland to Urfa]. *DCO* 11 (1910): 39-45, 55-56.

"Eine Reise im Orient während des Waffenstillstandes" [A Journey in the East during the Armistice]. *BA*, nos. 6-11 (1919).

"Reiseerlebnisse aus Mesopotamien" [Travel Experiences from Mesopotamia]. *NZB*, nos. 287-97 (1920).

"Letzte Erlebnisse in der Türkei" [Last Experiences in Turkey]. *DO*, nos. 6, 8 (1925): 60-64, 85-91.

"Ein Besuch in Ghazir" [A Visit to Ghazir]. *CVB*, no. 25 (1924): 225-99.

"Bei den Schützlingen des Völkerbundes" [Those under the Protection of the League of Nations]. *SRBN*, no. 278-80 (1928).

"Reise nach dem Innern Borderasiens" [Journey toward the Interiors of Asia]. In collaboration with Dr. B. Schütz. *OIB*, (1928 and 1929).

"Die Reise nach dem Libanon" [Journey to Lebanon]. *CVB*, nos. 20-26 (1932).

5. Charitable Activities

"Bericht über das armenische Hilfswerk in Urfa und Umgebung" [Report on the Armenian Relief Work in Urfa and Vicinity]. *MÜA*, no. 11 (1919): 126-31.

"Bericht an die Freunde Armeniens in der Schweiz" [Report on the Friends of the Armenians in Switzerland]. *MÜA*, no. 12 (1919): 145-47.

"Allerlei Rettungsarbeit" [Odds and Ends of Rescue Work]. *DO*, no. 8 (1921).

"Türkische Waisenhäuser" [Turkish Orphanages]. *DO*, no. 8 (1921).

"Die Waisenarbeit auf dem Libanon" [The Orphan Work from Lebanon]. *DO*, nos. 9-10 (1924).

Opfertag" [Sacrifice Day]. *ASB*, no. 42 (1924).

"Aus dem Leben von Jakob Künzler, Waisenvater in Ghazir" [From the Life of Jakob Künzler: Father of the Orphans in Ghazir]. *DO*, no. 1 (1925).

"Von unseren Waisenkindern in Ghazir" [About Our Orphan Children in Ghazir]. *DO*, nos. 2-3 (1925); nos. 1-2 (1926).

"Verlobung und Verheiratung der grösseren Waisenkinder" [Betrothal and Marriages of the Older Orphan Children]. *DO*, nos. 9-10 (1925).

"Die Gedächtnisfeier in Ghazir" [The Commemorative Celebration in Ghazir]. *DO*, no. 3 (1926).

"An die Pflegeeltern der Ghazir-Waisen" [On the Foster Parents of the Ghazir Orphans]. *DO*, no. 3 (1926).

"Zum Jahresanfang in Ghazir" [From the Beginning of the Year in Ghazir]. *DO*, nos. 5-6 (1926).

"Berichte über die Waisenkinder in Ghazir" [Report on the Orphan Children in Ghazir]. *DO* (1926).

"Ein Gedächtniswaisenhaus" [A Memorial House for the {Ghazir} Orphanage]. *OIB*, (1928).

"Der Geburtstag" [The Birthday]. *OIB* (1929).

"Der Camp-Jammer" [Camp Misery]. *OIB*, no. 4 (1928).

"Das Weihnachtsfest in Ghazir auf dem Libanon" [Christmas in Ghazir, Lebanon]. *MMCF* 26 (1928): 27-28.

Die Siedelungen für die Armenier" [Settlements for the Armenians]. *OIB*, no. 3 (1930).

"Die Nöte der armenischen Emigranten im Baradenlager von Beirut" [The Hardships of the Armenian Emigrants in the Barada Camp of Beirut]. *MÜA*, no. 52 (1931).

"Zum Häuschenbau" [About the Little House Construction]. *MÜA*, no. 54 (1931).

Photographs

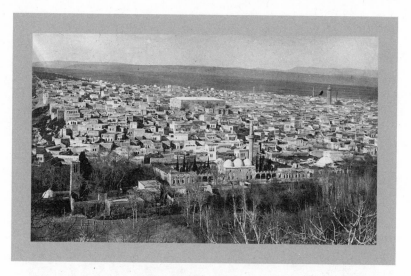

Urfa seen from Kale (hill fortification), at the beginning of the 20th century. In the center is the great Armenian Apostolic Cathedral. In the right hand corner the striking tower of the Ulu Jami (dating from late antiquity) is visible. The tower of the Protestant church is in the lower left hand corner. (Sources: Im Lande..., *1999 German edition, Private archive.)*

Jakob Künzler as a young man carrying out an electric current treatment of an Arab Bedouin in the mission hospital in 1902. (Sources: Im Lande..., *1999 German edition, Private archive.)*

Young Jakob Künzler as an assistant in "Armenischen Hilfwerks,"
Urfa, 1900. (Basel Mission Archive. Source: Die armenische Frage
und die Schweiz, 1896-1923 = La question armenienne et la Suisse,
1896-1923. *Edited by Hans-Lukas Kieser. Zürich: Chronos, 1999.)*

Transporting the sick to the mission hospital in Urfa around 1912. Patients travelled up to eight days to be treated in the hospital. (Sources: Im Lande...*, 1999 German edition, Private archive.)*

The mission doctor Andreas Vischer (not visible in the picture) held his consultation hours in the village of Garmuj near Urfa around 1909. They were conducted in the church, in the foreground of which headstones can be seen. (Sources: Im Lande...*, 1999 German edition, Private archive.)*

Ali, the loyal servant of Künzler and Vischer around 1909. He transported many people to safety and despite torture betrayed no one. (Sources: Im Lande*..., 1999 German edition, Private archive.)*

The Armenian quarter, completely destroyed by the Turkish Army in the fall of 1915. In the following years of the war it was thoroughly looted. (Sources: Im Lande*..., 1999 German edition, Private archive.)*

Armenian patients of the "German Orient-Mission," officially renamed the "Swiss Hospital," in 1919.
(Sources: Im Lande..., *1999 German edition, Private archive.)*

In 1922, in eastern and central Turkey, where the Turkish national militias were conducting "ethnic cleansing," Jakob Künzler organized the evacuation of about 8000 orphans to Syria for the aid organization Near East Relief. The picture shows a mule convoy crossing a small stream. (Sources: Im Lande…, *1999 German edition, Private archive.)*

Transport of the blind and crippled orphans by truck, 1922. (Sources: Im Lande…, *1999 German edition, Private archive.)*

A part of a group of the 130 boys and girls in Urfa on the way to Aleppo. They have been marching for two days and are taking a break at a watering hole. (Sources: Im Lande...*, 1999 German edition, Private archive.)*

The first group of these orphans taking their first longer break in a han (hostel, caravansary) in the Kurdish village of Suruj, southwest of Urfa. (Sources: Im Lande...*, 1999 German edition, Private archive.)*

Elisabeth and Jakob Künzler-Bender as grandparents with their grandchild, together with the Swiss consul Carl Lutz and his wife Gertrud in Jaffa (Palestine) in 1937. For Carl Lutz, Jakob Künzler was a role model for taking responsibility in a situation of genocide. Carl Lutz later became famous in 1944 for his aid efforts on behalf of tens of thousands of Hungarian Jews. Both men came from Walzenhuasen in Appenzell. (Sources: Im Lande..., *1999 German edition, Private archive. State Archive of Appenzell Ausserhoden.)*

The Künzler family photo. (left to right). Rosa [Alahaydoian], an Armenian orphan adopted by the Künzlers, Arnold, Ida, Marta, Jakob Künzler, Elibet, Elisabeth Künzler and Marie. (Switzerland, ca. 1919/1920) Courtesy of the Künzler family archive.

The Künzler family photo taken in Ghazir, Lebanon (ca. 1925-1930). (left to right) Marie, Marta, Marie Maas (Elisabeth Künzler's sister), Dr. Andreas Vischer, the director of the German Mission Hospital in Urfa preceding Jakob Künzler, Elibet, Elisabeth Künzler, Jakob Künzler and Ida. Missing from the photo is Arnold, their son.

(Near East Foundation organization Archive, and Missak Kelechian, photo archive, Beirut, Lebanon.)

General view of Ghazir Lebanon (ca. 1925-1930).
(Missak Kelechian, photo archive, Beirut, Lebanon.)

The American orphanage in Ghazir also known as "Mizar"
orphanage where over 1400 Armenian orphans, predominantly
girls, were sheltered under the care of Jakob and Elisabeth
Künzler. (Missak Kelechian, photo archive, Beirut, Lebanon.)

The Near East Relief medical staff, Beirut, Lebanon in 1927. Seated from left to right, are Elisabeth and Jakob Künzler on the front row. Behind them Mr. Theodore Wieser, director of the School for the Blind in Ghazir, Lebanon. (Missak Kelechian, photo archive, Beirut, Lebanon)

Map of Historical Armenia

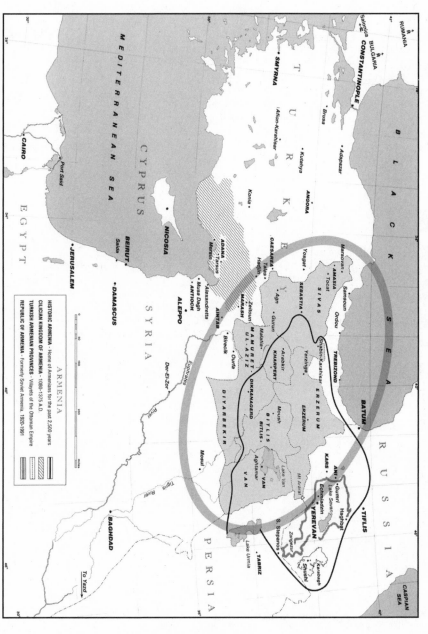

2. Map of Historical Armenia. The shaded area showing historic Armenian-populated provinces of Ottoman Empire.

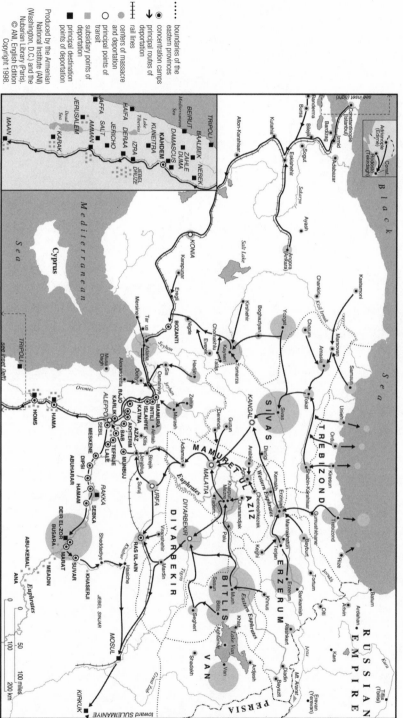

The 1915 Armenian Genocide in the Turkish Empire

Legend:
- ▪▪▪▪ boundaries of the eastern provinces
- ◉ concentration camps
- ↓ principal routes of deportation
- ⊢⊣ rail lines
- ○ centers of massacre and deportation
- ● principal points of transit
- ▪ principal points of deportation
- ▪ subsidiary points of deportation
- ▪ principal destination points of deportation

Produced by the Armenian
National Institute (ANI)
(Washington, D.C.) and the
Nubarian Library (Paris).
© ANI, English Edition
Copyright 1998.

3. The 1915 Armenian Genocide in the Turkish Empire. Produced by the Armenian National Institute (ANI) (Washington, D.C.) and the Nubarian Library (Paris).

Orphan Transport Routes

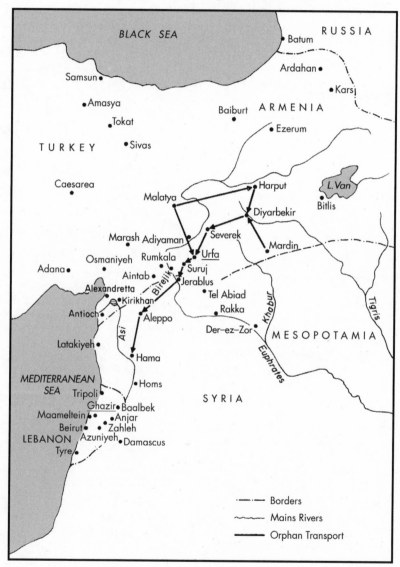

4. Transportation and relocation routes of the Armenian orphans
through the Near East (1922–1923). (Source: *Papa Kuenzler and the
Armenians* by Ida Alamuddin. London, 1970).